THE INNER CIRCLE

THE
INNER CIRCLE

Large Corporations and the Rise
of Business Political Activity in the U.S. and U.K.

Michael Useem

New York   Oxford
OXFORD UNIVERSITY PRESS
1984

Library of Congress Cataloging in Publication Data

Useem, Michael.
The inner circle.

Bibliography: p.
Includes index.
1. Corporations—United States—Political activity.
2. Corporations—Great Britain—Political activity.
3. Big business—United States.   4. Big business—
Great Britain.   I. Title.
HD2785.U85   1984   322'.3'0973   83–2163
ISBN 0–19–503344–2

Printing: 9 8 7 6 5 4 3 2 1

Printed in the United States of America

ACKNOWLEDGMENTS

Resources of several kinds were indispensable for the completion of this investigation. Generous financial assistance was provided over several years by a research grant from the U.S. National Science Foundation (grant number SOC77–06658); institutional housing and associated services have been furnished by Boston University, University of California at Santa Cruz, and Imperial College of Science and Technology, London; and grants to present this research at several international conferences and symposia were furnished by Boston University, the European Group for Organizational Studies of La Maison des Sciences de l'Homme, Paris, the Wenner-Gren Foundation for Anthropological Research, New York, and the Joint Spanish-North American Committee on Educational and Cultural Affairs.

Research assistance on a considerable scale and in many forms has been rendered by Francine Miller and Susan Sorensen of London; by Arlene McCormack, Gladys Delp, Carmenza Gallo, John Hoops, Carol Keller, Randy Nehila, Linda Trenholm, and David Swartz of Boston University, and Thomas Moore of the University of Wisconsin-Parkside. Several individuals were a source of leads, ideas, and contacts nearly throughout the project; these were Paul DiMaggio of Yale University, G. William Domhoff of University of California, Santa Cruz, Jerome Karabel of Harvard University, and S. M. Miller of Boston University. Numerous valuable suggestions for improving an earlier version of this manuscript were provided by Jerome Karabel, Gary T. Marx of M.I.T., and David Vogel of the University of California, Berkeley.

A number of other people contributed to the study in ways too diverse to describe individually, but whose suggestions, recommendations, and invitations were of inestimable value. In Europe and abroad, these include: Arthur Francis, Dorothy Griffiths, and Aubrey Silberston of the Department of Social and Economic Studies, Imperial College of Science and Technology, London; Dorothy Wedderburn of Bedford College, University of London; Elina Almasy of the European Group for Organizational Studies, Paris; Dennis Bradley, London; Martin Bulmer, London School of Economics; John Fidler, London; Hano Johannsen of the British Institute of Management; Sir Donald MacDougall of the Confederation of British Industry; Gavin Mackenzie, Cambridge University; Jane Marceau, Liverpool University; Richard Melville and Sandra Melville, London; Ralph Miliband, London and Brandeis University; Yoram Neumann and Dan Soen, Ben-Gurion University of the Negev, Israel; Victor Perez-Diaz, Complutense University, Madrid; Philip Stanworth, University of York; Richard Whitley, Business School, University of Manchester; Jack Winkler, Cranfield Institute of Technology; Janet Wolff, Leeds University; and Stephen Wood, London School of Economics. In the United States, these individuals are: Howard Aldrich, University of North Carolina; Dane Archer, University of California, Santa Cruz; Russell Epker, Boston; Sylvia Fleisch, Boston University; Louis Goodman, Yale University; Rodney Hartnett, Battelle Memorial Institute; Paul Hirsch, Business School, University of Chicago; John Kitsuse, University of California, Santa Cruz; Joel Levine, Dartmouth College; Roland Liebert, University of Illinois; Judy Locke, Boston University; Peter Mariolis, University of South Carolina; Arlene McCormack, Boston University; Henry M. Morgan, School of Management, Boston University; Lita Osmundsen, Wenner-Gren Foundation for Anthropological Research, New York; Donald Palmer, Business School, Stanford University; Richard Ratcliff, Syracuse University; Joel Schwartz, College of William and Mary; Michael Schwartz, State University of New York, Stony Brook; David Swartz, Boston University; David Vogel, Business Administration, University of California, Berkeley; Maurice Zeitlin, University of California, Los Angeles; and James Zuiches, Cornell University.

Finally, I would like to express my deep appreciation to some 150 individuals intimately familiar with the politics and organization of the largest American and British corporations, a familiarity derived from their roles as senior managers and directors of major companies, or, in some instances, as business journalists, government officials, or business-association staff members. Their willingness to guide a prying visitor into some of the more remote recesses of an invisible society shrouded in a mixture of discretion and secrecy proved invaluable. They generously shared their time, as well as their knowledge of, and insight into a world ordinarily closed to all but bona fide participants. Individual acknowledgment of each should be offered here were it not for the guarantee of confidentiality that necessarily accompanied all such discussions.

CONTENTS

TABLES

ONE

Organizing Business

This book offers a new thesis concerning the nature of contemporary political activity by large business firms. I will argue that a politicized leading edge of the leadership of a number of major corporations has come to play a major role in defining and promoting the shared needs of large corporations in two of the industrial democracies, the United States and the United Kingdom. Rooted in intercorporate networks through shared ownership and directorship of large companies in both countries, this politically active group of directors and top managers gives coherence and direction to the politics of business. Most business leaders are not part of what I shall term here the *inner circle*. Their concerns extend little beyond the immediate welfare of their own firms. But those few whose positions make them sensitive to the welfare of a wide range of firms have come to exercise a voice on behalf of the entire business community.

Central members of the inner circle are both top officers of large firms and directors of several other large corporations operating in diverse environments. Though defined by their corporate positions, the members of the inner circle constitute a distinct, semi-autonomous network, one that transcends company, regional, sectoral, and other politically divisive fault lines within the corporate community.

The inner circle is at the forefront of business outreach to government, nonprofit organizations, and the public. Whether it be support for political candidates, consultation with the highest levels of the national administration, public defense of the "free enterprise system," or the governance of foundations and universities, this politically dominant segment of the corporate community assumes a leading role, and corporations whose leadership involves itself in this pan-corporate network assume their own distinct political role as well. Large companies closely allied to the highest circle are more active than other firms in promoting legislation favorable to all big business and in assuming a more visible presence in public affairs, ranging from philanthropy to local community service.

The inner circle has assumed a particularly critical role during the past decade. Evidence we shall examine indicates that the 1970s and early 1980s were a period of unprecedented expansion of corporate political activities, whether through direct subvention of candidates, informal lobbying at the highest levels of government, or formal access to governmental decision-making processes through numerous business-dominated panels created to advise government agencies and ministries. This political mobilization of business can be traced to the decline of company profits in both the United States and the United Kingdom and to heightened government regulation in America and labor's challenge of management prerogatives in Britain. As large companies have increasingly sought to influence the political process, the inner circle has helped direct their activities toward political ends that will yield benefits for all large firms, not just those that are most active. This select group of directors and senior managers has thus added a coherence and effectiveness to the political voice of business, one never before so evident. The rise to power of governments attentive to the voice of business, if not always responsive to its specific proposals, is, in part, a consequence of the mobilization of corporate politics during the past decade and the inner circle's channeling of this new energy into a range of organizational vehicles.

Both the emergence of the inner circle and the degree to which it has come to define the political interests of the entire business community are unforeseen consequences of a far-reaching transformation of the ways in which large corporations and the business communities are organized. In the early years of the rise of the modern corporation, self-made entrepreneurs were at the organizational helm, ownership was shared with, but limited to, kin and descendents, and the owning families merged into a distinct, intermarrying upper class. It was the era of family capitalism, and upper-class concerns critically informed business political activity. In time, however, family capitalism was slowly but inexorably pushed aside by the emergence of a new pattern of corporate organization and control—managerial capitalism. Business political activity increasingly came to address corporate, rather upper-class, agendas, as the corporation itself became the central organizing force. If family capitalism was at its height at the end of the nineteenth century and managerial capitalism was ascendent during the first half of the twentieth, both are now yielding in this era to institutional capitalism, a development dating to the postwar period and rapidly gaining momentum in recent decades. In the era of institutional capitalism, it is not only family or individual corporate interests that serve to define how business political activity is organized and expressed but rather concerns much more classwide—the shared interests and needs of all large corporations taken together. Increasingly a consciousness of a generalized corporate outlook shapes the content of corporate political action.

The large business communities in Britain and America have thus evolved, for the most part without conscious design, the means for aggregating and promoting their common interests. While government agencies add further coherence to the policies sought, the inner circle now serves to fashion, albeit in still highly imperfect ways, the main elements of public policies suited to serve the broader requirements of the entire corporate community. This conclusion is not in accord with predominant thinking, nor with those theories about business-government relations more fully described below. Of these, most fall into one of two opposing schools. According to the first, corporate leadership is presumed to be either too-little organized to act politically at all, or, as the second goes, so fully organized that it acts as a single, politically unified bloc. This book rejects both schools of thought and argues for a new perception, a new theory of the nature of the politics of big business in contemporary British and American society.

A new conception of the business firm is also needed. Most corporate business decisions are viewed, correctly, as a product of the internal logic of the firm. Yet when decisions are made on the allocation of company monies to political candidates, the direction of its philanthropic activities, and other forms of political outreach, an external logic is important as well. This is the logic of classwide benefits, involving considerations that lead to company decisions beneficial to all large companies, even when there is no discernible, direct gain for the individual firm. The inner circle is the carrier of this extracorporate logic; the strategic presence of its members in the executive suites of major companies allows it to shape corporate actions to serve the entire corporate community.

The power of the transcorporate network even extends into the selection of company senior managers. In considering an executive for promotion to the uppermost positions in a firm, the manager's reputation within the firm remains of paramount importance, but it is not the only reputation that has come to count. The executive's standing within the broader corporate community—as cultivated through successful service on the boards of several other large companies, leadership in major business associations, and the assumption of civic and public responsibilities—is increasingly a factor. Acceptance by the inner circle has thus become almost a prerequisite for accession to the stewardship of many of the nation's largest corporations. Our traditional conception of the firm must accordingly be modified. No longer is the large company an entirely independent actor, striving for its own profitable success without regard for how its actions are affecting the profitability of others. While it retains its independence in many areas of decision-making, its autonomy is compromised. And this is especially true for company actions targeted at improving the political environment. Through the agency of the inner circle, large corporations are now subject to a new form of collective political discipline by their corporate brethren.

Finally, our thinking about democratic politics in Britain and America requires revision as well. The theory of democratic political practice rests on the traditional assumption that individual voters, special-interest groups, and political parties are the fundamental building blocks of the political order. Yet individual action is increasingly structured and mobilized through large-scale institutions nominally apolitical in purpose.[1] Large corporations, through their ability to expand, contract, or simply redefine employment opportunities, productive capacity, and other of society's resources have become among the most important of these large-scale institutions. When these corporations are feuding and atomized, their political impact tends to be inconsistent, at times contradictory, and thus neutralized. When less divided and better organized for collective action, however, they can be very effective in finding and promoting their shared concerns.

Certainly a common awareness among those with wealth, those with economic power, those with titles or in positions of authority has always existed. They have long shared the presumption that by virtue of ownership or performance they had the right to run their own firm or institution, and certainly to veto or compromise reform and other legislative measures aimed at undermining their ability to rule and protect their own organization. Notwithstanding the continuing jealousies between old company money and new corporate wealth, financiers and industrialists, self-made entrepreneurs and professional management cadres, among those at the very top there is now a far stronger sense of an imperative to act together. Rather than defensively protecting only their own company's interests, those in the highest circles of corporate leadership now share a clearer understanding that what divides them is modest compared to what separates them from those who would presume to exercise power over economic decisions from bases other than those of private economic power.

So while a sense of class affinity based on company stewardship can hardly be said to be new, the strength of the bond has increased, and a select circle of those in corporate power are now far more willing to work toward goals that serve all large companies. Through the advancement of consensually determined positions on the issues of the day, this community of corporate leaders has been able to acquire a special role in the democratic process. While voter preferences and prejudices have not suddenly become impotent and special-interest lobbying remains decisive on many issues, a vastly powerful new institution, with organizational skills to match its economic power, has joined the political fray.

THE UNITED STATES AND THE UNITED KINGDOM

The choice of corporations in the United States and the United Kingdom as the subjects for this study came about as a product of two considerations. A tension between business and state is generic to all capitalist democracies. Disparate industries face a single government, and precisely how the former take their point of view to the latter can be decisive for both the economic climate and the political course adopted for the nation. I will argue not only that this problem is common to advanced industrialized democracies, but that the solution, how the business point of view is promoted, is generic as well. The rise of institutional capitalism and classwide forms of social organization within the business community are a natural product, it will be suggested, of the unpredictability of circumstances facing all large corporations in industrial democracies. In moving to solve the immediate problems of monitoring and influencing their environment, companies have unintentionally and without coordination gravitated toward very similar perceptions of where safety might be. They have done so for reasons that are unique to no capitalist democracy, and indeed for reasons that are common to most.

To substantiate this convergence thesis, I have chosen to examine contemporary business organization in both the United States and Great Britain. If, despite their distinct economic histories, political institutions, and cultural traditions, these two corporate communities display many of the same elements of social organization and political behavior, the case for convergence is strengthened. It would be further enhanced if other nations were included in the study and similar findings emerged among these others. This general confirmation, if it did come, however, would be at the expense of undertaking a more intensive analysis of the smaller sample. Since the complex inner structure of the corporate community requires an in-depth study if it is to be properly characterized, I have adopted the strategy of concentrating on the U.S. and the U.K. only.

While demonstrating convergence, it is important at the same time to examine divergence. A full understanding of the rise and structure of business political activity in the U.S. and the U.K. requires that one focus on areas of difference as well as similarity. Despite comparable levels of economic development and relatively similar political systems, the American and British business communities offer more than the requisite degree of contrast. The higher levels of British business, especially finance, are notable for their fusion with elements of the British aristocracy, while the American community is relatively free of pre-industrial traditions. American companies face a less organized labor movement than do their British counterparts, but a more regulated political environment. Entry into the senior levels of British management depends more on "sponsored" mobility, that is, a system in which there is an early identification of those destined to succeed, while ascent up the American corporate ladder is more a product of "contest" mobility, a competition continued till the end. The British "public schools" (what Americans would call "prep schools"), have played a more influential role, and the British universities and professional schools a less influential role, than their respective counterparts in America. Higher proportions of British managers have had an exclusive secondary education than have American managers, while the reverse is true regarding university and professional training.[2]

Corporate behavior is different as well. Productivity and profit levels of U.K. companies are generally lower than those for similar U.S. firms. British enterprises rely more upon informal systems of internal control and evaluation, American corporations on more formalized and bureaucratic hierarchies.[3] Distinct political customs are evident too: British companies give company money directly to political parties, while American firms use the intermediary of the political-action committee. The British public servant and company director are from a similar "social catchment" and thus speak the same language, while the diverse origins of the American federal administrator and corporate managers place them at arms length. A "frank exchange of views" is the prescribed form of business contact with senior civil servants in London; aggressive "lobbying" of federal officials is normative corporate practice in Washington.

Such contrasts help sharpen our image of how business is organized in both America and Britain. The distinguishing features are, nonetheless, largely overshadowed by the presence of high similar elements of transcorporate organization. Diversity is selectively analyzed in what follows, but emphasis is placed on the parallel political responses of large corporations on both sides of the Atlantic to their declining fortunes.

My primary focus is on social organization, less on process and impact. The guiding agenda is to map the complex inner byways of the newly emergent forms of organization in the two business communities and to identify how these forms shape the rise and thrust of contemporary political practices of large corporations and their leadership. By giving this stress to the investigation, two implications follow. First, no attempt will be made to evaluate the impact of the new corporate politics on public policies and the business climate. Second, assessment of the *process* by which classwide business power is exercised as well receives comparatively little attention. A number of effects and elements of process are touched upon in the course of the analysis, but our central focus is on the organization of American and British corporate politics.

The analysis is based on a range of information sources. These include intensive personal interviews that I conducted with one hundred and fifty directors and senior executives (chief executive officers in many instances) associated with the largest industrial and financial corporations, primarily in New York and London, the centers of commercial activity in both countries; extensive statistical analysis of the careers, political activities, and intercorporate connections of several thousand senior executives and directors of four hundred large British and American companies; numerous documents, many unpublished, obtained from business associations, antibusiness groups, government agencies, and the corporations themselves; and other analytic and historical studies of large corporations, those who run them, and their political activity. The integrated use of these varied information sources permits me to synthesize research compiled over a number of years by a range of American and British investigators.

IMAGES OF BUSINESS UNITY

The ease with which large corporations are able to pursue their joint interests depends, as for any set of political actors, first on their social cohesion and common commitment. Although no informed observer of large enterprises in America and Britain would deny that such enterprises aggressively promote their political interests, whether or not they do this jointly, or in competition with one another, is still a matter of enduring dispute.

Recent studies of the politics of big business could hardly be more divided on the extent to which the corporate community is socially unified, cognizant of its classwide interests, and prepared for concerted action in the political arena. In a number of original investigations, for instance, G. William Domhoff finds "persuasive evidence for the existence of a socially cohesive national upper class."[4] These "higher circles," composed chiefly of corporate executives, primary owners, and their descendents, constitute, in his view, "the governing class in America," for these businesspeople and their families dominate the top positions of government agencies, the political parties, and the governing boards of nonprofit organizations. Drawing on studies of the U.S., Great Britain, and elsewhere, Ralph Miliband reaches a similar conclusion, finding that " 'elite pluralism' does not . . . prevent the separate elites in capitalist society from constituting a dominant economic class, possessed of a high degree of cohesion and solidarity, with common interests and common purposes which far transcend their specific differences and disagreements."[5]

Yet other analysts have arrived at nearly opposite conclusions. In an extensive review of studies of business, Ivar Berg and Mayer Zald argue that "businessmen are decreasingly a coherent and self-sufficient autonomous elite; increasingly business leaders are differentiated by their heterogeneous interests and find it difficult to weld themselves into a solidified group."[6] Similarly, Daniel Bell contends that the disintegration of family capitalism in America has thwarted the emergence of a national "ruling class," and, as a result, "there are relatively few political issues on which the managerial elite is united."[7] Leonard Silk and David Vogel, drawing on their observations of private discussions among industrial managers, find that the "enormous size and diversity of corporate enterprise today makes it virtually impossible for an individual group to speak to the public or government with authority in behalf of the entire business community."[8]

Observers of the British corporate community express equally disparate opinion, though the center of gravity is closer to that of discerning cohesion than disorganization. Drawing on their own study of British business leaders during the past century, Philip Stanworth and Anthony Giddens conclude that "we may correctly speak of the emergence, towards the turn of the century, of a consolidated and unitary 'upper class' in industrial Britain."[9] More recently, according to John Westergaard and Henrietta Resler, "the core" of the privileged and powerful is "those who own and those who control capital on a large scale: whether top business executives or rentiers make no difference in this context. Whatever divergences of interests there may be among them on this score and others, latent as well as manifest, they have a common stake in one overriding cause: to keep the working rule of the society capitalist."[10] The solidity is underpinned by a unique latticework of old school ties, exclusive urban haunts, and aristocratic traditions that are without real counterpart in American life. Thus, "a common background and pattern of socialization, reinforced through intermarriage, club memberships, etc. generated a community feeling among the members of the propertied class," writes another analyst, and "this feeling could be articulated into a class awareness by the most active members of the class."[11]

Yet even if the concept of "the establishment" originated in British attempts to characterize the seamless web at the top that seemed so obvious to many, some observers still discern little in British business on which to pin such a label. Scanning the corporate landscape in the early 1960s, for instance, J. P. Nettl finds that the "business community" is in "a state of remarkable weakness and diffuseness—compared, say, to organized labour

or the professions," for British businessmen lack "a firm sense of their distinct identity, and belief in their distinct purpose."[12] The years since have
brought little consolidation, according to Wyn Grant: business "is neither
homogeneous in its economic composition nor united on the appropriate
strategy and tactics to advance its interests." Thus, "businessmen in Britain
are not bound by a strong sense of common political purpose."[13]

Scholarly disagreement on this question, not surprisingly, is reflected
in the textbooks used in university social-science courses. Every year American undergraduate students enter courses whose main textbook declares
that business leaders have "a strong sense of identity as a class and a rather
sophisticated understanding of their collective interest on which they tend
to act in a collective way."[14] But students on other campuses find themselves studying textbooks with entirely different conclusions. They will be
taught that the capitalist class has ceased to exist altogether or, at the
minimum, that the received wisdom is, at best, agnostic on its degree of
cohesion. The required reading in some courses asserts that "the question
of whether [the] upper class forms a unified, cohesive, dominant group is
still the subject of unresolved debate."[15] The correct view according to the
assigned textbook in still other courses is that "until more data are gathered
the question of whether national power is in the control of a power elite
or veto group remains moot."[16] Still other students, especially those enrolled
in management courses, are informed that fragmentation rather than cohesion now prevails. "A great deal of evidence," asserts a text for business
school instruction, "suggests that our society is leaning toward the plural-
istic model" rather than the "power-elite" model. "Few, if any, books are
written about an 'establishment' anymore, suggesting that if one did exist
it either has disappeared or is not influential enough to worry about."[17]
The theory of the "power elite" is, according to another widely used textbook on business and society, "a gross distortion of reality and the conclusions derived from it are largely erroneous."[18]

Social theory itself divides along this very line. Both traditional pluralist
thought and a neo-Marxist strand sometimes labeled "structuralism" have
generally argued that the parochial concerns of individual firms receive far
greater expression in the political process than do the general collective
concerns of business. Competition among firms, sectoral cleavages, and executives' and directors' primary identification with their own enterprise all
inhibit even the formation of classwide awareness, let alone an organizational vehicle for promoting their shared concerns. Business disorganization, it is argued, prevails. Arguments based on pluralism and those on
structural Marxism radically diverge in the implications they draw from
the presumed disunity. To the pluralists, the corporate elite is far too
divided to be any more effective than any other interest group in imposing

its views on the government, thus enabling the state to avoid having its prerogatives co-opted by business. But for structural Marxism, it is precisely because of this disorganization of big business that the state can and does (for other reasons) assume the role of protecting the common interests of its major corporations.

Counterposed to both of these theoretical perspectives is an equally familiar thesis, advanced by what are now known as "instrumental" neo-Marxists and by many non-Marxists as well: that the government is more responsive to the outlook of big business than to that of any other sector or class, certainly of labor. According to these theories, this responsiveness is the result, in part, of the social unity and political cohesion of the corporate elite. With such cohesion and coordination, business is able to identify and promote successfully those public policies that advance the general priorities shared by most large companies.[19]

Resolution of these opposing visions of the internal organization of the business community is essential if we are to understand how, and with what effect, business enters the political process, or, in Anthony Giddens's more abstract framing, how we are to comprehend "the modes in which . . . economic hegemony is translated into political domination."[20] But the resolution offered here is not one of establishing which of these competing views is more "correct," for either answer would be, as we shall see, incorrect; in their own limited and specific fashions, both descriptions are also partly true.

Precisely where and how the descriptions are appropriate, and the unique political consequences that result, is much of the story that follows. Developing a more accurate picture of business political activity required going beyond available research and information, for as rich as it already was, essential elements were missing. A customary alternative avenue of settling the question through more abstract theoretical deduction would obviously not suffice either. However valuable such theorizing might be for establishing some conclusions, there could be no substitute for a direct effort, in W. D. Rubinstein's calling, "to comprehend the complexity and diversity of the capitalist elite."[21]

It is this complexity and diversity, or what we have already termed social organization, that is the subject of our inquiry. The analysis is concerned with the puzzle of how such seemingly contradictory descriptions of the business community can be so forcefully maintained in both scholarly and informed thinking. Yet the inquiry is far more than a matter of puzzle-solving. Our task is that of identifying whether large corporations are capable of promoting their classwide political stakes in contemporary America and Britain.

PRINCIPLES OF SOCIAL ORGANIZATION

To facilitate our inquiry, it may be useful to describe several competing forms of internal social organization of the business community. In both countries, the organization is simultaneously structured by a number of distinct principles, of which three are of overriding importance.[22] Each contains a fundamentally different implication for the ways in which business enters the political arena.

The *upper-class principle* asserts that the first and foremost defining element is a social network of established wealthy families, sharing a distinct culture, occupying a common social status, and unified through intermarriage and common experience in exclusive settings, ranging from boarding schools to private clubs. This principle is the point of departure for virtually all analyses of the British "establishment," or the group that has sometimes been more termed "the great and the good."[23] Yet the lesser visibility and heterogeneity of an American "establishment" has not discouraged scholars from treating the U.S. circles in terms analogous to those applied to the British upper class. This is evident, for instance, in E. Digby Baltzell's studies of the national and metropolitan "business aristocracies"; in G. William Domhoff's inquiries into America's "upper-social class"; in Randall Collins's treatment of the pre-eminence of upper-class cultural dominance in America; and in Leonard and Mark Silk's study of what they have simply called "the American establishment."[24]

Many, if not most members of the upper class also occupy positions in or around large companies. But from the standpoint of this principle, these corporate locations are useful but not defining elements. Individuals are primarily situated instead according to a mixture of such factors as family reputation, kinship connections, academic pedigree, social prominence, and patrician bearing. As the upper class enters politics, this principle supports the conclusions that its main objectives would be to preserve the social boundaries of the upper class, its intergenerational transmission of its position, and the privately held wealth on which its privileged station resides. Control of the large corporation is only one means to this end, though in the U.S. it has emerged as the single most important means. Thus, one "of the functions of upper class solidarity," writes Baltzell, "is the retention, within a primary group of families, of the final decision-making positions within the social structure. As of the first half of the twentieth century in America, the final decisions affecting the goals of the social structure have been made primarily by members of the financial and business community."[25]

A parallel movement into British industry is suggested by other analysts. "Without stigma," writes one observer, "peers, baronets, knights and country squires [accepted] directorships in the City, in banks, large companies and even in the nationalized industries." But the entry into commerce, necessitated by political and financial reality, was not at the price of assimilation, it is argued, for the upper class moved to rule business with the same self-confident sense of special mission with which it had long overseen land, politics, and the empire. Aristocratic identity ran far too deep to permit even capitalist subversion of traditional values: "Heredity, family connections, going to the same schools, belonging to the same clubs, the same social circle, going to the same parties, such were the conditions that enabled 'the charmed circle' to survive all change, unscathed, whether economic, political, religious or cultural."[26] Business enterprise is simply the newest means for preserving upper-class station, and, as such, is largely subordinated to that project.

The *corporate principle* of organization suggests by contrast that the primary defining element is the corporation itself. Location is determined not by patrician lineage, but by the individual's responsibilities in the firm and the firm's position in the economy. Coordinates for the latter include such standard dimensions as company size, market power, sector, organizational complexity, source of control, financial performance, and the like. Upper-class allegiances are largely incidental to this definition of location, for the manager is locked into corporate-determined priorities no matter what family loyalties may still be maintained. This is the point of departure, of course, for most journalists covering business, corporate self-imagery, and analysts working within the traditional organizational behavior paradigm.[27] Not only are upper-class commitments viewed as largely incidental, but loyalties to the corporate elite as a whole are taken to be faint by comparison with the manager's single-minded drive to advance the interests of his own firm ahead of those of his competitors. By implication, corporate leaders enter politics primarily to promote conditions favorable to the profitability of their own corporations. Policies designed to preserve upper-class station or the long-term collective interests of all large companies receive weak articulation at best. Capitalist competition and its political spillover might be described as one of the few remaining illustrations of Hobbes's infamous state of a war of all against all.

The *classwide principle* resides on still different premises about the main elements defining the social organization of the corporate community. In this framework, location is primarily determined by position in a set of interrelated, quasi-autonomous networks encompassing virtually all large corporations. Acquaintanceship circles, interlocking directorates, webs of interfirm ownership, and major business associations are among the central strands of these networks. Entry into the transcorporate networks is contingent on successfully reaching the executive suite of some large company, and it is further facilitated by old school ties and kindred signs of a proper breeding. But corporate credentials and upper-class origins are here subordinated to a distinct logic of classwide organization.

The relative importance of these three principles in shaping the social organizations of the business community has a major bearing on a fundamental question of corporate politics in both countries: To what extent does the corporate community formulate and promote public policies that are in accord with the broader, longer-range concerns of all large corporations? Neither the upper-class principle nor the corporate principle would suggest that the interest aggregation could be effectively achieved, for neither principle organizes company interests in a suitable fashion. The upper class may inveigh against confiscatory inheritance policies, burdensome capital-gains taxes, and state-mandated invasions of its club sanctuaries, but a positive, detailed program for economic growth and profit expansion will not be a foremost priority. Indeed, the presumed continuing supremacy of upper-class British "gentlemen" over corporate "players," even when the former have donned the hat of company manager, is an oft-used interpretation of why government policies are seemingly incapable of rescuing the British economy from increasing stagnation. The source of what American commentators have fearfully diagnosed as the "British disease" has been attributed to the fact that as "businessmen sought to act like educated gentlemen, and as educated gentlemen . . . entered business, economic behavior altered. The dedication to work, the drive for profit, and the readiness to strike out on new paths in its pursuit waned."[28]

Yet if one does not embrace this thesis, and corporate players do not aspire to be taken for upper-class gentlemen, the advance of class rationality is by no means then ensured. If corporate managers all aggressively lobby for policies most favorable to their own enterprises, uninhibited by any gentlemanly ethos, the resulting programs may serve business little better in the long run. This is because "businessmen tend to act irrationally from the point of view of the economic and political viability of the business system," in the succinct phrasing of David Vogel, since what is "rational from the perspective of the individual firm [is often] irrational from the perspective of the economic interests of business as a whole."[29] The thrust of both structuralist neo-Marxism and pluralism are surely on the mark here. The "liberation" of the general interests of business from the "fragmented, stubborn, and shortsighted empirical interests of single capital units" cannot be anticipated if business enters politics on the basis of purely corporate principles, however much these may have supplanted upper-class rationality.[30]

Classwide rationality, by contrast, should foster public policies far more coincident with the reconciled and integrated vision of most large corporations. Whatever the independent role of the government in liberating the broader needs of business from its atomized units, the extent to which corporate managers and directors are organized around the classwide principle will determine whether they can also independently contribute to the process. If some managers and directors are in a position to help appreciate and identify the public-policy issues of concern to large numbers of firms, not just those paramount to their own company, there is a kind of aggregated voice for the business community. And if they promote these concerns, both individually and through select associations, government policy-makers will hear, though of course not always heed, a point of view far more indicative of the general outlook of business than representatives of individual companies could ever provide.

Upper-class, corporate, and classwide principles of social organization distinctively shape the basic thrust of business political activity. Thus, their relative importance is of fundamental interest for comprehending contemporary corporate activity—from the orchestration of public opinion on behalf of "reindustrialization" to renewed assaults on organized labor and government regulation. The underlying theme of the present analysis is that the relative balance long ago shifted in the U.S. from upper-class to corporate principle, and that American business is currently undergoing still another transformation, this time from corporate to classwide principles of organization. By the middle of this century, family capitalism had largely given way to managerial capitalism, and in recent decades managerial capitalism itself has been giving way to institutional capitalism, bringing us into an era in which classwide principles are increasingly dominant. In the U.K., the corporate principle never quite so fully eclipsed the upper-class principle, but both logics are now yielding there as well to the rise of classwide organization within the business community. This transformation has profound implications for the power and ideology of big business in both countries, and it constitutes a central subject of this book.

CLASSWIDE CORPORATE LEADERSHIP

This study is, in part, about business leadership, but business leadership in a special and unique sense. This term conventionally refers to the role of managing a company. Business leaders are those who occupy the apex of the corporate pyramid; they have arrived there because they possess exceptional decision-making, planning, and communication skills. Our central concern here, however, is neither with how their power is obtained nor with how it is structured and exercised within the corporation. Rather, our focus is on how a leadership cadre has emerged whose powers extend far beyond the individual firm, whose responsibilities are those of managing no less than the broadest political affairs of the entire big-business community. The evident absence of any formally defined roles for the conduct of such leadership should not be taken to imply its actual absence, for informal organization has a habit of creatively achieving what formal arrangements could not produce. It is contended here that classwide informal organization—unincorporated, unnamed, and uncharted—but organization nonetheless, has indeed been formed, not through conspiratorial design but as an unintended byproduct of other forces playing themselves out.

It is this informal and thus seemingly invisible character that has made transcorporate leadership so elusive. Believing it absent but knowing it essential, observers have increasingly taken to urging a filling of the void. *Business Week*, for instance, partly attributes the alarming decline of the U.S. economy to the "tunnel vision pervading executive suites," for "today's corporate leaders are . . . business mercenaries who ply their skills for a salary and bonus but rarely for a [broader] vision."[31] Without such vision, the future of free enterprise may even be in doubt, according to an assessment of the Business Roundtable, an association of nearly two hundred chief executives of America's largest firms. "Little in [executive] education or business experience prepares them for participation in the untidy and often bruising public policy process," concludes a Roundtable committee. But the need for such experience is essential, the committee asserts and filling that void is a matter of "top priority":

> Large corporations are highly vulnerable targets for public criticism and government control. Survival in their present form will depend . . . upon the efforts of chief executive officers to make certain that their successors and the oncoming generation of executives develop the ability to participate in the public policy process and to manage the evolving role of the large corporation as effectively as executives must manage the other aspects of their work.[32]

With the assistance of the *Wall Street Journal*'s mass circulation and a little hyperbole, Herbert Stein elevates the concern to a clarion call: "Businessmen of the World Unite." More specifically, contends the former director of research for the Committee for Economic Development and a member of the Council of Economic Advisers under Presidents Nixon and Ford, a militant classwide vanguard is needed now:

> We need a businessman's liberation movement and a businessman's liberation day and a businessman's liberation rally on the monument grounds of

Washington, attended by thousands of businessmen shouting and carrying signs. We need a few businessmen to chain themselves to the White House Fence—and do it themselves, not have it done by their Washington reps.[33]

Though not sharing Mr. Stein's tactics, the business-liberation front has already taken form. An analysis of its inner structure follows.

The analysis proceeds in these steps. The economic and social foundation of the classwide principles of social organization and the formation of the inner circle are developed in Chapter 2. Of particular importance here is the continuing concentration of corporate resources and the formation of extensive transcorporate networks of ownership and shared directors. Then, in Chapter 3, we explore the special organizational features of the inner circle, including its close ties to the traditional upper class and its leadership role in the major business associations. This is followed in Chapter 4 by an examination of the inner circle's unique political role on behalf of the business community, especially in its advisory service to the national government, involvement in the governance of nonprofit organizations, support for political parties and candidates, activist use of the media for communication with the public, and the screening of business access to the highest circles of government consultation. Chapter 5 considers the reactive effect of the inner circle on corporate behavior: though rooted in large corporations, this transcorporate network has acquired an autonomy and power of its own, and it, in turn, can influence company decisions, especially those involving political outreach activities. We show that companies more tied to the transcorporate network also tend to be more socially and politically active. The decisions of companies whose top management is centrally involved in the inner circle, we find, are increasingly subject to the dual criteria of both corporate and classwide logics. The social organization of the inner circle is rooted in its corporate foundation but shaped by events beyond it, and in Chapter 6 we examine how external political pressures, particularly those coming from labor and government, and the problems of a continuing decline of company profits, have added to the cohesion and activism of the inner circle. Finally, in Chapter 7, the rise of the inner circle and classwide principles of organization are related to the broader transformations in modern business accompanying the displacement of family capitalism by managerial capitalism, and alongside the latter, the rise of institutional capitalism.

SOURCES OF INFORMATION

The complexity of the inner structure of the two corporate communities has required the synthesis of a range of evidentiary sources. For the finer texture of the political culture and social organization of the inner circle, our primary information source is a set of personal interviews with senior corporate managers in America and Britain. For illustrative material on the byways and actions of the inner circle, a wide array of documentary and business press sources are utilized. For systematic analysis of large corporations and their leadership, we rely upon four large-scale bodies of data specially assembled for this inquiry.

Interviews and Documents

Since the boundaries of the inner circle are unfixed, its rules unwritten, and its relations informal, it operates quietly and escapes notice. Systematic data sets are required to reveal the otherwise largely invisible contours of the internal social organization of business. Yet even they cannot fully capture the complex informal mores and principles of operation that structure the political work of the inner circle, and for this there could be no substitute for direct contact. To this end, I conducted personal interviews with seventy-two directors of large British companies and fifty-seven executives and directors of large American corporations. The interviews required approximately one hour on average, though they ranged in length from forty-five minutes to well over two hours. All were undertaken in London during December, 1979, and January, 1980, and in Boston and New York City during May, June, and August, 1980.

Interviews were requested with 164 British directors and 162 American directors sampled from two large-scale systematic data sets described in the next section.[34] The British and American interview samples were designed to be as parallel as possible, recognizing that the structure of top management, corporate boards, and business sectors are not identical in the two countries. Half of the directors initially approached were on the board of at least two of the corporations included in the larger samples, and the other half were matched for company sector and size but only served on a single board. An additional geographic constraint was imposed to control the high cost of personal contact: the work place of eligible British directors was limited to greater London, and the American directors were to have office locations in the metropolitan regions of Boston and New York city. Of those contacted for the interview, approximately two-thirds responded to the initial written query. Of these, 58 percent of the Americans and 61 percent of the British were interviewed, 31 percent of the Americans and 18 percent of the British declined the request, and the remainder could not be interviewed for a variety of reasons. Some had retired to residences far outside the metropolitan region, while others agreed to the interview but were traveling abroad during the period of the interviewing. For one British director, a prolonged absence from the office necessitated by the "shooting season" ultimately prevented an interview; for a second, illness and surgery led to indefinite postponement. For still another, an interview was finally completed, but only after long delay due to an extended mountaineering expedition to the Himalayas.[35]

Entry into the executive suite for the interview provided its own preliminary archaeology on the higher corporate circles. Before a single question can be asked, the itinerant observer recognizes distinct national qualities in the everyday organization of otherwise similar decision-making environments. Corporate hierarchy in the U.S. is encoded architecturally, with the chief executive's suite typically located on one of the uppermost floors of a commanding tower. Spacious windows on two sides of the corner office offer magnificent perspectives on the three-dimensional Manhattan landscape. In the U.K., such physical representation of the chain of command is less requisite, for a second- or third-floor office with no special view in the intimate maze of the "City"—the commercial district surrounding St. Paul's—quite suffices. If power is the subliminal message offered the New York visitor, class is the London ambiance. Express elevators whisk the interviewer to the upper floors for the American appointment; ancient lifts for "directors only," with room for scarcely more than two, deliver senior managers and their special guests to the third floor. The outer room in which visitors await escort into the American executive's inner office is not uncommonly adorned with the plaques and awards received as "businessman of the year" and for "outstanding service" on a range of civic associations, trade groups, and foreign governments. Alongside these plaques and awards are photographs of the principal of the company in the company of instantly recognizable political personalities, Henry Kissinger and Richard Nixon among them. The visitor to the British executive's office meets no such signposts of power. The most recent issue of *Country Life* is often all the visitor is provided to occupy the waiting moments. Tea and, as a concession to an American visitor, coffee, arrive on a silver service once the interview commences; no refreshments of any kind, save an occasional styrofoam cup of coffee, will appear during the American discussion. The difference in cultural style, trivial in itself, is indicative of the emphasis each places on symbols, whether as trappings of corporate power or quiet suggestions of upper-class tradition.

Adding to the interest and at times the substance of the study were those revealing incidents and moments that always accompany personal interviewing. One British manager arranged for the interview to be conducted in his company's comfortable and well-appointed directors' dining room, a setting whose unobstructed view of the outdoor sculpture at the Tate Gallery, the flow of the Thames, and the classic London skyline made for momentary distraction of the first-time guest. The four-course serving had opened with port and paté and would close with quality cigars, Cuban included. It required two and a half hours to complete and four staff members to serve, and one could not but wonder about the managerial efficiency that must have later compensated for such lengthy noon-time interludes. The conditions made for an unusually expansive discussion. The tape recorder placed near the center of the table, unfortunately, proved more effective at recording the movement of silverware than the passage of conversation. Another British executive, a managing director of a very large firm with global operations, offered a glimpse of how managers can make up for the generous time so often invested in the business luncheon. He left his home soon after 5 A.M. every business day; while his driver negotiated the two-hour trip into London, he negotiated the company's business from the desk and telephone in the back seat of the company Rolls Royce, taking advantage of the early hours to talk with his African and Asian plant managers, who were already well into their work day.

One of the lighter moments occurred when I arrived on the executive floor of one of America's leading airlines. Muffled laughter seemed to emanate from several directions at once. The public-affairs director who was accompanying me to the interview with the airline's president inquired about the unusual ambiance on this normally very subdued floor. He learned that the chairman of the board had just arrived from Kennedy International airport in a grim mood. He had been a passenger on one of his airline's widebodied flights across the Atlantic. Also on board this fully booked flight were some one thousand laboratory mice. Their crate had been damaged in loading, but the European groundcrew felt that its taping of the fractured section would surely suffice. It did until high over the Atlantic. There the freezing temperatures in the cargo hold sent the mice scurrying for the warmth of the passenger cabin, the tape presenting only a momentary barrier. In the pandemonium following the sudden eruption of a thousand mice into the passenger cabin, the chairman is said to have found reason to sink low in his seat and to doze for the remainder of the trip. The executive staff appeared to be relishing the story, but the same could not be said for the man whom I had come to interview and who reported directly to the chairman. As the president sat in his office during the interview that afternoon, behind a desk dominated by half a dozen giant models of his air fleet, he seemed preoccupied by even more than the fact that his company was operating deeply in the red.

There were also moments when the validity of the entire enterprise seemed in doubt. On several occasions, as I was departing from the office of one executive, an executive of another company whom I had already interviewed was arriving. This was of some substantive interest since it suggested the small world in which members of the inner circle traveled. But in one instance even more was learned. A British director had accompanied me to the elevator, and just as we arrived a previously interviewed director stepped out. The visiting director chuckled to himself and warned me that the man I had just spent an hour with was wholly unreliable and that I should not believe a word he said. The latter director responded that the cautionary advice was entirely warranted, if applied to the former. Both went off agreeing that they had probably contradicted each other on all major points.

For additional background information, informal interviews were also conducted with several dozen well-placed, informed observers. Included in these British discussions were an executive with the London office of an American oil company, the public-affairs directors of two large manufacturers, a former director of one of the key nationalized industries, a top official of the Confederation of British Industry (the major association of British business), the executive director of a large trade association, and one of the Conservative government's current ministers, whose contact with business was extensive. Included in the background interviews in the U.S. were several senior executives who consented to discussions of great length, a financial journalist, the community-affairs director of a large company, staff members of the Business Committee for the Arts and the Business Roundtable (a key association of American business), and the staff of several organizations devoted to research on business.

Complementing the interviews in both countries is a wide assemblage of documents that capture still other facets of these worlds. Among the most valuable are reports and studies, many unpublished, that were obtained through direct contact with such organizations as the Business Roundtable and the Confederation of British Industry; studies produced by organizations that service business, such as the Conference Board in New York, or that service unions, such as Labour Research in London; and, of course, the business press, especially the *Financial Times* of London and the *Wall Street Journal*. Finally, other analytic studies of corporations and corporate managers, now increasingly available because of a revival of research interest in both countries, provide still other elements on which the overall portrait is constructed.

Information on Corporations and Their Managers and Directors

Four systematic bodies of data on large American and British firms and their managers and directors have also been analyzed as part of this inquiry. They are briefly described here.

(*1*) *American Corporate Executives and Directors and Their Firms.* The first systematic source of information consists of 3,105 senior executives and directors of 212 of the largest American corporations. These companies were selected for intensive examination according to their sector and size at the end of 1977. The annual *Fortune* magazine compilation of America's largest companies was used to identify the firms.[36] The sampled companies included manufacturing firms ranked 1 to 60 and 451 to 500 according to their sales volume; commercial banks numbered 1 to 25 and 41 to 50, insurance companies from 1 to 15 and 41 to 50, diversified financial firms numbered 1 to 10 and 41 to 50, utilities numbered 1 to 5, all by assets; retail firms ranked 1 to 5 by sales; and transportation companies from 1 to 5 by operating revenue. Six to eight of the senior-most officers and ten of the nonexecutive directors for each company were selected for detailed study, yielding a total of 3,105 executives and directors, or about 14 per company.[37]

More than fifty sources were scoured to gather information on the careers, intercorporate connections, and political activity of the executives and directors. In addition to the usual biographical references,[38] our sources included annual company reports, alumni directories for elite preparatory schools and universities, compendia of philanthropic-foundation trustees, lists of presidential campaign contributors, business-association rosters, and media indexes. Approximately forty other sources yielded information on the 212 corporations; in addition to the usual economic measures, these references provided data on a range of noneconomic features, including philanthropic contributions, investments in South Africa, illegal and questionable corporate payments, support for electoral referenda, and directorship links with other corporations.[39]

(*2*) *British Corporate Executives and Directors and Their Firms.* Paralleling this American data set is a range of information assembled for 1,972 directors of 196 large British companies. From the standard sectoral rankings of the largest U.K. firms prepared by the London *Times* for 1977, a set of companies was drawn as similar as possible in size and sector to the American corporations, though precise comparability could not be achieved because of the differing structures of the two economies. The 25 largest American commercial banks out of several thousand, for instance, are included in the study, but the consolidation of British banking over the past century has resulted in the survival of only seven separate clearing banks. We selected the 60 largest manufacturing companies, 50 somewhat smaller manufacturers appearing in the middle range of the top 1,000 list, the 7 clearing banks, the 23 largest life insurance companies, the 15 largest accepting houses (merchant or investment banks), the 11 largest discount houses, 10 large investment trusts, 10 large real estate companies, the 5 largest retail firms, and the 5 largest finance houses.[40] These 196 corporations are a reasonably representative set of the largest British-owned firms spanning all major sectors of industrial and commercial activity.[41]

A total of 2,211 board positions were associated with the 196 corporations, though 418 of the directors serve on two or more of the boards simultaneously and, thus, the seats were filled by only 1,972 individuals. Merchant banker Philip Shelbourne, then chairman and chief executive of the fourth largest accepting house, Samuel Montague & Co., bears the singular distinction of serving on no less than six: in addition to his own company, he is a director of Allied Breweries (30th largest manufacturer), Dunlop Holdings (16th largest industrial), Eagle Star Insurance Company (8th in insurance), English Property Company (number 1 in property), and Midland Bank (the 4th largest clearing bank). Like Mr. Shelbourne, virtually all the directors are top managers of at least one large company.[42] Examined in another way, two-thirds of the directors on the typical company board are themselves also the senior management of the same company. To obtain information on the directors' careers, intercompany ties, and political activity, we consulted nearly twenty separate sources, including *Who's Who, Who's Who in Finance, Directory of Directors,* company annual reports, records maintained by the British Institute of Management and Confederation of British Industry, and a roster of the trustees of grant-making trusts. Some fifteen additional sources provided information on both the economic and noneconomic characteristics of the 196 companies.[43]

(3) *U.S. Corporate Directors in 1969.* To untangle the temporal sequencing of certain events in corporate managers' careers, it will also prove useful to have a set of directors on whom longitudinal information is available. Accordingly, we have included a special set of American business leaders who were directors of America's 797 largest corporations in 1969. The largest firms are those identified by the standard annual ranking compiled by *Fortune* magazine.[44] Companies were ranked for 1969 in seven general groups: 500 largest industrials and 50 largest retail corporations ordered by sales; 50 largest commercial banks, 50 largest life insurance companies, and 50 largest utilities ranked by assets; 50 largest transportation companies ranked by operating revenues, and 47 other large firms not readily classed with the previous groups. Investment banks and privately held firms are not included on the list, but otherwise the compilation is a reasonably complete roster of the largest U.S. companies. Two or more of the directorships of these companies were simultaneously occupied by

1,570 individuals; 61 percent served on two boards, 22 percent occupied three, and 17 percent held four or more directorships. These multiple directors are selected for intensive study, and, for comparative purposes, a one-in-twenty sample (433 individuals) of the remaining 6,053 directors of only a single firm is included as well.[45] Information on the outreach of these 2,000 corporate directors is obtained from the standard biographical reference source, a directory of members of national government advisory committees and original membership lists for a number of major business associations and exclusive metropolitan clubs.[46]

(4) *American Corporate Executives and Directors Who Serve as University Trustees.* The involvement of corporate leadership in the affairs of nonprofit organizations constitutes a seldom acknowledged but highly important part of business's political outreach. The programs of universities, arts organizations, medical centers, and civic institutions can have a critical bearing on the business climate. The technology of many companies, for instance, is advanced by university-based research, and business depends on a supply of well-trained university graduates for its technical labor force.[47] Moreover, the public image and legitimacy of private enterprise can be significantly shaped by what students learn in the classroom. Efforts by corporate managers to shape university policies, through service on a university governing or advisory board, should thus be viewed as one element of a broader company strategy to better shape its environment. The absence of sufficient detail on this activity in the other data sets dictated the inclusion of one additional representative sample of business leaders—those who are involved in the governance of higher education in the U.S. In 1968 a survey was conducted of more than 5,000 trustees of a cross-section of American colleges and universities; because business executives are frequently sought for university governing boards, a large number of these trustees—1,307—are executives or directors of large corporations. The survey itself yielded extensive information on the trustees' corporate connections, educational philosophies, fund-raising activities, and influence on the policies of their universities. To this has been added extensive information on the characteristics of the institutions themselves, including the social composition of the student bodies, alumni success in corporate careers, and contributions received from business.[48]

TWO

The Economic and Social Foundation

Corporate Ownership, Concentration, and Interlocking Directorship

Classwide business organizing has, in the first instance, been made possible by the rise of a favorable economic infrastructure. Both America's and Britain's economies are increasingly dominated by a relatively small number of large companies linked in inclusive and diffusely structured networks.[1] Inclusive refers to the fact that most large companies are now joined into the networks, and diffuse signifies that the network ties are spread widely rather than localized within small cliques. The fact that there are comparatively few corporate units, each united by numerous strands of interdependency enhances the evolution of a common political culture and social organization among those who manage the companies and who enter into politics on their behalf. A foundation is thereby provided for a group of business leaders whose vision can transcend the parochial concerns of their own companies and even of their own industries.

Before turning to this transcorporate infrastructure, it is important to identify the central interests of the corporations that support it. It has long been argued that large publicly owned corporations have ceased to enshrine the growth of company profits as their overriding objective. Senior managers of these firms are no longer disciplined, this thesis suggests, by the same profit imperatives that had so narrowly directed the founding entrepreneurs. By implication, corporate leadership is now better characterized as managerial than entrepreneurial. The distinction is far more than semantic, for the political role of the former would be radically different from that of the latter. Unlike the founding entrepreneur's unswerving commitment to growth in company profits, management's political objectives, dictated by company priorities, would be based on a mix of objectives that includes more than profitability: perhaps company growth or bureaucratic efficiency, maybe employee welfare or the public interest, or possibly just "getting by," depending on the particular brand of revisionist thought.[2] If short- and long-term profitability are now subordinate to one or another of the alternative priorities, the main directions of corporate politics would be as transformed as the control of the corporation itself.

A number of studies on this question in both America and Britain are fortunately now available, and their conclusions all point toward a business community that is as centrally concerned with profit growth as ever. Company management is obviously far more complexly organized now than was the management that once guided the formation of the modern corporation half a century ago. Still, when the leading edge of this group enters politics, it does so primarily on behalf of entrepreneurial, not managerial interests.

THE SEPARATION OF OWNERSHIP AND CONTROL

Most research on this issue has been framed by the debate over whether a fundamental separation of ownership and control has occurred in large companies. Adolf Berle and Gardiner Means' 1932 landmark study, *The Modern Corporation and Private Property*, established the main themes of a dispute that has continued with virtually undiminished vigor for half a century. They correctly asserted that corporate leadership had become divided into the two distinct wings of owners and managers. By definition of their relationship to the corporation, owners placed primary emphasis on the profit criterion in business decision-making, but their actual control over the decisions of the large corporation was gradually but inexorably passing into the hands of the nonowning professional managers who ran the firm on a day-to-day basis. This quiet managerial coup could be traced to both the growth and dispersion of corporate stock. When few owners held all or most of a corporation's stock, they readily dominated its board of directors, which in turn selected top management and ran the corporation. Now that a firm's stock was dispersed among many unrelated owners, each holding a tiny fraction of the total equity, the resulting power vacuum allowed management to select the board of directors; thus management became self-perpetuating and thereby acquired de facto control over the corporation. In the summary line of Berle and Means, "ownership of wealth without appreciable control and control of wealth without appreciable ownership appear to be the logical outcome of corporate development."[3]

To this transfer of power, other analysts have added the proposition that the interests of the managers differ in kind from those of the owners. The nonowning managers are presumed to have noncapitalist interests, or "utility functions," ranging from stable growth of the firm to technical efficiency and "soulful" protection of the public interest.[4] Indicative of the conclusions reached by many, Talcott Parsons, for years one of the deans of contemporary social theory, positioned his analysis of American society on what he perceived to be one of the fundamental transformations of the twentieth century: the "basic phenomenon" he writes, "seems to have been the shift in *control* of enterprise from the property interests of founding families to managerial and technical personnel who as such have not had a comparable vested interest in ownership."[5] Management no longer seeks simply to ensure the owners a high return on their investment, for now, according to another prominent analyst, economist Carl Kaysen, "management sees itself as responsible to stockholders, employees, customers, the general public, and perhaps most important, the firm itself as an institution."[6] Thus, those who manage the affairs of large companies are no longer motivated to act solely as capitalist owners. The owners themselves have been transformed into passive investors whose fragmented influence on corporate policies is minor if not negligible. In other words, writes Parsons, "we can clearly no longer speak of a 'capitalistic' propertied class."[7]

This characterization of corporate management had become so accepted as to constitute a pillar of the conventional wisdom of the social sciences, an axiom of scholarly, textbook, and popular writing alike. Re-publication of the Berle and Means book on the subject in 1967, more than a third of a century after its first appearance, provided the occasion for Gardiner Means to elevate their postulate to a theorem of contemporary thought: "The fact of the corporate revolution is now so widely accepted that statistical evidence is no longer needed to establish its occurrence."[8] The emergence of "postcapitalist" industrial organization implied a corresponding appearance of postcapitalist business politics as well. John Kenneth Galbraith, whose accessible books have widely shaped popular economic thinking, adopted this logic as a foundation of his own thesis on the rise of what he called the new industrial state. "The decisive power in modern industrial society," he finds, "is exercised not by capital but by organization, not by the capitalist but by the industrial bureaucrat."[9] Though not always accompanied by all the corollaries, the central assumption of a managerial triumph has come frequently to color official thought as well. An extensive report on British financial institutions, commissioned by the prime minister and issued in 1980, exemplifies the idea's official acceptance: "The wide dispersal of shareholding in the UK, and the increasing complexity of decision-taking," the report asserts, "has in the past given many managements a substantial degree of independence from outside control."[10]

Despite the widespread acceptance of the managerial-revolution thesis, and despite Gardiner Means' denial of the need for, if not of the value of, further "statistical evidence" for it, the thesis has remained a subject of continuing inquiry by a number of scholars. Their studies have generally focused on three central tenets of the thesis. The first is that the largest corporations are now more often than not controlled by managers, not owners; the second is that managerial incentive systems are more closely tuned to criteria other than company profitability; and the third is that, as a result of the first and second changes, most large firms are now oriented toward objectives beyond strict profit maximization. While the now considerable evidence supports the first tenet for the U.S., the results are mixed on the first tenet for the U.K. and they lead to the rejection of the latter two tenets for both countries. We will examine the evidence on each of these in turn.

The Proportion of Managerially Controlled Large Corporations

The separation of ownership from control is theorized to be most advanced in the largest corporations, where stock dispersion is presumably greatest. At least thirteen American studies conducted over a period of nearly fifty years are available on the control of large firms; they generally concentrate on the 100 to 500 largest nonfinancial companies. In part, because the results are highly sensitive to the methods of firm classification—and the methods do vary considerably from study to study—the research has produced little agreement on the proportion of firms now in the hands of management. One study concluded that some three-fifths of the companies are still closely owner controlled; three studies find that clear ownership interests can be found in only one-fifth to one-half of the largest firms; seven studies report evidence that one-fifth to one-half of the companies are management dominated; and three studies conclude that two-thirds or more of the largest firms are management controlled.[11] The most recent and most comprehensive study, by economist Edward Herman, however, finds that more than four-fifths of the largest 200 nonfinancial corporations were under management control by 1974 (up from the 24 percent of a comparable set of firms under management control in 1900 and 41 percent in 1929).[12] A cautious conclusion, based on the studies prior to Herman's, is that at least one-fifth and perhaps half of the largest American corporations are clearly controlled by inside management. Herman's findings are persuasive, however, and a final conclusion is that the great majority of large U.S. firms are now in the hands of professional management.

The proportion of British companies dominated by management appears still to be a minority, according to parallel inquiries there. The most recent study of the largest 250 U.K. manufacturing companies in 1975, for instance, yields the conclusion that slightly more than half are still under proprietary control, and just under half under management control.[13]

The Ownership Incentives of Managers

That managerial control has arrived in many companies is certain, even if this transformation of control is less complete than some proponents of the managerial-revolution thesis would have preferred. Yet whatever the fraction of firms unambiguously now under the decisive guidance of inside officers, the question remains whether the presumed autonomy of the officers in insider-controlled firms permits them to deemphasize the search for profits in favor of satisfying other measures of company performance instead. A careful reading of the evidence on this question reveals that such deemphasis of profits is not prevalent.

First of all, managers themselves hold large quantities of stock in their own companies. In 1974, for instance, the median value of company shares held by officer-directors of the 100 largest U.S. manufacturing companies exceeded $900,000.[14] Most managers own only a tiny fraction of their company's shares, but in terms of the individual manager's portfolio the investment is very large. Such investment is deliberately encouraged by a variety of company policies. Most large American companies, for instance, maintain stock-option plans, which allow senior executives to acquire company shares at prices below market value.[15] These plans, year-end bonuses, and other schemes within which compensation to the manager depends on the firm's profits, ensure that a significant proportion of the managers' total income derives from serving an ownership-oriented interest in the company. Further, by one estimate, the proportion of managers deriving significant parts of their incomes from their ownership roles is very high: a study of the remuneration of the top executives of fifty large American manufacturing enterprises during the early 1960s reveals that their after-tax incomes from stock-based compensation schemes, capital gains, and stock dividends were six times as large as their salaries. Thus, the investigator concludes, "the observably high degree of separation of ownership and management *roles* in the modern corporation has not been accompanied by a significant separation of their respective *self-interests*."[16]

Second, as should follow from this managerial income pattern, total after-tax income is found to be more dependent upon the firm's profit rate than its growth rate, scale of operations, or other plausible determinants. It has been suggested by some analysts, for instance, that executives' salaries are more closely linked to company sales than to profitability, and the results of several American studies would appear to confirm this thesis.[17] These investigations, however, use pre-tax salary as the income measure, and they exclude compensation from stock options, dividends, and capital gains—all forms of ownership-based income known to comprise more than half of most managers' total income. Studies that have included more precise measures of true income yield the contrary conclusion, that, in the words of one analyst, "profits still appear to be the key variable determining the level of executive remuneration in large corporations."[18] Thus, to the extent that financial compensation acts as an incentive in corporate decision-making, the manager is strongly encouraged to make corporate decisions as if he were an owner.

Third, research has also shown that the ultimate form of negative incentive—dismissal—is itself predicated on criteria directly tied to firm profitability. If manager-controlled firms are less profit constrained than owner-controlled firms, as is postulated by proponents of the managerial-revolution thesis, then downturns in profits among the manager-controlled companies should less often result in removal of top executives than among the owner-controlled firms. Owners unhappy with the declining profits of the companies they control should presumably quickly intervene to install new leadership. Manager-controlled companies, by contrast, should less swiftly act to axe their own to restore high profit margins. Yet a study of involuntary turnover in the presidency and board chairmanship of 300 large American industrial corporations over a two-year period in the mid-1970s reveals no such difference. A decline in profits during the preceding several years is found to be a strong predictor of which firms dismiss their top management, but it is no less a determinant in manager- than owner-controlled firms.[19]

There is some evidence that managers may be even more profit disciplined than owners. In a comparison of chief executive officers of large American corporations who hold very large blocks of stock and those who are without sizable investments, the nonowning managers are found to be more promptly replaced during a period of profit decline than are the owner-managers.[20] Furthermore, according to other research, dislodged managers have not simply been made the scapegoats for conditions beyond their control. In examining the immediate and delayed effects of changes in the president or board chairman of 167 large American corporations during a recent twenty-year period, two analysts concluded that the impact of changes in top management on the companies' profit margins was substantial, even taking into account fluctuating economic conditions; and, the impact of introducing a new management team following a top dismissal was far greater on profits than on company sales.[21]

Corroborative evidence comes from an intense study of the directors of nineteen large British companies; information was acquired by interviewing directors, through informal discussions with groups of directors, and by direct observation of each director's work. The investigators, Ray Pahl and Jack Winkler, conclude that, if anything, the professional manager "represents a return to the values of hard, unameliorated, unconstrained capitalism." Moreover, the "professionals' orientation to profit was not only explicitly recognized by the family owners and the new, employed managers themselves, but both expected the managers to be *more* profit conscious."[22]

Claims of distinct managerial and proprietary corporate goals are further contradicted by direct study of the managers' own definitions of their priorities. Nearly 190 senior executives and directors of eighteen large U.K. firms were interviewed during the mid-1970s, in a study by Arthur Francis, and they were asked to identify the primary objectives of their own firms. The two priorities receiving highest overall ratings were those of "maximizing growth of total profits" and "maximizing rate of return on capital"; ranked far below in importance were maximizing growth in sales, growth in assets, and other objectives, including the "provision of service to the community at large." Moreover, when forced to make a choice between these various competing objectives, the managers generally report that their company would stress growth in total profits over growth in sales or assets.[23] Similarly, drawing on their extensive observations of private, informal discussions among American industrial executives, two investigators discern little inclination to reorient large corporations to serve interests other than those of stockholders.[24]

If public speeches by corporate executives can serve as an imperfect but indicative measure of how this issue is treated when corporate leaders enter the political domain, the sanctity of profits would appear to remain unquestioned. From a study of the lectures of U.S. executives over a forty-year period, one analyst concluded that the nonowning managers are "mystified" by the thesis of the managerial revolution, and there is a prevailing belief that "professional management acts just as the owner-entrepreneur did, that is, in the best interests of the owners."[25] Still another investigator compared the content of speeches by top officers of large American corporations under the two major forms of control, and he concluded that "managerial-controlled firms develop and express the same ideologies as owner-controlled corporations" on the question of profits versus more soulful behavior. A comparatively low stress on corporate priorities other than return on investment characterizes the speeches of executives of all companies, regardless of the locus of control.[26]

Corporate Behavior

The thesis that the managerial revolution has led to the creation of a new set of missions for large corporations receives definitive rejection from studies of the financial performance of the corporations themselves. If manager-controlled firms are, indeed, freed in part from the profit discipline of ownership control, manager-controlled companies should be observed to report lower average profitability rates than matched sets of owner-dominated firms.

Four American studies do in fact report statistically significant, though substantively modest, differences in the predicted direction.[27] One inquiry, for instance, reports that manager-controlled firms are approximately one-fifth less profitable than owner-controlled firms.[28] Ten other U.S. studies and two U.K. studies, however, find no significant differences.[29] One additional U.S. investigation finds that the expected difference does occur but only among firms with a high degree of market power. This result is consistent with a plausible extension of the managerial-revolution thesis: the latitude of the management-controlled firms to avoid strict profit discipline should be possible only when they are somewhat shielded from the strictures of a highly competitive market. Even this extension does not find consistent corroboration, however, for another analysis, using an improved measure of corporate control, revealed no substantial difference in profit rates even among those firms operating in highly concentrated markets.[30] A proponent of the managerial-revolution thesis might still contend with a modicum of persuasiveness that expected differences might yet be found in nonfinancial areas of corporate behavior. Manager-controlled firms, even without cutting into their profits, might be more responsive to the demands of constituencies other than stockholders. Compared with owner-controlled firms, they might tend to maintain safer and more healthful conditions for their employees, operate their plants in ways less damaging to the environment, take greater care to protect consumers against faulty and unsafe products, and contribute more money to charitable purposes. Studies of these elements of corporate behavior as a function of the type of corporate control are, regrettably, not available. Still, since the results of the many studies of the area where the greatest difference is expected—financial performance—are so negative, it can be inferred with some confidence that little significant difference in nonfinancial areas of corporate behavior are likely to exist.

The empirically founded conclusion that the displacement of owners by professional managers has not displaced the importance of profits in company decision-making is of fundamental importance for understanding business politics. A long-held assumption, derived from the managerial-revolution thesis, contained an implicit image of a political process largely devoid of capitalist, though certainly not bureaucratic, pressures; "the decisive power in modern industrial society," Galbraith asserted, is exercised "not by the capitalist but by the industrial bureaucrat."[31] Control systems today are vastly more differentiated and complex than in the era when entrepreneurs held direct command over the enterprises they had created and still owned. Yet the central criterion of these systems is largely unchanged. The "triumph of management control in many large corporations has not left them in the hands of neutral technocrats," concludes Edward Herman in the most exhaustive recent study of the subject. "The control group of these organizations seem as devoted to profitable growth as are the leaders of entrepreneurial and owner-dominated companies, past and present."[32] When corporations and company managers enter the political process, therefore, it is fair to infer that among their overriding concerns is a search for public policies favorable to profitable growth. This conclusion about the central thrust of business politics resides on a deduction from largely nonpolitical evidence, and its foundation would be stronger were more direct evidence available. Still, the inference is drawn from a sufficiently solid data base that it can be embraced with considerable confidence.

It must be kept in mind, however, that the preeminence of the profit criterion in corporate decision-making in Britain and America is based on a calculus located at the level of the individual firm. Aggregation of the single firm's resulting perspectives on matters political can be achieved according to both corporate and classwide principles, and their relative importance has a critical bearing on the public policies sought. Policies favorable for a firm's profitability are often not the same as those favorable for collective profitability. The evidence that follows indicates that in both the U.S. and the U.K., the classwide principles are increasingly ascendent.

ECONOMIC FOUNDATION: THE CONCENTRATION OF CORPORATE RESOURCES

Comparatively few corporate units enhance the evolution of a common culture and organization among those directing corporate activities. Coordinated and self-conscious political action is by no means assured, but the concentration of more economic activity in fewer hands should facilitate the formation of networks of communication and action among those whose decisions count. The inexorable trend in both Britain and America has been for fewer companies to orchestrate ever-greater shares of total economic activity, even as the economies have vastly expanded.

In 1909, the 100 largest British manufacturers accounted for only 15 percent of the net output of all such companies, but the fraction steadily climbs to 23 percent by 1939, 33 percent by 1958, and 45 percent by 1970.[33] Even greater concentration is apparent if net assets are considered instead: the share of all quoted (publicly traded) companies' assets held by the 100 largest quoted British firms stood at 47 percent in 1948 but had reached 68 percent only two decades later.[34] Financial concentration is even more advanced. The commercial banking sector has undergone vast consolidation, with just four London clearing banks—Barclays, Lloyds, Midland, and National Westminster—now accounting for virtually all retail banking in the country. These four banks alone are responsible for nearly half of all employment in the entire financial sector.[35]

Though there is still less overall concentration, American companies are following much the same path.[36] The share of total manufacturing assets held by the 200 largest manufacturing firms has been increasing by approximately 0.5 percent per year since the turn of the century, and there is no sign of any slackening of the pace in recent decades. The top 200 are now in control of approximately three-fifths of all manufacturing assets.[37] Other measures of corporate concentration evidence similar trends: the 750 largest U.S. firms, industry and finance included, accounted for 39.7 percent of private-sector employment in 1955, but 50.5 percent in 1965 and 55.3 percent in 1974.[38] The progressive overall concentration of the economy is not matched by a corresponding trend in many areas of manufacturing. Indeed, there is no intensification of concentration in most sectors. The explanation for these seemingly inconsistent trends lies in the diversification of large firms: in the past, the top corporations in a sector confined their products to that one sector; now, the dominant firms in one sector are often the leading firms in several other sectors as well.[39] In some product areas, notably automotive manufacturing, the rise of foreign competition is leading to some deconcentration. Foreign multinational firms, however, are relatively less active in American politics than are domestic manufacturers. Their intrusion into the U.S. market thus does not significantly alter the conclusion that there are fewer important political actors in the American business community now than in the past.

Finance is still far less concentrated than in the U.K., but U.S. banking activity is also in the control of ever-fewer hands: the 200 largest financial institutions now account for over half of all financial activity.[40] Indicative of the overall level of concentration and the opportunities it can present for political coordination, a single business association with fewer than 200 members—the Business Roundtable—brings together those who are responsible for corporate decisions affecting a vast portion of the economy. The 196 chief executive officers who participate in Roundtable deliberations on public policy are collectively responsible for making decisions for firms whose annual revenues are in the aggregate equivalent to nearly half of U.S. gross national product.[41]

Thus, the great bulk of the private economy in both countries is now overseen by managers and directors of fewer than a thousand large companies. And the trends suggest even fewer hands in the future. In one whimsical extrapolation, the managing editor of *Fortune* is foreseen to have quietly decided in 1998 to still retain the famous "Fortune 500" appellation for a list for which only 479 corporations could by then be found. Even L. L. Bean and *The New Yorker*, companies whose extraordinary growth might otherwise have provided the editor with at least two entries to help complete her 500 list, had already been long absorbed by MCA, a *Fortune* 479 firm that by then had acquired a virtual monopoly on entertainment in America. The authors of the British *Times 1000* might well be faced by the same dilemma in 1998, though even some two decades earlier the extreme concentration in British banking had already negated any possibility of paralleling the somewhat lesser known "Fortune 50's," the listings of the fifty largest U.S. companies in commercial banking and other nonindustrial sectors. Only seven U.K. clearing banks could be found by 1983, and insurance had already become so consolidated that it made little sense to list more than the top 25.

Accompanying concentration, particularly in recent years, has been product diversification, paced by the so-called conglomerates but pursued to varying degrees by most large firms as well. Not only are large enterprises in control of a dominant and still-expanding share of all economic activity, but most are also increasingly familiar with a range of disparate market conditions, labor forces, and business climates. The extent of this diversification is illustrated by changes in a sample of more than 270 *Fortune* 500 firms between 1949 and 1974. By one accounting scheme, the percentage of companies in a single line of business declined from forty-two to fourteen. Conversely, the percentage of corporations involved in several related or unrelated lines of manufacturing grew over the same period from thirty to sixty-three. Only one-in-twenty of the companies could be considered conglomerates in 1949; one-in-four could be so classified by 1974.[43]

At the same time, networks of economic relations among the largest firms are becoming more inclusive. Among the most significant trends is the rise of intercorporate ownership. Once again the U.K. is ahead of the U.S., but the developments are very much the same. The proportion of the market value of U.K. company stock held by financial institutions, the primary source of intercorporate ownership, stood at 21 percent in 1957 for ordinary shares and 36 percent for preference shares. But individual shareholding is being rapidly displaced by company holding in the years since, with financial institutions' share rising to 33 and 59 percent for the two types of shares by 1967, and to 50 and 76 percent by 1978. Over the same period, ordinary shares held by persons declined from 66 to 32 percent.[44] The analogous figures for U.S. holdings, in this case for the share of all outstanding corporate shares owned by financial institutions, are 23 percent for 1958, 24 percent for 1968, and 33 percent for 1974.[45] Although corporate shareholding in American companies is still a minority in the aggregate, the high degree of concentration of corporate investments has meant that the dominant stockholders of most large companies are other, primarily financial, corporations. Typical of the present-day ownership profile is that of Mobil Oil Corporation, the fourth largest American industrial firm. Of the top ten shareholders in 1973, possessing in the aggregate some 20 percent of the voting rights for Mobil, nine are other corporations; all but one are banks or insurance companies. Included among Mobil's ten largest shareholders are Bankers Trust, Morgan Guaranty Trust, Chase Manhattan Bank, Northern Natural Gas Company, and Prudential Insurance. Only a single noncorporate owner is present among the top ten owners—the Rockefeller family interests, represented via several Rockefeller foundations and Rockefeller University.[46] This transformation in stockholder composition is repeated in the shareholder profile of virtually all major firms.[47] The proverbial orphans and the widows have largely given way to the institutions.

Patterns of intercorporate ownership have received extensive attention in connection with the question of bank influence over industrial corporations.[48] Yet despite the rapid expansion of intercorporate shareholding in recent years, no systematic evaluation of the overall configuration has been undertaken in either country. Even brief examination of ownership profiles, however, suggests the hypothesis that the intercorporate ownership network now embraces nearly all large companies, and it is little based on purely particularistic ties between pairs or small cliques of firms. Some intercorporate ownership does reflect an interest on the part of one corporation in pressuring, co-opting, controlling, or even acquiring another company or set of firms. But the bulk of such shareholding is the product of investment strategies that treat large blocs of companies as largely equivalent; the acquisition of stock in one enterprise rather than another is most typically the product of a return-on-investment decision rather than an effort by the investing company to secure the services or the control of the other firm. Institutional investors usually favor the rule of selling shares rather than pressuring management when they become unhappy with a company's performance. In other words, they attach far greater importance to the welfare of their own funds than to the well-being of any company in which the funds may be momentarily placed.[49] The "Wall Street Rule" prevails: if a company in which an investment is held becomes troublesome, exercise neither voice nor loyalty, but quick exit.

The spread and structure of the intercorporate network of ownership, in short, is both inclusive and diffuse. The spread of this network in the past few decades has created a context in which decisions taken by one large company are necessarily of increasing concern to many other large corporations. The same is true for political factors that may retard the growth of company profits. Corporations not directly affected by a problem confronting a single firm or sector nonetheless may have their own prospects dimmed by virtue of the indirect dependency. Political challenges to one become, in attenuated but real ways, of concern to all.

SOCIAL FOUNDATION: THE INTERLOCKING DIRECTORATE

To the economic foundation for a classwide aggregation of corporate interests is added a distinct social foundation. Its logic is related, but not reducible, to the economic foundation. Probably the most important single element, and certainly the most prominent one, is the network of shared company directorships, often called the "interlocking directorate." This network is constituted of those company directors who simultaneously serve on the boards of two or more large companies. Three qualities of the interlocking directorate in both America and Britain make it a particularly effective informal organizational vehicle for the aggregation of pan-corporate political concerns. First, the bulk of its members are fulltime senior managers of large corporations; second, the network encompasses nearly all important companies; and, third, the links are dispersed in a fashion favorable to classwide integration.

Multiple Directors Are Senior Managers

The interlocking directorate is, first of all, a network whose members are deeply rooted in the concrete practice of running big business. Though a few attorneys, university presidents, retired civil servants, foundation officials, titled nobility, and even church ministers appear on corporate boards, each represents little more than a token presence. The addition of the president of the United Auto Workers' union, Douglas Fraser, to the board of Chrysler Corporation in 1980, is one of those exceptions without precedent whose special prominence has only served to reaffirm the rule.[50] For most board positions, corporations seek individuals who can offer information and advice drawn from their own direct experience in managing a large organization. Though preferably this would be another business firm, it need not always be; running a university or a foundation can provide a nearly equivalent base. Two American chairmen whom I interviewed had only entered business after distinguished academic careers that had culminated in university presidencies. Both individuals observed that overseeing a large corporation had more similarities with, than differences from, running a university. Still, managing a large corporation is considered the quintessential prerequisite for effective contribution to a board. This principle is illustrated by the experience of outside directors once they have retired from their managerial position. Unless they remain active in business in other ways or bring unique qualities to the board, they are often quietly dropped from their nonexecutive directorships. Extensive but dated experience offers no certain protection, nor does family wealth or social prominence. In one case, for example, an outside director of an American insurance company lost his presidency of a retail company when it was acquired by another firm. One of his colleagues on the insurance board describes the consequences:

> The president suddenly was without a job; he devoted his time to working with the local art museum, but he didn't keep up with the business community because he hadn't any base. He was dethroned by a takeover. We tolerated that for about a year on the [insurance] board. Then the nominating committee, all outside directors, came up with nominations. We said, John has gone into working with the arts, he's got money, he's not tuned in. His being on the board does not add anything. There is nothing wrong with his morals, his ethics, but he is no resource to the board. There is no point in sitting with him. He's using the board rather than bringing something to the board.

Despite a record of longstanding service to the board, and a social prominence bred of old wealth, he was not renominated.

Systematic figures bear out this preference. Approximately two-thirds to three-quarters of what are referred to in the U.S. as outside directors—and in the U.K. as nonexecutive directors—are themselves top-ranked officers of still other large companies. A sample survey of outside directors for Fortune 500 firms in 1977, for instance, finds that half are president, chairman, or chief executive officer of their own companies.[51] Half of the outside directors elected to major U.S. boards in 1978, according to another study, also hold one of these three positions; of the remainder, 7 percent are with law firms, 10 percent are educators, and 14 percent find employment in other noncorporate settings.[52] Similarly, our own analysis of the main positions of the directors of the 797 largest corporations in 1969 reveals that more than three-quarters are executives of a business firm, and half are senior managers of one of the 797 top corporations themselves.[53] A comparable employment profile characterizes the directors of the 196 large British firms selected for examination as part of this study: of those directors who constitute the interlocking directorate—defined here to consist of those who serve on the boards of two or more large enterprises—three-fifths are large company managers and another fifth are senior managers of smaller firms.[54]

An Inclusive Intercorporate Network

The interlocking directorate, secondly, draws together nearly all important corporations into a single network. Though the British network has been far more divided and diverse than its American counterpart, recent decades have witnessed the formation of shared directorships directly or indirectly linking nearly every important company. This is evident, for instance, in time-series data compiled on the 85 largest manufacturing and financial companies from 1906 to 1970. At the start of this period, fewer than half of the firms were united by shared directorships; by the end, better than four-fifths were so joined.[55] Moreover, bridges across the great divide between industry and finance have grown as well. Directorship links between similar samples of large manufacturing firms and banks increased nearly seven-fold between 1906 and 1970.[56] The resulting network is now highly inclusive. Directorship ties among 40 large industrial and 27 large financial companies in 1970, for instance, were examined in one study: 56 of 67 firms are linked to at least one other company in the set, and if indirect connections through other corporations are taken into consideration, 62 of 67 companies are ultimately linked.[57] A more recent study of the directors of 235 of the largest manufacturing and financial firms for 1976 reveals comparable levels of network spread.[58]

Network density has not grown in the U.S. during this same period, but the present level of inclusiveness is much the same as for the U.K. According to an investigation of the interlocking directorate among the 167 largest American firms at seven time points between 1904 and 1974, no secular trend appears in the overall frequency of shared directorships. There is, however, progressive equalization of the number of interlocks per firm, signifying the entry of nearly all large firms into the network.[59] Geographic concentration adds a modest cliquing structure to the network, and the higher rates of shared directorships displayed by the boards of large commercial banks adds some hierarchy to the system. Still, geographic boundaries have been diminishing over time and are now only faintly discernible,[60] and although banks add disproportionately to the overall connectedness of the interlocking directorate, the inclusiveness of the network does not intrinsically depend on banks. Their removal from the network does not significantly reduce its breadth or spread. As a result, nine-tenths of America's

1,131 largest companies were directly or indirectly linked in 1962, according to one study; another reports that better than nine-tenths of the 797 largest firms were joined in 1969.[61] Depending on the precise number of large companies considered, the typical firm is no more than three steps in the interlocking directorate from three-fifths to nine-tenths of all other substantial corporations.[62] Thus, connectivity among the largest corporations is nearly complete.

A Diffusely Organized Intercorporate Network

The third quality of important political implication is the extent of diffuseness in the shared directorship network. Diffuseness refers to whether the directorships shared by corporations are largely the product of specific ties among pairs or cliques of firms, or derive instead from processes unrelated to such specific relations. The degree of diffuseness is of critical significance, for if diffuseness is low, the interlocking directorate is unlikely to serve as an effective vehicle for communication and political mobilization among the nation's largest companies. If diffuseness is high, however, those who are part of the interlocking directorate are well positioned to comprehend the issues vexing numbers of large firms, and to play a leading role in seeking general solutions. This question requires special attention since most previous analysis has viewed the interlocking directorate as the product of highly specific dyadic ties among pairs or small cliques of firms. Shared company directorships are seen as an instrument for reinforcing intercorporate resource exchanges, and, as such, they are taken to be little more than an extension of such relations. Companies are motivated to share directors, according to this perspective, as a means of securing and routinizing the buying and selling of products, the borrowing of money, the formation of joint ventures, and other forms of economic interchange, influence, or cooptation. One of the leading proponents of this resource-dependence perspective, Jeffrey Pfeffer, offers a characterization typical of many:

> Cooptation can be implemented by using the board of directors as an instrument for dealing with important external organizations, by putting representatives of these institutions on the board. . . . Business organizations . . . use their boards of directors as vehicles through which they coopt, or partially absorb, important external organizations with which they are interdependent.[63]

Thus companies create shared directorships as an instrument for influencing or controlling other corporations whose actions are potentially significant and uncertain in outcome, a point underscored by Michael Allen, another advocate of this approach:

Interorganizational elite cooptation, in the form of interlocking corporate directorates, represents a response to environmental uncertainty and constitutes a cooperative strategy for anticipating or controlling potentially disruptive unilateral actions by other organizations.[64]

Moreover, a number of U.S. studies have produced findings consistent with this thesis of particularistic interlocking ties. Manufacturing firms, for example, maintain disproportionately high numbers of ties with commercial banks, presumably as a means for ensuring access to a line of credit; companies disproportionately interlock with companies in other sectors in which products are bought and sold, presumably to reduce uncertainty in supply and price; and larger firms construct more shared directorships with other companies, even taking into account variant board sizes, presumably because they have more intercompany relations that require reinforcement.[65]

If this interpretation of the origins of the interlocking directorate is correct, the overall network would be without an essential quality if it is to serve as an effective channel of transcorporate communication and mobilization. The localized, parochial concerns of the active participants would cement pairwise corporate relations, but would discourage the emergence of overarching concerns affecting broad sections of business. The multiple directors' role would largely be the narrow one of promoting the joint interests of pairs of cliques of firms that have formed economic alliances, or advancing the interests of one firm at the expense of another, as would be suggested by the theses that companies use shared directors to coopt one another and that banks use them to facilitate their "control" of industrial firms.[66]

Several lines of argument, however, suggest that although this type of organization does characterize a fraction of the network, most ties are in fact generated on a far different basis. Let us return, for a moment, to the studies concluding that the interlocking directorate is, in large part, the result of corporate strategies to influence other firms. While such studies have utilized data identifying the specific pairs of corporations that share interlocking directors, they have not been able to obtain firm-specific data on the pairs of firms that actually exchange resources. This latter information is generally not publicly available, and analysts have resorted by necessity to inferring such relations from aggregate-level data. The resource-exchange thesis, for instance, found support in the research conclusion that large manufacturing firms maintain an exceptionally high number of ties with major commercial banks. It is inferred from this aggregate pattern that industrials must maintain directorship ties with the banks with which they wish to protect large credit lines. Alternatively, it is sometimes inferred that banks maintain these directorship ties to help protect their investments and loans in specific industrial firms. Either way, an assertion is made that pairs of corporations are interlocked by their directors to serve the specific economic relations between them. Yet this can only be an inferential assertion, since company-level information on loans is not generally a matter of public record. Similarly, the finding that industrial sectors buying from and selling to each other also maintain higher rates of shared directorships has been used to support the resource-exchange model. But again such support rests on the inference that specific pairs of buyers and sellers, not just broad classes of firms, share directors, a micro-level extrapolation for which directly corroborating information has been unavailable. This is not to suggest that the resource-exchange thesis is necessarily or entirely incorrect, but rather to suggest that there are other factors underlying the creation of many, perhaps even most, interlocking directorships, factors that could give rise to the same observed aggregate patterns. Two questions, thus, require attention: what fraction of the interlocking directorate can be attributed to the factor of resource exchange? and, to the extent that space remains for other generating factors, what are the most important other sources of interlocking directorates?

The Repair of Broken Interfirm Directorship Ties

Several recent American studies provide reasonably compelling evidence that the predominant source of the interlocking directorate is something other than economic interchange between pairs or among cliques of companies. The first of these studies examined the consequences for network connectedness of the death of an interlocking director.[67] The investigators studied those board members who linked the 797 largest U.S. firms in 1969. Using the obituary section of the *Wall Street Journal*, they found that forty-five directors held two or more seats on these boards just prior to their death. Since nature's disruption of the intercorporate links is presumably unrelated to any changes in the pairwise economic ties among these firms that might otherwise explain the cessation of a given interlocking directorship, most of the broken ties should be repaired reasonably soon if the resource-exchange thesis underlies the formation of most shared directorships. This does not occur, however. Only 6 percent of the severed ties are reestablished within a year of their interruption.

It might be argued that it can require more than a year to reestablish most such broken directorship ties, but a second study using a longer time frame revealed a comparably low rate of repair. This study, by Donald Palmer of the Stanford Business School, focused on those who were multiple directors of the 1,131 largest American corporations in 1962, 1964, and 1966.[68] Interlocking directorships in this study are classed as "accidentally" broken if they are severed due to changes in the director's personal circumstances rather than changes in the economic relations between the companies that the director connects. Relevant changes in the multiple directors' situations leading to accidental severance include retirement, acceptance of a new place of employment, and, once again, death. In cases where two firms shared *two* directorships in common and one is accidentally broken, there is a pronounced tendency for the fractured tie to be quickly repaired. Double directorships between two firms and their immediate restoration are, however, the exception. The vast majority of the other ties are not reestablished, even after the passage of as much as four years. Utilizing a complex procedure of analysis, Palmer concludes that no more than 15 percent—one in seven—of the interlocking directorships among large U.S. corporations are vehicles of interfirm coordination. The resource-exchange factor would appear to be responsible for a fraction of the shared directorships, but the bulk of the network is generated by other factors.[69]

This conclusion is reinforced by the results of a different form of analysis that focuses on the behavioral consequences predicted by the resource-exchange model. This thesis leads to the expectation that industrial firms sharing directors with a specific bank should display economic behavior distinct from that of similar firms without such bank ties. If a shared directorship is designed, in part, to secure credit lines for the industrial firm and to facilitate a bank's influence over the decisions of a manufacturer to which loans might be extended, industrials with such ties to banks should be at least modestly more likely than companies without such ties to have assumed bank debt. But in examining the degree of bank indebtedness for 84 primary-metals manufacturers, as a function of their shared directorships with large individual commercial banks, no such pattern is discerned, again implying that directorship links are not, on the whole, established to coordinate, coopt, or otherwise influence practices between specific pairs of corporations.[70] Participants themselves report the same thing. A majority of chief executives and directors of nearly 250 large U.S. firms, interviewed by the Conference Board, say they are opposed to the inclusion of any suppliers of products and services on their own boards.[71]

An Alternative Thesis

In place of the resource-exchange thesis, or at least alongside it, an alternative thesis on the origins of much of the interlocking directorate is set forth here. It is primarily derived from information acquired during my personal interviews with the 129 American and British executives and directors. The thesis must be regarded as tentative, but so many separate elements of evidence point toward the same hypothesis, and participants in the interlocking directorate so consistently describe their own world in ways that accord with and support the hypothesis, that considerable confidence can be placed in it. This new interpretation of the origins of most shared director-ships comes from an attempt to understand why the resource-exchange thesis consistently did not fit with the information that was acquired during the interviews with the corporate executives and directors who are part of the interlocking directorate.

In asking the executives, for instance, why they had appointed specific outsiders to their boards, and in inquiring of the multiple directors why and how they had joined the several boards on which they served, it quickly became apparent that resource-exchange considerations were of minor, though not negligible, importance.

In some cases, firms did share directors for reasons identical to those postulated by the resource-exchange thesis. When I asked several British merchant bankers (executive directors of accepting houses), for example, why they were on the boards of several industrial companies, it was evi-dent that their appointment was largely a product of the fact that these in-dustrial firms had long been special clients of the banks. In fact, in these instances, previously broken ties had been repaired precisely as the re-source-exchange model would have predicted. The present interlocking ties had been created only when earlier senior managers at the banks had mo-mentarily broken the close formal linkages by retiring from active work and from the boards of both companies. But these were the exceptions, or minor variations, on the general finding that specific economic ties between pairs of large corporations are of very little moment in the forging of most shared directorships.

The logic of the interlocking directorate, I found, was not reducible to particularistic, pairwise ties between firms, but rather originated in an en-tirely different business consideration, and one that is far more likely to generate a diffusely structured network. The central dynamic lies instead in efforts by the large companies to achieve an optimal "business scan" of con-temporary corporate practices and the general business environment.

THE INTERLOCKING DIRECTORATE AND BUSINESS SCAN

The scale of large companies makes their effective management dependent on a continuous monitoring of new developments in government policies, labor relations, international tensions, markets of many kinds, technology, and business practices ranging from stock options to charitable contribu-tions. Large corporations rely upon many procedures for enhancing their scan of these developments, including the maintenance of public affairs of-fices and special staffs responsible for assessments of domestic and foreign political environments and risks.[72] Aside from these formal staff functions, among the most important means that senior managers use to keep themselves informed, according to previous studies, is reliance on their own personal contacts and direct presence. A study of American companies operating abroad concludes, for instance, that "knowledge of foreign economic affairs came either from the most general news sources or, more vividly, from correspondence and personal experience."[73] And Henry Mintzberg, in a detailed study of the daily activity of top managers, finds that the typical executive "perpetually scans his environment for information, interrogates his liaison contacts . . . and receives [a wide range of] unsolicited information, much of it as a result of the network of personal contacts he has developed." This "soft," personally acquired information is often preferred, Mintzberg concludes, over information acquired through management information systems and other more formal channels.[74]

Few experiences, according to both British and American executives, were more useful for current intelligence on domestic corporate practices and the business environment than service on the board of directors of another major corporation. Learning about the practices and experiences of another large company, and hearing about the policies of still other companies from other outside directors, proves invaluable according to virtually all those multiple directors (those serving on two or more major boards) with whom interviews were held. The chairman and managing director of one of Britain's twenty-five largest manufacturers was asked about the value to his own company of his service as a nonexecutive director for another, larger manufacturer and a diversified financial company:

> The biggest impact really is on me, as chairman. [The larger manufacturer] is a premier company, a highly sophisticated matrix organization. Watching how they run so massive an organization, how investment decisions are taken and so on, is of tremendous input to me as an individual chief executive. [The other outside board] is fascinating, because it is a financially orientated company, it's a holding company, a conglomerate: [I value] watching that take a totally sharp-nosed approach to buying, selling, or keeping; gradually watching it having to come to terms with the fact that there are people there; seeing it meeting up with more and more of the problems that we all know about. One [company] is a destroyer, the other is a battleship, and I'm running a light cruiser in the middle. These have given me tremendous insights for use here.

Similarly, the chairman and managing director (the chief executive officer) of another major British industrial firm, who also held a seat on the board of an industrial company operating in an entirely different area, asserted that his presence there was unrelated to any relations between the two companies but was of considerable general value nonetheless:

Constantly one gets alerted to problems that the company whose board you may be attending had in a particular area. As to the possible applications, it's useful to get some information of use to one's own company. There are prompts, there are alerts that go through one's mind. Often I will be sitting at a board meeting and I'll think, "By gosh, you know, that's something that relates to where we stood." I'll put a scribble on a piece of paper, three lines, and I'll put it in my briefcase—"check 'so and so' when I get back."

For the deputy chairman of one of the London clearing banks and an outside director of a major construction firm, the directorship provided what he considered indispensable knowledge about two important sectors of the economy. Learning about the specific firms was far less important than what one might learn about broader trends:

[As a result of the directorship], I am reasonably well informed, for instance, about the construction industry. Simply because you're making concrete, you know an awful lot about the ebbs and flows of the tide in the construction industry, the impact of government cuts, and their seriousness in the totality in one major industry in this country.

The president and chief executive of a large American manufacturing firm, who also served on the board of two other large industrial companies among the nation's top 500, attributed the central value of the directorships to their vantage point for viewing other firms operating in divergent markets—and for learning of the problems faced by still other firms directly from their presidents, who joined him as other outside directors on his boards:

I think the most important benefits of serving on the [outside] board are input you get from the board and from the other board members as well as the CEO [chief executive officer] of the board you serve on. And the manner in which that corporation addresses similar policy making areas versus the way you address them in your own company—such things as strategic planning, personnel development, budgeting, internal controls, managing pension funds under ERISA [Employee Retirement Income Security Act]—you are getting a significant, valuable, diverse opinion on very timely subject matter which can help you make better judgments in your own business. That's really the most significant thing. It's the exposure of being on a board of directors and being in the company of those who are your equals or betters in many areas of expertise.

Summing up an evaluation universally expressed, the executive offered a final judgment: "If you want to just bottomline it, it's a hell of a tool for top management education." Said another American executive: "You're damn right it's helpful to be on several boards. It extends the range of your network and acquaintances, and your experience. That's why you go on a board, to get something as well as give. You get a more cosmopolitan view—on economic matters, regional differences, and international questions these days. It just broadens your experience, the memory bank that you have to test things against."

OUTSIDE DIRECTORSHIPS AND UPWARD PROMOTIONS

Recognition of the importance of business scan is deeply encoded in company promotion policies. Executives who are being groomed to rise up to the most senior company positions are encouraged to take on outside directorships as a means of enhancing their awareness of the company's business environment. Several British managing directors and American chief executive officers, for instance, report that upon receiving offers to become outside directors at a time when they already held several such positions and could afford time for no more, they recommended that the inquiring company consider appointing another senior executive in their company who showed considerable promise for eventual promotion to chief executive or managing director. In one major British company, rising senior managers are even offered a more formal preparation for such outside service. "I have had the managers that I have wished to see get on some directorships," and the chairman, "put into a nonexecutive director management development program." The program's visibility had indeed successfully attracted nonexecutive-director headhunters searching for new talent.

It is viewed as essential that an aspiring manager have the proper character and temperament for successful service as an outside director. A blemished reputation for this kind of external service weighs against a candidate aspiring to the apex of the company hierarchy. Several company chairmen reported that they considered it indispensable for a chairman to take on the role of continuously listening to the business environment of his company through service on other boards, and that a person who could not do this effectively could not make an effective chairman. As a result, nearly all the topmost executives of large American firms also serve as outside directors with at least one other firm. A *Fortune* survey of more than half of the chief executive officers of the 800 largest companies in 1975 revealed that six out of seven served on at least one board and that the typical chief executive held two-to-three directorships.[75]

Another indicator of the corporate value placed on outside directorships is that despite the considerable internal costs such service imposes, it elicits universal corporate support. Senior managers experience extremely heavy demands upon their time, and any absence from the day-to-day operations of a firm obviously requires compelling justification. Effective service on another board may consume as much as one day per month, or even more. Though comparable British data are unavailable, American statistics are indicative: the typical outside director of a large corporation in the U.S. attends eight board meetings per year for each company on whose board he or she serves, requiring approximately two work weeks annually. For those executives who hold two or three outside board positions, an average of four to six weeks per year are taken up by the outside service.[76] This level of what might be called released time must have some recognized compensations. Few of the interviewed executives could point to specific gains in enhanced relations with the interlocked companies; virtually all did point to enhanced company intelligence regarding the environment.

As might be anticipated, then, it is also reported that a decision of a manager to join another board is not his or her decision alone. An offer is always discussed with a manager's senior colleagues and often with the board as well, and the final decision is a company, not personal, one. In many companies, an invitation is scrutinized with great care for its informational value—and, on the negative side, for potential conflicts of interest—before acceptance. The response of one American chief executive to a query about why he had cleared with his own board of directors an invitation to join another manufacturing board is typical: "Since it will involve some time away from the business, which the board will expect the individual to benefit from and bring back something to the business as a result, I think the board ought to make the judgment as to whether that particular company and industry and that amount of time would be beneficial to the corporation."

In Britain, the logic here extends to the disposal of the fees that a non-executive director collects for his services. An outside director's compensation can exceed £5,000 per year, and the total personal income from service on several boards may thus be considerable. Although nonexecutive directors technically represent no outside organization or constituency save that of the shareholders, in practice their employing companies consider outside board service as an extension of company duties, and most managers do not retain their directorship fees for personal disposal. The compensation is simply passed through to the employing corporation, on the widely shared premise that outside directorship time is intrinsically part of the manager's obligations, and is thus already compensated by regular company salary. Formalization of this premise is not common in the U.S., however, where directorship income is normally retained by the individual, though even here there are exceptions. American directorship fees can also be quite substantial. More than two-thirds of the outside directors of the largest 200 industrial corporations were paid at least $18,000 in 1980 for their services; since two-to-three directorships are typically held by topmost American managers, total annual remuneration frequently exceeds $50,000.[77]

THE SOURCES OF INVITATIONS
TO JOIN A CORPORATE BOARD

Senior managers are expected to join the boards of other large firms. Yet from their own company's standpoint, it does not matter which ones, so long as the inviting firms fall within broadly required categories. The same is true from the perspective of the inviting firm: what counts is not so much the specific company of the prospective director as the general class in which his company falls. Invitations to join a particular company board thus do not generally follow preexisting relations between firms. Rather, they tend to move along the networks of ancient friendships and personal contacts. Without the guidance of a strict intercompany logic, an interpersonal logic has come to govern the flow of invitations.

Specific interfirm considerations are not always without influence in decisions on which outside executives to invite on a board, or which outside board positions an executive would seek. In some instances, the recipient of an invitation desired and anticipated an offer to go on a board with which his or her own company maintained an important relationship. An investment bank manager, for instance, had long been the chief financial advisor for an industrial enterprise, and in time he was brought on the board, a position he desired, though never openly sought, to facilitate his work with the client. Such experiences, however are not typical.

When I inquired whether outside directors anticipated the invitations to join the boards on which they now serve, the great majority reported that they did not. Only rarely did they have special reason to expect that the invitation would be extended by one company rather than another. Usually the invitation came as a complete surprise. Only after joining the outside board did the directors learn why they had been selected, and then it was typically discovered that their name had come to the fore through connections and for reasons entirely unrelated to any contact between their own firm and the inviting company. An American industrial corporation and a bank, for example, share two directors, one primarily affiliated with the manufacturer, the other with the bank. Double appointments of this type would appear to indicate some kind of enduring economic relationship between the firms. Yet even here, such an inference would be mistaken.

The banker stressed the complete absence of any such interests and offered instead the following story of how the shared directorships came to pass:

> I got there on a reciprocal basis, although that isn't the way it started. I met a fellow . . . who was the head of [an investment bank] out at the Bohemian Grove, and he said, "Frank, do you know Sam [X]?" Sam ran [the industrial firm]. And I said I knew him, though I didn't know him well. He said, "Well, sometimes you're looking for board members, and he'd be a good guy to look at." So I looked at him the next time around we needed a board member, and I decided to invite him. So he came on the board of the bank. And I guess somewhere along the line he was looking for a board member too . . . and there I am.

When managers holding outside directorships were asked to describe how at least one of the directorships was initiated, in more than three out of four instances they identified factors unrelated to trade or any other strictly business relation between the companies. Commonly, the manager was already personally acquainted with the chairman or other directors on the board he was asked to join. Such contacts stemmed from a range of sources. Often, they had a prior business relationship—but not as a product of any dealings between the two companies. The individuals might have served together, for instance, on another corporate board, or perhaps on a business association task force. One instance is generically descriptive of many: The chief executive of a large U.S. utility company had become personally involved in his firm's project to develop an educational movie on the problems of nuclear power from the industry's point of view. In the course of producing this film he came to know the top people of a major broadcasting corporation. The personal chemistry seemed right, and the utility executive was called and readily accepted an invitation to go on the broadcaster's board.

Less often but not infrequently, the acquaintance originated in social or other entirely nonbusiness circumstances. The individuals had known each other since attending Eton or Harrow; or they had first met at an exclusive metropolitan club, perhaps Links or the Carlton; or it was through family circles that they had become familiar; or perhaps it was during their joint work on behalf of the local symphony orchestra that they had first impressed one another. Several such circumstances can be seen, for example, in an account of an American media executive who was invited to join the board of a major airline; I asked him to describe the origin of the airline invitation:

> At the time of the invitation, I knew about four or five directors. One of them was [W], who had become head of a [large manufacturer], but before that had been a publisher of [a newspaper]. And there was a man

named [X], who's head of [another company], who I had known through my wife's family. And I met [Y] on a trip to South America, about three years before he had become chairman [of the airline], and I had seen him from then on, two or three times a year socially. [A rival airline] had invited a bunch of people to fly from Houston to South America and back all in about five days. [Y] was on the trip, the first time I had met him, and we became pretty good friends. I met [Z], a banker, through my wife's family. He was strictly a social friend of theirs; I had met him at their home. I don't know that he was responsible, but it's reasonable to assume at least he knew who I was, and whoever suggested me, [Z] would certainly have said "I know him," and apparently he didn't say don't put me on.

A British multiple director traces one industrial board appointment to his acquaintance with the deputy chairman, a contact dating to the former's earlier service as a government minister, and a contact since renewed through their joint service on the board of an insurance company. How his name came to the attention of the insurance company he has never learned, though he suspects the company called because they had been seeking a lawyer for the board, and somehow his name had been recommended.

The predominance of such indirect origins in outside directorships is not the pattern that should have prevailed if intercorporate resource exchange were a major determinant of the makeup of the network. Instead, we should have learned that the last mentioned British director had joined the two boards because the industrial company was seeking investment in its stocks by the insurance company; or because the insurer had already obtained a major position in the industrial and sought to protect its investment; or because of any number of other specific reasons that the two companies needed a top-level formal tie between themselves—and not with other corporations. Rarely, however, were such considerations reported, despite repeated probing.

The pattern actually observed, on the other hand, is consistent with the business-scan thesis on the origin of the interlocking directorate. Corporations, according to this thesis, encouraged their senior managers to join the boards of other large companies. Yet within the general constraint of the need to have good spread across all major business sectors, it does not greatly matter for which specific firms they ultimately come to serve as outside directors. Nor is it of great moment how these ties are created, so long as their breadth is adequate. General business and social acquaintances among senior managers, connections that only rarely paralleled specific economic linkages between pairs of firms, are thus a perfectly suitable informal network through which to create the formal directorship network. And, as we have seen, this is indeed how much of the interlocking directorate actually comes about.

THE INTERLOCKING DIRECTORATE
AS A COMMUNICATIONS NETWORK

With nearly all major companies involved in an exchange of directors, the interlocking directorate forms a national transcorporate network overarching all sectors of business. Moreover, the network is far more diffusely structured than if it were built largely around intercorporate exchange relations. Corporate reciprocity requires shared directorships between specific pairs or cliques of firms, while the element of external business scan leads to shared directorships only between large classes of firms. While it is useful for a company to have one of its managers on a bank board to remain abreast of general financial trends, the major banks offer roughly equivalent informational opportunities, and thus an interlocking tie with any bank serves much the same purpose. An executive of an American retail corporation offered a characteristic assessment in describing the value of his two outside directorships, one with a major insurer, the other with a high technology firm:

> I'm concerned with financial problems, for instance, and I get a much broader view of these problems from sitting on other boards. You could read about insurance policies on loaning money, but in my service on an insurance company board I learn about the real climate of lending, and this is very useful when it comes time to borrow money. You also learn about people's thinking about savings when you sit on the insurance company board. It makes no difference [which insurance board you sit on]. The important thing is to learn about the insurance business.

In addition, since outside directorships are primarily accepted as a means of learning about the general business environment, it is not surprising that informal discussion before and after board meetings is devoted to just that rather than to cementing relations between particular firms. Even discussion during board deliberations is generally steered away from any reference to specific business relations that the company may have with an outside director's own firm. There are exceptions, of course, but the multiple directors almost uniformly report that it would be an egregious impropriety if they used one board position to promote another company's interests. One director of a British manufacturing firm was asked if his position on the board of a clearing bank ever yielded information of specific value to the manufacturer:

> If there were detailed pieces of information, I wouldn't use them. I would feel that was wrong. If I thought they were important to be known here, I would get the chairman [of the bank] or somebody else to authorize me to tell them.

There is a self-conscious effort to segregate the roles, a posture that is rooted in widespread norms about personal and company conduct in these matters. These can be seen in the observations of one high-ranking officer of a British clearing bank. He had been asked to comment on potential conflicts of interest arising from his simultaneous service on the boards of an insurer and an industrial firm. He cautioned:

> One has to be very careful how you use specific information gleaned from one quarter in another quarter. Very often it comes, and it must be a matter of conscience, and in my experience people adhere to this strictly. You just keep quiet when there is anything arising [related to the relations between two companies]. Many people have the experience of wearing different hats, and they know just how far they can properly go. Suppose I knew that [the industrial company] were getting into real trouble, and it hadn't become public knowledge yet, and I went round to my insurance company and they were contemplating investing [a] quarter of a million in it. I could not say anything, and the insurance company would not ask a question specifically relating to one's experience [at the industrial firm].

When relations between two firms unavoidably do come before a board that includes an individual who is a director of both, propriety often dictates the absenting of the multiple director from any discussion of the relations. For instance, one British director served on the boards of two companies that were at times competitive in certain markets. A related decision came before the board of the firm for which he was an outside director: "I remember [the chairman] was talking about this. He said we have a very clear policy—'we trust our nonexecutive directors completely, we just don't send them the papers.'" As further reinforcement for the policy of trust, the linking director also withdrew from the board room whenever the issue arose. For those few who transgress the unwritten mores of discretion, the sanctions can go as far as complete expulsion from the network. Thus, one experienced chairman and outside director observed that discussions in and around board meetings are "candid, off the record, personal—and if you violated that, you're dead, because you get a reputation of not being discreet personally. You don't get invited into the club, you've misbehaved. If you are being suspected of using inside information or self-dealings, when you come up for renomination and there is a poll, informal or otherwise, you would be considered an outcast," and, thus, unceremoniously dropped from the board.

A minority of firms in both countries, especially the very largest and those that have many corporate customers or suppliers, have explicit policies against interlocking directorships with companies where there could be any appearance of a conflict of interest. One American corporation that provided major services to several firms in the chemical industry, for example, decided it could not, for appearance sake alone, invite an executive from any chemical firm to serve on its board. It feared that other firms would make unwarranted but nonetheless damaging inferences about the consequences of such a tie. Similarly, an oil company maintained a board policy that excluded drawing outside directors from any of its numerous corporate buyers. Another American petroleum firm followed an identical practice, applied to both incoming and outgoing directorships, as described by one of its senior executives:

> Most of the outside boards that [our top officers] are involved with are in totally different industries. And of course all our outside board members are from totally different industries. We forbid [directorships with customers or suppliers]; it's such a sensitive issue that we don't want to have any sort of board membership on our board or our board on other boards that would in any way be involved with an association that could be called clandestine or privileged.

His company does nonetheless insist that its top people sit on outside boards in highly unrelated industries: "What we get back is what other businessmen think, taking the longer view particularly. We're just as interested in General Foods' general economic forecast for the next ten years as we are in our own, given that we are in totally different industries."

NETWORKS AND CLASSWIDE SOCIAL ORGANIZATION

As a communication network, then, the interlocking directorate discourages the specific and fosters the general. The comments of one veteran multiple director captured the essential features of how specific interfirm information is downplayed and general business information is played up. He was asked, as the managing chairman of a large British industrial enterprise, to describe the value to his own company of his time-consuming service as an outside director for one of the country's preeminent banks, a major manufacturing firm, and several other companies:

> I'm a great believer in the theory of the part-time nonexecutive director. The benefit is watching quite different organizations work in different spheres of activity. [Q. It's not a specific kind of information transfer so much as a general transfer?] Oh yes, I would be totally worried if I found I was ever getting specific information of value to [my company]. I would wash my young man's ears if I ever found anything of special interest to us from any other company I am involved in. But the bank board, for instance, is involved in general discussions of economic circumstances, and it's helpful background information. Put it this way: direct involvement in other company's affairs replaces an awful lot of reading.

Though localized in formation, the interlocking directorate has the qualities of a transcendent network: participants are directly and indirectly placed in contact with a large number of other participants. Multiple directors are cognizant of the fact that there are important informational gains, for example, from the regular rubbings of shoulders with other multiple directors. Outside board service opens access not only to the specific companies' experience, but also to the collective wisdom of the many other directors from other companies, whose outlook has been influenced by the experiences of still other directors with still different companies. One British company chairman, managing director, and nonexecutive director for a half dozen other corporations described it this way:

> If you serve on, say, six outside boards, each of which has, say, ten directors, and let's say out of ten directors, five are experts in one or another subject, you have a built-in panel of thirty friends who are experts who you meet regularly, automatically each month, and you really have great access to ideas and information. You're joining a club, a very good club. You can sit down with [another outside director], and you can say, "well what do you do about this kind of pension fund, what do you do about this kind of profit sharing, or what do you do about this or that."

It is commonly recognized that traveling in multiple-director circles, because these circles include so many well-informed persons facing such vastly different business circumstances, is invaluable for top corporate management, and because the information transmitted is of such high value to just such persons. One British chairman offered his own variation on a familiar definition of a business leader's worth: "I think a chairman is as valuable, really, as the number of expert, influential personal friends he has." And there is no swifter means of creating influential friendships than sharing the responsibility of running a company, for "once you've served on a board with somebody, you break the barriers, you become very swiftly accepted as a colleague, a confidant."

In sum, then, the interlocking directorate is largely structured in a way that favors the flow of information throughout the network about the practices and concerns of most large companies, companies that are operating in virtually all major sectors of the economy and facing the full range of economic and political problems confronting business generally. This diffuse structure has been evident in the kind of company benefits that multiple directors acknowledge as motivating their service; in the corporate policies that reinforce their pursuit of generic information about common business practices and the environment; in the network norms and company policies that discourage or prohibit the use of shared directorships to facilitate intercorporate business; and in the factors unrelated to specific, reciprocal interfirm relations that largely account for why specific individuals ultimately join particular boards.

There is no question that a fraction of the directorship network is structured in a way favorable to the flow of more parochial and localized information between pairs or among small cliques of firms. Many shared directorships are created expressly for the purpose of cementing resource-exchange ties between two firms. Yet most are not. Donald Palmer's previously described quantitative study of broken directorship ties between U.S. corporations found that no more than one-sixth of the shared directorships among large corporations are related to resource-exchange considerations. A qualitatively based estimate drawn from the present interviews yields a fraction close to this as well. Still other sources, unexplored here, account for at least some of the remaining five-sixths of the shared directorships in the network. There are cases, for example, in which the managing director of one company joins another company board solely because he is the largest single shareholder in the latter. But again, this explains only a tiny portion of the overall network. The predominant mode of organization is built instead around the dynamics of business scan, and as such the resulting network is not connected to specific intercorporate relations. Though any specific figure must remain tentative because of its qualitative base, from the interview patterns it can be estimated that at least two-thirds, and perhaps more, of the ties composing the interlocking directorate among the largest British and American companies derive from corporate strategies related to business scan.[78] The interlocking directorate is not self-consciously or explicitly created to transcend all large firms, for, as we have seen, it largely originates in the commonly shared but individual firm-defined need to have better information about the business environment. The unplanned consequence, however, is the formation of a communications network that defines an inner circle of the business community in each country that can rise above the competitive atomization of the many corporations that constitute its base and concern itself with the broader issues affecting the entire large-firm community.

When the inner circle enters politics, its capacity to act, and its central concerns, are decisively shaped by the economic and social foundation on which it rests. The overriding and undiminished corporate stress on the growth of profits necessarily dominates the vision of all who enter politics on behalf of the business community. Their first priority could not be otherwise. Just how this imperative is translated into specific public policies at a given moment, however, is subject to many interpretations. However, if the principle of individual corporate focus in business politics prevailed, each major corporation would express, through its leadership, its unique

vision of what the government and nonprofit institutions should do on
behalf of business and a cacophony of demands, often contradictory, would
be heard coming out of the corporate community. Corporate demands are
at times so expressed, but not always so, and not entirely so. The inclusive
and diffusely structured economic and social foundations described here
have created a special form of social organization within the business communities of both America and Britain, an inner circle whose unique qualities equip corporate leaders to enter politics on behalf of consensually
arrived at classwide interests rather than narrow, individual corporate
interests.

THREE

Inner Circle Organization

Rarely, if ever, does big business act collectively to promote its political interests, classwide or otherwise, for as a bloc it lacks even the most rudimentary means for identifying and agreeing on its common needs, let alone a vehicle for pursuing them. The inner circle, by contrast, is opportunely situated to overcome these lacks. As we have seen in the previous chapter, it possesses the intercorporate connections and organizational capacities to transcend the parochial interests of single companies and sectors, and to offer a more integrated vision of the broader, longer-term needs of business. This chapter details the social organization of the inner circle; the next considers the inner circle's entry into politics. We explore both subjects with a range of information sources, primarily those assembled directly for this inquiry. The guiding purpose is to describe and explain the unique characteristics of the inner circle, and then to show how these special characteristics shape and focus the political activities of the corporate managers in the network.

THE POWER ELITE

Business, military, and the government—these were the three pillars of C. Wright Mills's famous American "power elite."[1] Since publication of this classic study in 1956, several generations of university students have been required to master its elements, even as, or perhaps because, they were soon themselves to become part of one of the three pillars. As contested as it was, Mills's thesis was assimilated into the shared perception of most educated circles, a touchstone for informed conversation about how our society governs itself, if not proven fact. In opening an article profiling the chief executives of the largest U.S. corporations some two decades after *The Power Elite* first appeared, *Fortune* magazine could still frame a question whose reference most readers were certain to comprehend: "Is [the chief executive], as often supposed outside the business world, an aristocrat of what C. Wright Mills called the Power Elite?"[2]

Less remembered than the general thesis, but more useful for understanding corporate politics, is Mills's prescient insight regarding why business had become a pillar of the establishment. American capitalism, he observed, has been marked by continuously increasing centralization and concentration. This process, in Mills's view, had led to the emergence of a new breed of corporate executives committed to industry-wide concerns reaching far beyond the interests of their own firms. Moreover, a fraction of these executives took an even broader view of business problems: "They move from the industrial point of interest and outlook to the interests and outlook of the class of all big corporate property as a whole."[3]

Mills identified two features of business organization as primarily responsible for the change in outlook. First, the personal and family investments of top managers and owners had become dispersed among a number of firms. As a result, he wrote, "the executives and owners who are in and of and for this propertied class cannot merely push the narrow interests of each property; their interests become engaged by the whole corporate class."[4]

Second, the emergence of an extensive network of interlocking directorships among the major corporations also meant that a number of managers had assumed responsibility for the prosperity of several corporations, and thus those holding multiple directorships constituted "a more sophisticated executive elite which now possesses a certain autonomy from any specific property interests. Its power is the power . . . of classwide property."[5] It is this power that had so well positioned the business elite to serve as a dominant pillar of the American power elite.

Surveying much the same landscape, other analysts have offered kindred hypotheses. Maurice Zeitlin has suggested that centralizing tendencies akin to those discussed by Mills are creating an overarching unity within the business community. Prominent among such tendencies is "the establishment of an effective organizational apparatus of interlocking directorates" cutting across both financial and industrial sectors. Such interlocking directorates may be very important in any effort to maintain the "cohesiveness of the capitalist class and its capacity for common action and unified policies."[6] The number of owners and managers holding diversified corporate investments and positions is viewed by both Zeitlin and Mills as a potentially dominant political segment of the business community, one that is increasingly in a position to impose its outlook as it recognizes itself as the national network that it is.

The growing concentration of economic power in this network has been recognized in official circles as well, with equanimity in some, alarm in others. A U.S. congressional study of shared directorships warns, for instance, that "the interlocking management device" could lead to a situation in which "inordinate control over the major part of the U.S. commerce would be concentrated in the hands of [a] few individuals," creating the possibility that "an 'inner group' would control the destiny of American commerce."[7]

Central to these analyses is the potentially critical political role played by top managers holding multi-firm connections. Executives with ties to several, often disparate, companies necessarily become concerned with the joint welfare of the several companies. Their indirect ties to other firms through the interlocking directorate further enlarges the scope of their concern. "Even more than other large corporation executives," writes one group of analysts, "those who sit at the center of the web of interlocking directorates must have an outlook and executive policies that, while yet serving particular and more narrow interests, conform to the general interests of the corporate community and of the principal owners of capital within it."[8] The inner circle, in short, constitutes a distinct, politicized business segment, if a segment is defined as a subset of class members sharing a specific social location with partially distinct interests.[9] Though members of the inner circle share with other corporate managers a common commitment to enhancing company profits, their heightened sensitivity to business interests more general than those that look solely to support individual company profits also sets them apart.

THE FUNDAMENTALS OF INNER-CIRCLE ACTION

Those with multiple corporate connections are expected not only to share a vision distinct from that of other business leaders, but also to take a far more active role in promoting their politics. Compared with the one-company managers, this power network should be at the forefront of corporate outreach to government, political parties, nonprofit institutions, and the media. This is anticipated for four interrelated reasons: (1) the inner circle's multiple company connections place its members in exceptionally powerful positions within the corporate community; (2) the inner circle's multiple connections generate a degree of social cohesion absent elsewhere among the business elite, a factor facilitating the mobilization of resources on behalf of positions generally favored within the circle; (3) the inner circle's close ties with the traditional upper class add further to its stature and influence; and (4) the inner circle's pervasive presence among the leadership positions of the main business associations provides a special vehicle for political expression. We will consider each of these in turn, drawing primarily on the systematic information sets on large companies and their management compiled for this study.

THE POWER OF MULTIPLE CORPORATE CONNECTIONS

The multiple company connections of those who constitute the inner circle provide these leaders with a unique stature within the corporate community. Compared with other corporate leaders, inner-circle members possess special powers that derive from three distinct factors. The first relates to the inner circle's ability to mobilize corporate resources on behalf of its own entry into politics. By virtue of their ties with several firms, members hold an edge over other corporate managers who might otherwise be equally prepared to join the fray.

The second factor derives from the integrative role of the inner circle in linking firms facing different circumstances. Companies confronted with different problems would be inclined to seek equally different solutions. In searching for suitable ambassadors to represent the general views of business to government and elsewhere, the inner circle provides an attractive source of compromise candidates holding positions that appeal to a broad base of business interests and seriously offend few. Because of their great understanding of the needs of a diverse group of companies, multiple directors would tend to be the logical choice of the business community when seeking a voice to trust to carry its message to the political sector.

Finally, from the standpoint of the government and other institutions, the multiple-director network is an appealing source of counsel. The varied connections of these managers lend them a special aura of stature, legitimacy, and influence that is but faintly shared by directors of single companies, however eminent they may be within their own company or sector. Moreover, an imputed capacity of the inner circle to better comprehend the general concerns of large corporations make it a preferred voice when the prevailing perspective of business is sought. Its ability to transcend the parochial interests of specific firms and sectors makes its members particularly attractive for outside appointment. Together, these three factors—the special ability to mobilize corporate resources, to emerge as the compromise representative, and to express the general outlook of business—result in a heightened capability of the inner circle to enter the political process, compared with other corporate leaders, and to speak with greater authority when it does so.

The inner circle has been primarily defined as those who serve on the boards of several large corporations. This is a useful point of departure for a study of this group, but it offers neither a full description of the inner circle nor a precise definition of its boundaries or membership. It has been initially defined this way in part as a matter of substantive emphasis, but also in part as a matter of technical convenience. Technically, use of multiple directorships to define a person's membership in the inner circle brings distinct research advantages. Inner-circle status of large numbers of business leaders can be readily determined, while the use of more complex standards would be cumbersome and costly, though at certain points in the analysis that follows it will prove necessary to introduce other standards as well. Still, in much of the ensuing discussion it should be kept in mind that the multiple-directorship standard is serving only as a proxy for a far broader and more intricate set of informal social relationships within the British and American business communities. So too, it is well to remember that there is no sharp cleavage between the inner circle and the rank-and-file of corporate leadership. Rather, it is a matter of fine gradations, of pales within pales. Some business leaders are at the core, others beyond the periphery, with those in between displaying some of the qualities of both of those inside and out. Such a system of classification without sharp division is typical of the informal organization of power in politics, the professions, and other fields of social activity.

THE SOCIAL COHESION OF THE INNER CIRCLE

The inner circle's special ability to mobilize political resources is enhanced to the extent that it is more socially cohesive than the remainder of corporate management. Social cohesion implies that the inner circle is truly a circle: acquaintanceship networks are dense, mutual trust and obligation are widespread, and a common sense of identity and culture prevail. All these features are embodied and reinforced in a variety of social institutions, ranging from clubs to intermarriage. While social cohesion is not a necessary precondition for mobilization, it is a powerful facilitator. It is often along pre-existing lines of personal connection that the first mobilization of many partisan movements first occurs; there is no reason not to expect the same in corporate mobilization.[10] Furthermore, it is to be anticipated that the lattice of personal ties is likely to be especially highly concentrated within the inner circle. This is so for several reasons. Studies of city-based multiple-position holders show that they are far better acquainted with one another than are comparable sets of single-organization leaders.[11] And my own interviews yield evidence of the same. Recall from the previous chapter that an oft-cited benefit of nonexecutive directorship service is contacts, frequently transformed into friendships, with other nonexecutive directors. Most participants in the interlocking directorate report that their acquaintanceship circles had been richly expanded.

Systematic data can be used to corroborate the multiple directors' perceptions. To do this, we utilize an imperfect, but indicative, measure of a manager's social network—membership in one of the major exclusive metropolitan clubs. Among the first names are Brook's, White's, Pratt's, and the Carlton in London; the Century Association and Links in New York; and Pacific Union and the Bohemian Club in San Francisco. Though many clubs have been traditionally attached to the British aristocracy or the American upper class and are still imbued with their customs, in recent decades even these have generally come to be favored within, and to favor, business cadres as well.[12] The clubs can be viewed as nodes in which members of informal social networks of the corporate elite concentrate. Initiation of a company manager into a club signifies a measure of social acceptance, an acceptance further extended by the unending rounds of club life. Accordingly, if our expectations are correct, inner-circle executives should more often belong to the great metropolitan clubs than should top executives without the special connections of multiple directorships. If so, on the reasonable assumption that club memberships are a serviceable measure of mutual acquaintanceship, such a finding would indicate that members of the inner circle are, on average, better known to one another than are other corporate managers.

To examine this, we turn to the U.K. and U.S. data sets. Central to our analysis is a measure of the managers' proximity to the inner circle. Since this dimension will recurrently appear in the analysis that follows, a note on its operational definition is introduced at this point, first for the British, then the American data. The inner circle is specified here to consist of those who serve on the *main* boards of two or more *large* corporations.[13] Of the 1,972 British directors associated with the 196 large companies in this study, 1,554 sit on only one main board and are designated *single directors*. Multiple directors include 262 who serve on two large-firms boards (*double directors*), and 154 on three or more boards (*many-board directors*).[14] Thus, slightly more than one-fifth (21 percent) of the total set of company directors comprise the British inner circle, as specified here.[15]

An analogous definition of location is used with the American information.[16] Of the 2,799 American executives and directors occupying 3,116 positions associated with 212 of these companies, 2,306 sit on none or one main board of one of the large corporations; these are designated single directors.[17] The American multiple directors consist of 267 who serve on two large-firm boards, and 267 who occupy three or more board positions. Together, these double and many-board directors constitute the American inner circle, again approximately one-fifth (18 percent) of the entire set of corporate managers and directors.

In the ensuing analysis, it will be useful to retain a distinction between the double- and many-board directors, for it will frequently provide a stronger means of evaluating the thesis advanced. Not only is club membership expected to be greater for multiple directors than single directors, but the logic of our thesis would also imply that the rate of membership should be an increasing function of the number of directorships held. The many-board directors should constitute an innermost ring within the inner circle.

Drawing on several standard biographical sources, we find that our British company directors have joined more than fifty prominent clubs. Preferences are nonetheless highly concentrated among a small, highly select set of preeminent associations favored by the "great and the good," led by MCC (Marylebone Cricket Club), Brook's, White's, Pratt's, Boodle's, City of London, and the Carlton. Each of these included at least fifty of the company directors within its ranks.[18] The rate of membership in at least one of these leading clubs, as a function of inner-circle location, is displayed in Table 3.1. Two estimates based on alternative assumptions are given for the British Clubs; the true rate is probably closer to what is

Table 3.1 Percentage of corporate directors who are members of at least one exclusive social club, by Inner-circle location

Number of large-company directorships	British Clubs[a]		American Clubs[b]	(Number of directors on which successive column figures are based)		
	A est.	B est.				
One	24.6%	8.9%	10.9%	(564)	(1554)	(2306)
Two	41.4	26.5	31.5	(169)	(264)	(267)
Three or more	37.4	31.8	46.9	(131)	(154)	(226)
Ratio, 3+/1 bd.[c]	1.5	3.6	4.3			

SOURCE: Data collected by author.

[a] MCC, Brook's, White's, Pratt's, Boodle's, City of London, and the Carlton.

[b] Bohemian (San Francisco), Brook (New York), California (Los Angeles), Century (New York), Chicago, Detroit, Duquesne (Pittsburgh), Links (New York), Metropolitan (Washington, D.C.), Minneapolis, Pacific Union (San Francisco), Rolling Rock (Pittsburgh), Somerset (Boston), Union (Cleveland), and Union League (Philadelphia).

[c] The "Ratio, 3+/1 bd." figures in this and subsequent tables represent the ratio of the rate for those with three or more directorships to the rate for those with one directorship. Thus, the figure of 4.3 in the third column is obtained by dividing 46.9 percent by 10.9 percent, and it signifies that the American multiple directors are some four times more likely than are single directors to have been invited into one of the exclusive clubs.

termed the A than the B estimate.[19] Similarly, though the American executives and directors are active with more than one hundred clubs, they tend to concentrate in several dozen, and the fifteen with largest numbers are considered here. They include the Bohemian (sponsor of the Bohemian Grove), Century, Duquesne, Links, Metropolitan, and Pacific Union.

It is apparent that club rosters are disproportionately occupied by those most central to the inner circle. The rate of involvement using the A estimates is 25 percent for single British directors, but 37 percent for many-board directors; the B estimates are 9 and 32 percent. Similarly, the American rates are 11 percent for single directors, 32 percent for double directors, and 47 percent for many-board directors. This pattern is readily explicable: the more company boards on which a senior manager sits, the more forthcoming are invitations to join the clubs of which the manager's fellow directors are members. But the implication goes beyond the cause: compared with most senior managers, members of the inner circle are more often personally familiar with each other. Both national inner circles thus possess an important rudiment of transcorporate social organization, and one that is far better developed than elsewhere within the corporate communities.

THE UPPER CLASS AND THE INNER CIRCLE

The third factor facilitating the inner circle's political leadership is its close alliance with the upper class. The upper class consists of the social network of established wealthy families whose status is preeminent, whose culture and identity are distinct, and whose membership is closed to nearly all but those of proper descent. High rates of occupational inheritance at the highest levels of business are of course well known in both countries. Studies of the family origins of top officers of large U.S. corporations, for example, generally reveal that two-fifths to three-fifths of the officers were themselves raised in business families.[20] Descendants of truly patrician families are less often found in British manufacturing, yet they too have some presence here and they are especially prominent in British finance.[21] As we shall see in a moment, however, when scions of the upper class do enter business, they tend to reach the inner circle more often and more rapidly than those of more modest origins. Several political consequences follow. Borrowing a useful terminology from Pierre Bourdieu, the upper-class connection enhances three inner-circle qualities: the personal style, values, and educational credentials that Bourdieu terms "cultural capital"; the network of family-generated social contacts, or "social capital"; and the privately held financial assets, or "economic capital." Judiciously applied, all three elements should improve both the inner circle's contacts and its influence with those who count in the nonbusiness world. And to the extent that the latter derive from similar patrician origins, as has long been the case for the upper reaches of the British political system, an element of accessibility and trust is accorded the inner circle ordinarily denied all others who would seek a hearing, if not favor.[22] Finally, the fusion of the upper class with the inner circle can only further strengthen the latter's cohesion, as the networks of family loyalties and patrician connections crisscross and reinforce the matrix of interlocking directorships. This is well illustrated in one study of the directorship and aristocratic kinship ties in the early 1970s among 27 large British financial institutions, including Barclays, Lloyds, the Bank of England and Prudential Insurance. Shared directorships link twenty-six of the twenty-seven institutions; but so also do kinship ties, though the specific pattern is rather different. Moreover, in many instances companies not connected by shared board members are connected by relatives, and vice versa. Where members of the inner circle lack immediate interboard connections, family ties offer alternative channels of access.[23]

The inner circle's special affiliation with the upper class is evident in its educational origins, upper-class trappings, and personal wealth. Though attendance at one of Britain's exclusive public schools or America's preparatory schools is no certain mark of patrician pedigree, it has long served as a highly reliable indicator—for the upper class and its observers alike. Eton, the premier English school, "includes all kinds of boys," Anthony Sampson observes in his "anatomy" of British society, "stupid, clever, lazy, ambitious, creative or dull. But their parents are nearly all rich."[24] The graduates of Harrow, Rugby, Groton, and St. Paul's are also, with notably few exceptions, descendents of established families.[25] A convenient, albeit imperfect, measure of patrician origins can thus be constructed from the schooling record of the directors. A limited set of the most exclusive schools is employed in the analysis. Five British schools are included, all at the top of any list, and all the most frequently attended of any public schools by the business leaders in this study: Eton, Harrow, Marlborough, Rugby, and Winchester.[26] Thirteen American schools have been selected; they too are at the apex of the boarding school hierarchy, and are the first choice of the American business leaders: Andover, Choate, Deerfield, Exeter, Groton, Hill, Hotchkiss, Lawrenceville, Milton, St. George's, St. Mark's, St. Paul's, and Taft.[27] In the aggregate, these institutions are responsible for the secondary schooling of slightly more than 10 percent of both the American and British directors. It is anticipated that the inner circle's upscale origins would have channeled them toward these crucibles of upperclass socialization, and indeed this is the case, as can be seen in Table 3.2. While 6 percent of the British business leaders outside the inner circle

Table 3.2 Percentage of corporate directors who were graduated from an exclusive boarding school, by Inner-circle location

Number of large-company directorships	British School[a]		American School[b]	(Number of directors on which successive figures are based)		
	A est.	B est.				
One	10.5%	5.9%	9.5%	(564)	(1554)	(2306)
Two	17.2	14.0	16.5	(169)	(264)	(267)
Three or more	16.0	13.6	15.0	(131)	(154)	(226)
Ratio 3+/1 bd.	1.5	2.3	1.6			

SOURCE: Data collected by author.

  [a] Eton, Harrow, Marlborough, Rugby, and Winchester.

  [b] Andover, Choate, Deerfield, Exeter, Groton, Hill, Hotchkiss, Lawrenceville, Milton, St. George's, St. Mark's, St. Paul's, and Taft.

received the benefit of a public schooling (by the B estimate), 14 percent of the core of the inner circle—those with three or more corporate directorships—had been so privileged. The corresponding figures for the American business community are 10 and 15 percent.

An alternative American indicator of proper pedigree is the premier blue book of all blue books, the *Social Register*. With separate metropolitan editions dating to 1888, and a single, combined national edition in recent years, the *Social Register* has long been an accepted arbiter of established status, a definitive "metropolitan upper class index."[28] The appearance of a company manager's name in the 1978 or 1979 editions of the national *Social Register*, then, provides a convenient index of proper origins. A more restrictive but suitable British indicator of aristocratic descent is the possession of a title normally obtained only through inheritance. Duke, Baron, Earl, Marquess, Baronet, and Viscount lead the list, and these six are used here. Both these measures are, of course, imperfect; some members of the American upper class refuse entry into the *Social Register*, and some British title holders obtained entry more through the display of special influence than proper pedigree. Still, both are strong indices, and Table 3.3 reveals that the business inner circles are closely allied to their respective upper classes, if holding an honored title or a place in the register of high society are the markers of upper-class status. Double directors are twice as likely to hold either, and many-board directors are even more often so honored. Of the British, 4 percent of the single directors are titled, while 18 percent of the many-board directors are so distinguished. Of the Americans, 8 percent of the single directors but 20 percent of the many-board directors are recognized by the *Social Register*.

A final indication of upper-class penetration of the inner circle comes from an examination of the personal assets of the business leaders. Though

Table 3.3 Percentage of corporate directors who hold a hereditary title or are included in the American Social Register, by Inner-circle location

Number of large-company directorships	British Title[a]		American Social Register[b]	(Number of directors on which successive column figures are based)		
	A est.	B est.				
One	9.9%	3.6%	7.6%	(564)	(1554)	(2306)
Two	14.2	9.1	20.2	(169)	(264)	(267)
Three or more	20.6	17.5	19.9	(131)	(154)	(226)
Ratio 3+/1 bd.	2.1	4.9	2.6			

Source: Data compiled by author.
    [a] The aristocratic titles include Baronet, Baron, Duke, Earl, Marquess, and Viscount.
    [b] The 1978 and 1979 editions.

the compensation of top corporate officers is large enough to permit accumulation of substantial wealth during a successful career, extensive holdings are typically only the product of several generations' accumulated growth of diversified investments.[29] Information on the directors' total personal holdings is unavailable, but income can be used to estimate wealth, and it is available for the more than 1,300 American business leaders in the college and university trustee data set. This is the special set of corporate executives and directors who also served as university trustees. They are of particular interest here since, in response to a survey, they had provided information on both their corporate positions and their personal income. A fair proportion of these individuals served on the board of a large corporation but did not themselves hold an executive position, and it will prove useful in the following analysis to distinguish them from those who were executives.[30] All were asked to report their total annual income in 1967 from all sources before taxes, and the percent receiving incomes exceeding $100,000 is displayed in Table 3.4. Though there is obviously no

Table 3.4 Percentage of American executives and directors with annual family incomes exceeding $100,000 in 1967, by Inner-circle location

Number of large-company directorships	Manager of large company		(Number of individuals on which column figures are based)	
	Yes	No		
One	41.5%	27.6%	(199)	(291)
Two	61.3	37.2	(107)	(144)
Three or more	76.2	57.1	(151)	(125)
Ratio 3+/1 bd.	1.9	2.0		

Source: Data compiled by author.

one-to-one relationship between income and wealth, incomes in this range nearly always signify large personal assets. Of the general public, aged fifty-five to sixty-four with incomes of more than $100,000 in 1962, nine-tenths held assets whose total value exceeded $500,000.[31] Moreover, those with incomes in this range tended to derive the bulk of it from property ownership rather than from salary.[32]

Using the nine-tenths fraction, it can be estimated from Table 3.4 that approximately 37 percent of the single-directorship managers held at least half a million dollars in assets. By contrast, 55 and 69 percent of the inner-circle executives—the double and many-board directors—were worth more than $500,000. The possibility must be addressed that this wealth is more often a consequence than an antecedent of entry into the inner circle. The wealth disparaties observed among the directors who are not managers, however, suggest that this has not been the order of events. The remuneration of outside directorships is not sufficient to amass substantial wealth, and lacking the high levels of compensation managerial positions provide, most nonmanagers would have had little opportunity to create their own personal fortune. Yet it is observed that the income differences between the core of the inner circle and those outside its boundaries are equally pronounced for the directors who are not corporate managers, ranging from 27 to 57 percent.[33]

INNER-CIRCLE LEADERSHIP OF THE MAJOR BUSINESS ASSOCIATIONS

The fourth and final factor accounting for the inner circle's leading political role is the strategic location it has come to occupy in the councils of the major business associations. Trade associations abound in both countries, of course, and most are organized to defend the interests of a specific industry, whether banking, petroleum, or electronics, or to promote regional economic growth. Yet a few have been established to provide a forum for the discussion and articulation of policies affecting most large companies, regardless of sector or region. These organizations typically draw their most active members from the top ranks of a broad range of corporations scattered throughout the country. The first among these in the U.S. are the Committee for Economic Development, Business Council, Conference Board, Council on Foreign Relations, and, of particular interest, the Business Roundtable; the important U.K. associations include the Association of British Chambers of Commerce, the Institute of Directors, the British Institute of Management, and, above all, the Confederation of British Industry. Detailed studies of these organizations confirm what is well familiar to readers of the business press and denizens of the higher circles, namely that these organizations have assumed a central role in establishing common business positions on a range of contemporary public policy issues.[34]

The Confederation of British Industry (CBI), for example, numbers more than 13,000 companies and 200 trade associations among its ranks, and its working staff exceeds 400. It has been described as "the US Chamber of Commerce, the National Association of Manufacturers, and the Business Roundtable, all rolled into one."[35] And with a "level of access to the government decision-making process which few interest groups can equal," the CBI, since its founding in 1965, has assumed an undisputed role as the chief voice of industry: the CBI's growing enrollment of many leading financial and retail firms has further legitimized its claim to be the chief voice of business as well.[36] The CBI is in continuous negotiation with government ministers on practically all matters of any significance to business. The policies it puts forward are evolved through a complex governing structure that includes a ruling council of 400 members, a president's advisory committee of 25 company directors, and more than 25 standing and ad hoc committees responsible for the formulation of positions on everything from general economic policies to research strategies and environmental legislation.

Though dwarfed in political significance by the CBI, the British Institute of Management (BIM) also occupies an important niche in the constellation of general business representation. With some 65,000 individual members (the CBI accepts only company and trade-association membership), the BIM's traditional role has been to provide educational and informational services to management as a profession. More recently, however, it has also undertaken "to represent the collective views of the membership vigorously and forcefully" to the government on matters ranging from taxation to labor legislation.[37] It too evolves positions through a governing council and committee system, with the bulk of this leadership drawn from a select group of some 1,200 Fellows of the Institute.

No single American organization can claim the near monopoly over expression of the business viewpoint that the Confederation of British Industry has come to command. American business still speaks through diverse organizational voices. The fragmentation is not a competitive one, however, for the key associations perform largely complementary tasks. Foreign policy is the privileged domain of the Council on Foreign Relations (CFR), a private body of some 1,500 members, largely corporate but with foreign policy experts from a range of other institutions as well. Through its continuous round of seminars and discussions, position papers, publications that include its influential journal, *Foreign Affairs,* and access to the highest levels of government, the CFR is the unrivaled vehicle for private discussion of foreign affairs among those who count. The lesser known Conference Board and Committee for Economic Development (CED) are devoted to research, analysis, and policy development on matters of general interest to large business firms. The Conference Board emphasizes issues of corporate organization and operation, such as board structure and decision making, while the CED stresses policy formulation on matters of current economic debate, including, in recent years inflation, monetary policy, and unemployment. Made up of fewer than seventy active members, the Business Council has long operated as a direct, though in recent years unofficial, advisory body to the Department of Commerce. It facilitates informal dialogue between the highest levels of business and government by bringing representatives of both together in weekend retreats and other forums designed to encourage frank exchange. Along with the Business Roundtable, it is described as "the country's most elite business organization."[38] The Business Roundtable is the newest of the major American associations, and it has adopted the aggressive role of pressing for national legislation through direct participation of its nearly 200 members—each of whom is a chief executive officer of one of the nation's largest corporations. The personal involvement of these CEOs has more than compensated for the organization's comparative youth. Most observers would not fault the assessment of one writer that the "Roundtable represents more concentrated economic power and political clout than any other business organization in the country."[39]

Since these associations constitute the formal interface between the highest levels of government and large corporations in all sectors, those who guide their activities can have a decisive impact on the public policies collectively promoted or opposed by business. Given this organizational raison d'etre, association leadership should fall on those with a demonstrated ability to articulate the broader needs of business and to translate these into realistic policy alternatives. The continuous round of association meetings and conferences should provide members with ample opportunity to judge their mutual capacities at very close range. And in fact, this is precisely what does transpire, according to the staff members of several of the organizations and active corporate participants who were interviewed. Given the breadth of perspective already shared within the inner circle, its members should be among the first to receive invitations into the smaller, select associations, such as the Business Council, and be favored candidates for leadership roles within the broader membership organizations, such as the Confederation of British Industry. The participation rates are shown in Table 3.5, and once again it is evident that members of the inner circle occupy a leading position.[40]

Reaching the bureaucratic apex of the CBI and BIM is a direct function of proximity to the inner circle. Six percent of single directors, eight

Table 3.5 Percentage of corporate directors who are members or leaders of the major business associations, by Inner-circle location

Number of large-company directorships	British associations[a]		(Number of directors on which figures are based)
	Confederation of British Industry	British Institute of Management	
One	6.0%	11.5%	(1554)
Two	7.6	20.1	(264)
Three or more	20.1	39.6	(154)
Ratio, 3+/1 bd.	3.4	3.4	

	American associations[b]					
	Business Round-Table	Business Council	Committee Economic Develop-ment	Conference Board	Council Foreign Relations	(N)
One	2.9%	2.5%	2.9%	5.0%	4.0%	(2306)
Two	5.6	7.1	9.0	12.7	15.0	(267)
Three	15.0	19.0	12.8	23.0	15.0	(226)
Ratio 3+/1 bd.	5.2	7.6	4.4	4.6	3.8	

Source: Data compiled by author.
  [a] For the Confederation of British Industry, members of the 1980 council and committees; for the British Institute of Management, 1979 fellows and members of the council and committees.
  [b] For the Business Roundtable, 1979 members; for the Business Council, 1977 and 1979 members; for the Committee for Economic Development, 1978 trustees; for the Conference Board, trustees and officers in 1976, 1977, and 1979; and for the Council on Foreign Relations, 1978 members.

percent of the double directors, and 20 percent of the many-board directors were members of the CBI council or committees. The rate of participation of those in the core of the inner circle is better than three times that of business leaders outside the circle. An identical ratio in participation rates is observed for the BIM as well. Invitation into the highly select Business Council and Business Roundtable seems almost always to require inner-circle status, as does ascent into the leadership of the Committee on Economic Development, Conference Board, and Council on Foreign Relations. Ratios of the participation rates, comparing single and many-board directors, range from 3.8 for the Council on Foreign Relations to 5.2 for the Business Roundtable and 7.6 for the Business Council.

The leaders of the Confederation of British Industry and the members of the select Business Roundtable, then, are not cross-section communities, nor are association policy initiatives expression of a cross-section of business opinion. Rather, those who shape CBI and Roundtable positions, who guide their deliberations, and who enter as emissaries into regular meetings with senior government officials are a highly select lot, given to ideas that may promote the prosperity of all but are frequently at odds with, if not antithetical to, the momentary wisdom of most. To assert that the CBI and Business Roundtable are little more than instruments for inner circle politics would be an overstatement, but there is no doubt that they are closely guided by the concerns, if not always the interests of one small fraction of the business community. Of the British directors in our study who serve on the two most central governing bodies of the CBI, the president's advisory committee and the ruling council, fully half are members of the inner circle. Similarly, of the American executives and directors we have been closely following who are members of the Business Roundtable, more than two-fifths (42 percent) are inner-circle connected; more than half (52 percent) of our members of the Business Council are from the inner circle. To the inner circle's many other strategic political advantages is added, then, the stature and resources of the premier business associations. Moreover, the visibility and contacts in government circles generated by association leadership can only further heighten the inner circle's opportunities for special hearing.

INNER-CIRCLE ORGANIZATION

The business pillar of the establishment is indeed a pillar, but as powerful as those who occupy the pillar's base may be within their own large corporation, they lack the means and incentives for shaping classwide policy. The top of the pillar does not. It has the power to act through its umbrella of intercorporate connections. It has the unity to act by virtue of its shared social cohesion. Its upper-class connections opens doors when it chooses to act. And at its disposal are the business associations when formal representation is needed.

The inner circle is not all powerful, however. Nor is it seamless. The upper-class credentials are partial, the ability to control the associations imperfect. Yet in all these respects it is more prepared to act than are other individuals or groups of corporate managers and directors. The pluralist and structuralist claims of elite disorganization capture a relative truth when applied to the bulk of the corporate community. The claim of disunity is far less applicable, however, to the inner circle.

Even then the inner circle does not act as a committee of the whole. Political action is taken not by the inner circle, but by organized entities within it. Resources are actually mobilized through (1) the intercorporate and informal networks linking members of the inner circle, and (2) the formal associations over which the inner circle exercises substantial influence. The real unit of classwide corporate politics, then, is not the business elite as a whole, nor even this select stratum of the elite. As blocs, neither business nor the inner circle act on behalf of anything. But within the inner circle are a set of horizontally organized networks and vertically structured organizations that do act. These are the real motors of business political motion. The inner circle, then, refers not just to the company executive directors who constitute its membership, but also to the networks that constitute its internal structure. It is the power of these internal networks that propel members of the inner circle into leadership roles on behalf of the entire corporate community.

FOUR

The Leading Edge
of Business Political Activity

With a power supported by so many reinforcing strands of corporate, social, associational, and class connections, the inner circle should be expected to be found at the forefront of business political outreach, whatever the forum. And the forums are many. Corporate executives are called to counsel government and govern universities. They are a favorite target of inquiring journalists and campaign fund raisers. The opportunities for directly shaping government policies and indirectly shaping the political climate are many and varied.

The inner circle is well positioned to intervene in virtually any forum. This chapter will demonstrate that it does so, and that it does so far more often than the remainder of the corporate community. We will examine four distinct forms of intervention, selected for their political significance, diversity, and research tractability. They are: (1) advisory service to the national government; (2) assistance in the governance of nonprofit organizations; (3) financial support for political parties and candidates; and (4) appeals through the mass media for public opinion.[1] The inner circle's aggressive presence in each forum suggests that whatever the opportunity, it will be there first and in greatest force.

ADVISORY SERVICE TO THE NATIONAL GOVERNMENT

The American and British governments are assisted in the prolonged process of policy formulation by numerous advisory panels composed of outside experts. Sometimes representative, nearly always distinguished, panel members provide counsel to government agencies and ministries on virtually all major questions of public policy. The U.S. Department of Commerce draws upon the National Industry Energy Council; the Treasury Department hears from its National Advisory Committee on Banking Policies and Practices; and the Department of Defense is counseled by its Defense Industry Advisory Group. On somewhat more circumscribed matters, the Commerce Department also learns from its Advisory Committee on Fire Training, while the Defense Department is assisted by its Advisory Group on Utilization of Gravimetric Data. At the end of 1976, no fewer than 23,000 outsiders on 1,159 advisory committees, commissions, boards, councils, and other bodies added their thinking to the policy process, constituting a "major institutional method for linking private interests and private expertise to public authorities."[2]

Numerous boards, commissions, and advisory bodies have been temporarily or permanently created to assist in the formulation of British public policy as well. In 1978 some 360 minister-appointed "public boards" served the government.[3] Their service varied widely, from operation of quasi-autonomous agencies—the British Broadcasting Corporation is a familiar example—to the management of nationalized industries (British Steel Corporation), guidance of research and development programs (Science Research Council), and oversight of social service delivery (Regional Health Authorities of the National Health Service). The purpose of the boards is not to offer a democratic forum; expert guidance is the objective. In the case of the nationalized industries, for instance, the oversight bodies are there "to provide the industry with possible collective leadership and not . . . to secure the representation of certain interests, such as those of workers and consumers."[4] Business presence on nationalized industry boards comes as no surprise; less expected is its presence throughout the advisory apparatus. An assessment of the occupations of 272 members of 39 public boards in 1956—including the British Transporation Council, Central Electricity Authority, and Gas Council, among others—finds that two-fifths of the members are company directors (they constitute a fraction of 1 percent of the adult population), and at least one company director is placed on all but two of the boards.[5] The voice of business on such bodies, however, is not expected to be a cross section of corporate opinion.

To gauge which business leaders do indeed help govern, we draw upon comprehensive lists of the members of all U.S. federal advisory committees in 1975 and 1976 compiled by the U.S. Senate Committee on Governmental Affairs.[6] A comparable roster of all public-board members in Britain is unavailable, but we were able to identify the members of a large number of the most prominent boards for 1978 and 1979; included are the boards for the British Broadcasting Corporation, United Kingdom Energy Authority, and the National Bus Company.[7] Dividing our business leaders in much the same way as before, we see that the number of corporate directorships

Table 4.1 Percentage of corporate directors who serve on a U.S. federal advisory committee or U.K. public board

Number of large-company directorships	U.S. federal advisory committee 1975–76	U.K. public board 1978–79	(Number of directors on which figures are based)	
One	8.5%	2.6%	(2306)	(1554)
Two	17.6	6.1	(267)	(264)
Three	24.8	12.3	(226)	(154)
Ratio 3+/1 bd.	2.9	4.6		

SOURCE: Data compiled by author.

they held is a reliable predictor of whether they will be called to render public service (Table 4.1).

In 1975–76, only 9 percent of the American board members outside the inner circle (single directors) held appointment to a federal advisory committee, whereas 25 percent of the center of the circle (many-board directors) so served. The parallel figures for British managers serving on public boards appointed by the national government are 3 and 12 percent, for a ratio of better than four to one. Again, these results are little changed when age and other possibly confounding factors are taken into account. It is arguable that a fraction of this difference is due to a reverse causal ordering: managers become more attractive outside directors if they are demonstrably well connected in government circles. Other evidence, however, suggests this cannot explain most of the difference. If we first classify those who were directors of the 800 largest firms in *1969* according to their inner-circle location by criteria identical to that used in Table 4.1,[8] and they examine their federal advisory-committee participation rates in *1976*—seven years later—we find even greater disparity between single and many-board directors, with an odds ratio of more than three to one.[9]

Just how extensive can be the activities of the many-board company director/public-board member is well illustrated by the career of one merchant banker, Edwin Philip Chappell.[10] The bulk of his career has been with the sixth largest accepting house, Morgan Grenfell, where he was vice-chairman in 1980. But he also attended board meetings of Equity and Law Life Assurance Society (the 14th largest insurer), Fisons (approximately 100th in manufacturing), Guest, Keen & Nettlefolds (the 15th industrial), and International Computers Ltd. (the premier British computer manufacturer) of which he assumed chairmanship in 1980. His diverse banking, insurance, and manufacturing experience appealed as an asset to the government as well, for Mr. Chappell also served on one of the Treasury's Economic Development Committees (for the food and drink manufacturing industry) and as a governor of the British Broadcasting Corporation. Earlier he had lent his expertise by serving as chairman of the National Ports Council and as member of the Department of Education and Science's Business Education Council.

American business leaders are provided an additional opportunity denied their British counterparts. While the senior administrative positions in the British state are occupied by the governing party's own members of Parliament, the analogous American posts are given to whomsoever the White House may favor. And all presidents have favored leading figures from the world of business. Whether the administration is Republican or Democratic, majorities of the Cabinet and sub-Cabinet appointments have been of those from or close to large corporations whose full-time service to the government is viewed as purely transitory.[11] But here too inner-circle status is a decisive asset in securing the opportunity to shape government policy—in this case, very directly. The likelihood that the multiple directors in the U.S. data set had served in a senior government post is approximately twice that of single directors.

The seventeen Cabinet-level officials appointed by the Reagan administration in 1981 could claim better corporate roots than some previous Cabinets, yet their collective profile is not atypical and usefully illustrates the inner circle's privileged access. Four of the most important posts were filled by senior executives of large American corporations who also served on several boards of other major corporations: Defense Secretary Caspar Weinberger (from Bechtel Group, a large privately held construction and engineering company), Treasury Secretary Donald Regan (of Merrill Lynch, the number one Wall Street company), Commerce Secretary Malcolm Baldrige (Scoville Inc., the 300th largest industrial firm), and Alexander Haig (from United Technologies Corporation, the 25th largest manufacturer). Several other posts were occupied by senior partners of corporate-oriented law firms who also served on the boards of a number of blue chip corporations. These include William French Smith, the attorney general, and Samuel Pierce, the secretary of Housing and Urban Development. Before entering the administration, the latter had been a director of the First National Boston Corporation (the nation's 16th largest commercial bank), Prudential (the largest life insurer), General Electric (the 9th largest industrial firm), International Paper Company (the 57th manufacturer), and several other companies. He had also proven an attractive candidate for earlier government service, and his extensive experience had included membership on a national commission on wiretapping and an advisory committee to the U.S. comptroller of the currency. The reliability of such multiple corporate directorships in helping to discern the political leanings of each Cabinet member was widely used in media commentary at the time of the appointment.[12] In predicting the housing and urban policies of the only member of a racial minority appointed to the Reagan Cabinet, the *Wall Street Journal* comforted its readers with this final judgment on Samuel Pierce: "The fact that he is black explains less about him than the fact that he was, until taking office, a member of several corporate boards."[13] Later, when George P. Schultz and his new appointees replaced Secretary of State Alexander Haig and staff, *The New York Times* offered its readers similar assurance. "The State Department has been placed in the hands of a group of men noted for their calm, conservative and self-assured authority," the *Times* observed. "They are the consummate old boys of the country's political/corporate network."[14]

GOVERNANCE OF NONPROFIT ORGANIZATIONS

The policies of nonprofit organizations—the "third sector"—are often of no less significance to business than are those of government. The curriculum and research agenda of universities, the vitality of cultural organizations, and the programs of philanthropic foundations and grant-making trusts can all have a decisive impact on the business environment, a reality increasingly recognized by corporate leaders. "Business cannot survive and prosper unless the society in which it operates is healthy and vibrant," announced the chairman of the Business Roundtable, Clifton Garvin (also chairman of Exxon Corporation). "It is, therefore, in business's own self-interest . . . to engage in philanthropic activities which serve to strengthen the fabric of society." The Roundtable accordingly calls "on the business community to increase contributions for educational, health, welfare, and cultural activities and give philanthropy greater importance."[15] The third sector's potential value to business has received greater recognition by the nonprofit organizations themselves, for they have increasingly sought business subvention in the form of executive time, and, especially, financial assistance, as the rather long list of corporate sponsors for nearly any recent opera or ballet performance at Covent Garden or Lincoln Center illustrates.

The governing boards of nonprofit institutions in both countries typically include several top administrators from the institution and a dozen or more prominent outside citizens. The business presence on British governing boards of the nation's leading organizations is already a significant fraction and still growing; in America, business people now typically occupy one-third to one-half of the governing positions.[16] But once again, as anticipated, company appointees are drawn disproportionately from one highly select pool. Consider, for instance, the twenty-four-member governing board for one of England's premier institutions of higher education, the London

Business School. In 1979, four members of the school's staff were joined on the board by four outside educators and four government officials. The remaining twelve seats were occupied by highly successful corporate managers, and half of these executives were themselves on the board of directors of at least two major companies. Thus, the programs of the London Business School were guided by, among others, Sir Alex Jarratt, chairman of Reed International (24th on the London *Times* list of industrials) and director of Imperial Chemical Industries (4th largest industrial); Sir Brian Kellett, chairman of Tube Investments (47th industrial) and director of Unigate (42nd among manufacturers); and Sir John Pile, chairman of Imperial Group (6th largest industrial) and director of National Westminster Bank (2nd biggest clearing bank). All could speak with authority about the managerial training required for those wishing to enter business enterprise.

For a systematic assessment of corporate directors' involvement in the governance of nonprofit organizations, we focus on their role in overseeing three institutions: cultural organizations (e.g., as trustee for the Royal Opera House or the Metropolitan Opera Guild); universities (e.g., as chancellor of the University of Sussex or trustee of Princeton University); and grant-making trusts or philanthropic foundations (e.g., as trustee of the Rayne Foundation or Ford Foundation). Information on involvement in cultural organizations and universities is drawn from standard biographical directories,[17] and data on trusteeships of the British grant-making trusts and American philanthropic foundations are obtained from complete directories of the major trusts, foundations, and their overseers.[18] Rates of participation in the governance of these three areas of nonprofit activity appear in Table 4.2. It is strongly suggested that multiple directors are preferred over other business leaders when such appointments are considered. In the case of British cultural organizations, for instance, according to the A estimates, 9 percent of the single directors took part in the governance of at least one institution, but 14 percent of the double directors served, and 16 percent of the many-board directors were active, with even sharper differences indicated by the B estimates (the odds ratio is nearly 4). The disparity in probabilities of appointment are equally pronounced for higher education and grant-making trusts, where the odds ratio ranges from 2 to more than 6. The basic pattern is paralleled in the U.S. as well. Many-board directors are 3 to 5 times as likely to oversee third-sector organizations as are single directors.

It is also expected that inner-circle managers find it easier than other business leaders to mount resources for favored nonprofit organizations. Their exceptional ability to mobilize corporate support is a factor accounting for the inner circle's superior status within the business community; but it also makes them attractive candidates when financially strapped arts

Table 4.2 Percentage of company directors involved in the governance of three types of nonprofit institutions, by Inner-circle location

Number of large-company directorships	British nonprofit institutions[a]				
	Cultural		Universities		Grant-making trusts
	A est.	B est.	A est.	B est.	
One	9.0%	3.6%	7.6%	2.8%	8.9%
Two	13.6	9.1	13.6	8.7	15.2
Three or more	16.0	13.6	21.4	18.2	16.9
Ratio, 3+/1 bd.	1.8	3.8	2.8	6.5	1.9

	American nonprofit institutions[b]				
	Cultural		Universities		Philanthropic foundations
	A est.	B est.	A est.	B est.	
One	4.3%	3.0%	5.6%	3.9%	18.0%
Two	3.4	3.4	17.6	17.6	41.6
Three or more	13.7	13.7	20.8	20.8	51.3
Ratio 3+/1 bd.	3.2	4.6	3.7	5.3	2.9

SOURCE: Data compiled by author.

[a] The number of directors on which the British A estimates are based are 564, 169, and 131 for one, two, and three or more directorships, respectively. The base numbers for the B estimates and the grant-making trust percentages are 1554, 264, and 154.

[b] The number of directors on which the American A estimates are based are 1591, 267, and 226; the base for the other columns are 2306, 267, and 226.

organizations and universities compose their governing boards. Nonprofit administrators who cue on inner-circle location are indeed making discerning judgments, according to evidence from the study of American university trustees. The executives and directors in this survey were asked about the amount of money they had been able to raise during the preceding five years for the universities on whose governing boards they served. The amount included "contributions generated by [their] efforts through direct solicitation or contacts," but it excluded funds personally contributed by the trustee. The percentages mobilizing over $100,000 for their university is shown in Table 4.3, with corporate managers again distinguished from nonmanagers, and it is evident that inner-circle centrality is a strong predictor of resource mobilization. Twenty-two percent of the single-director executives obtained major financial backing for their university, while this proportion was raised to 55 percent among many-board executives. Moreover, it is apparent that nearly the same difference in fund-raising success is evident among those directors who are not themselves corporate managers. Indeed, whether a director is also a manager has virtually no bearing

Table **4.3** Percentage of American executives and directors raising at least $100,000 in 1963–68 for the university on whose governing board they serve, by Inner-circle location

Number of large-company directorships	Executive of large company		(Number of individuals on which column figures are based)	
	Yes	No		
One	22.4%	23.8%	(161)	(231)
Two	45.5	35.1	(88)	(114)
Three or more	55.1	51.0	(127)	(104)
Ratio, 3+/1 bd.	2.5	2.1		

Source: Data compiled by author.

on his or her ability to mobilize resources.[19] Thus, in predicting which business leaders would be most vigorous and effective in improving the financial security of a favored nonprofit organization, it is far more important to know their multiple-corporate connections than their managerial status in a single firm. Interorganizational position seems more the determinant than intraorganizational position.

Viewed from the standpoint of the nonprofit organizations, if obtaining financial support is of pressing concern, as it surely is for most, forging links with the inner circle is a better strategy than with specific companies or a cross section of the business community. This can be seen if we reorganize our data to make the university, rather than the individual trustee, the unit of analysis. We examine the success of 341 universities in raising corporate funds as a function of the business composition of their governing boards.[20] The annual level of business support for each university is assessed by calculating the average corporate contribution over a two-year period during the late 1960s.[21] The universities received from business enterprise, on average, more than $400,000 annually per institution, about 15 percent of the income received from all contributing sources.

In order to consider several alternative explanations for the observed patterns of business contributions, university governing-board composition is assessed using four distinct indicators, justified below, in addition to a measure of inner-circle presence (the rationale for their separate inclusion will become apparent in a moment). A university trustee is classed as (1) a member of the inner circle if the individual was a director of a large corporation and an executive of another big firm, or a director of at least two large companies; (2) an *industrialist* if he or she was an executive of a manufacturing or merchandising firm; (3) a *financier* if the executive position was with a banking, investment, or insurance firm; (4) a large-firm manager if he or she is an executive with a publicly traded corporation; (5)

Table 4.4 Level of corporate financial support for American universities, by business composition of university governing boards

Type of trustee[a]	(1) Average percentage of trustee type on governing board	(2) Average corporate contribution ($1,000s) Board < 11% of trustee type	(3) Average corporate contribution ($1,000s) Board > 30% of trustee type	(4) Ratio, (3)/(2)	(5) Correlation (of corporate contribution with trustee type)
Inner circle	14.9%	$196	$936	4.78	.353
Large firm manager	15.8%	$259	$874	3.38	.259
Industrialist	23.8%	$230	$556	2.42	.170
Business manager	35.4%	$112	$506	4.52	.155
Financier	11.6%	$374	$475	1.27	.018

SOURCE: Data compiled by author.

a See text for definition of trustee type. The figures for column 1 and 3 are based on 341 institutions. The figures in column 2 are based, in descending order, on 175, 140, 177, 135, and 176 universities. In column 3, the average amounts are calculated on the basis of 57, 54, 104, 193, and 29 institutions.

a business manager if he or she is an executive of any business firm, industrial or financial, large or small. The first column of Table 4.4 breaks down the composition of boards of trustees, showing the average percentage of trustees across the 341 universities in each of these classifications. Twenty-four percent are industrialists, 12 percent are financiers, 16 percent are large-firm managers, 15 percent are part of the inner circle; and, overall, 35 percent are business managers. Individual universities, of course, may have percentages far above, others far below, these overall averages.

At issue is the extent to which corporate contributions received by the universities increase with increasing fractions of inner-circle members or other types of business trustees on their governing boards. This can be viewed in two ways. First, we examine the average level of business support to institutions whose governing boards have 10 percent or less of each kind of business trustee, and we compare this with corporate contributions to schools with more than 30 percent of a given type of trustee. Second, we calculate the correlation between the level of company support and each of the measures of governing board composition (correlations vary from −1.0, indicating a perfect inverse relationship, to 0.0, implying no relationship between the two factors, to 1.0, signifying a perfect direct association between the factors). These figures are arrayed in Table 4.4, and again we see that it is the inner-circle composition that makes the greatest difference in business financial support.

Universities with one-tenth or less of its board composed of inner-circle trustees receive an average of $196,000 in annual business contributions, while institutions with more than three-tenths of their trustees from the inner circle raised an average $936,000 annually, a ratio of 4.8 (column 4 of Table 4). This ratio exceeds that for the other four composition measures. A more systematic measure of the association between business contributions and trustee type is the correlation coefficient, and here it is even clearer that inner-circle presence on a governing board is the best single predictor of business support for a university (column 5). The inner-circle correlation is .35, with the other four correlations ranging from .26 down to .02.[22] These figures indicate that bringing business executives onto a university governing board enhances the prospects of corporate underwriting; selectively inviting executives of only large corporations improves business funding even more; stacking the board with those having multiple corporate connections enhances it the most. Thus, we see that the most salient factor predicting contributions is the business trustees' involvement in the intercorporate directorship network, not their sector, company, the size of their firm, nor even whether they are business executives at all.

This finding contains an important cautionary implication as well. Because inner-circle members are affiliated with several large corporations, it would appear without careful analysis that the distinguishing factor in predicting corporate contributions to universities was simply whether or not the trustees were from business—or perhaps big business. Consequently, it might have been falsely concluded that it is business or big business as a bloc that is the relevant unit. If we are to have an accurate portrayal of corporate relations with nonprofit institutions, however, neither business nor even big business can be treated as if they are unitary or undifferentiated entities. The special role of the inner circle, as masked as it may be, must be acknowledged.

POLITICAL PARTIES AND CANDIDATES

Business political activity extends, of course, into the formal domain of party politics and candidate support. Direct company subvention in the U.S. is prohibited, though corporate political action committees (PACs), established in large numbers of major corporations in the late 1970s, operate on a company-wide basis to guide senior managers' personal contributions toward committee-selected candidates, generally influential incumbents and Republicans. During the 1978 election, more than two-fifths of the largest

500 industrials and 300 nonindustrial corporations had PACs in operation.[23] Company coffers are directly tapped for political financing in Britain, a legally permissible custom that the Conservative Party would be the very first to defend. Yet company financing of parties and candidates is only one facet of this form of business politics, for executives and directors take an active part in party politics as well. Corporate political contributions will be considered at a later point, and for the moment we concentrate on personal contributions.

Few senior business leaders ever enter the political fray as candidates themselves. Only 6 percent of the chief executive officers of more than half of the 800 largest American firms in 1975 had been elected to public office, according to one survey, though better than 90 percent indicated they would like to see business executives more active in electoral politics.[24] Less visible political activity is far more widespread, according to a Conference Board survey of four hundred chief executives of large American enterprises in 1979. Nearly half had publicly endorsed candidates for political office since becoming chief executives, and an equal proportion had actively campaigned or served as a fund raiser for a candidate.[25] Moreover, corporate managers are exceptionally fertile targets for campaign fundraising appeals. The degree of responsiveness to campaign solicitation, however, is neither uniform nor only a matter of personal predilection. It is, instead, crucially shaped by the business leader's proximity to the inner circle. To see this, we utilize American presidential campaign contribution data for the one year, 1972, for which the records, as a result of Watergate-associated scandals, became exceptionally public. A reasonably comprehensive listing of campaign contributors was published by the federal government, and, integrating these figures with the U.S. data set, it is evident that those within the inner circle were far more forthcoming than those outside it (Table 4.5).[26]

Of the single directors, 20 percent made contributions to the Republican presidential campaign, while 28 percent of the double directors and 45 percent of the many-board directors did so. The average contribution varied from $434 for single directors to $823 for many-board directors. Very few corporate directors gave any money at all to the campaign of George McGovern, but even here there was a slight tendency for those in the inner circle to be more active. Similar patterns are found if we examine 1972 contributions to all federal campaigns, including gifts to Republican and Democratic candidates in the presidential primaries, candidates for the U.S. House and Senate, and the two national parties.[27] Combining all forms of support for all campaigns for federal office, we find that 21 percent of the single directors gave at least some money to one or more Republican efforts, but 30 percent of the double directors and 47 percent of the many-board direc-

Table 4.5 Level of personal financial contribution to 1972 U.S. presidential campaigns, by Inner-circle location

Number of large-company directorships	Republican		Democratic		(Number of directors on which column figures are based)
	Percent of directors making some contribution	Average amount	Percent of directors making some contribution	Average amount	
One	19.8%	$434	3.1%	$52	(2306)
Two	28.1	$536	4.1	$25	(267)
Three	44.7	$823	4.4	$61	(226)
Ratio 3+/1 bd.	2.6	1.9	1.4	1.2	

SOURCE: Data compiled by author.

tors contributed. The parallel percentages for Democratic gifts are 4, 5, and 6 percent.[28] Inner-circle location structures not only national campaign financing, but local political giving as well. In a study of nearly 900 directors of 77 banks in the St. Louis area, analysis reveals that centrality to the local inner circle was the strongest single predictor of the level of the direct contributions to metropolitan, state and national candidates during the 1976–79 period.[29]

CONTACT WITH THE MEDIA

"Glib and glamorous spokespeople for the left have often succeeded in capturing the greatest share of attention while most business executives haven't yet mastered the necessary techniques," laments Willard C. Butcher, the successor to David Rockefeller as president and chief executive of Chase Manhattan Bank, but "we can't withdraw and whine over biased reporting. We have a right and obligation to hit back." His message is one to which business executives on both sides of the Atlantic are increasingly sympathetic, despite a personal shyness many of them have about contact with the public: "We must take our message directly into American homes, to the people, to the ultimate deciders of our society's fate. We need nothing less than a major and sustained effort in the marketplace of ideas."[30] Other top corporate officials agree. More than half of the chief executive officers of four hundred large American corporations surveyed in 1979 felt they should take their "views on public policy issues" to "the people" through personal media appearances.[31] "The day is gone when the top of an organization chart permitted a private life style," observed Irving Shapiro when he served as chairman of E. I. du Pont de Nemours. "A generation or two in the past, you could get by in business by following four rules: stick to business, stay out of trouble, join the right clubs, and don't talk to reporters."[32] For the current generation, the first and fourth rules no longer apply.

Corporate public affairs offices have of course long devoted themselves to promoting a proper corporate image, but Mr. Butcher is referring to a very different kind of message. Defense of "American capitalism" is the issue, according to Butcher, a defense that necessarily transcends his or any other firm's public relations agenda. It is recognized that successful corporate contact with the media can often contribute to the promotion of both firm and system interests. Still, the balance varies, and if company interests are the first, and usually only, priority for most executives, the system's interest are the concern of a select few, generally the seniormost managers whose linkages to the broader corporate community are well developed. Their efforts on behalf of system interests assume many forms, according to the American and British managers and directors interviewed for this study. An open-door policy is followed by some. They accept virtually all invitations to deliver speeches at meetings and conventions likely to receive any media coverage, appear as guests on radio and television programs devoted to general economic or political affairs, and make themselves available to be interviewed by journalists and financial writers.

It is this policy, as several managers directly acknowledged to me, that accounted for the willingness of some executives to receive me for an interview. It also helps explain why seniormost managers more often accepted my interview request than did their subordinates. They generally felt greater responsibility for getting the business point of view across to the public, and communication with visiting researchers was one more means to that end.[33] More explicable too was the offer by some managing directors and chief executives to have me back for further questions and discussion should the need arise (it sometimes did), an accessibility rarely extended by their subordinates.

A number of the managers reported that they had evolved a policy of meeting reguarly but informally with a handful of journalists, often around a luncheon at the company, offering frequent opportunity not only to explain company business but also to provide commentary on problems common to all business. The final product still remains in the journalists' hands, however, and some executives expressed dismay with what they ultimately read. Proposals abound for overcoming what is perceived to be the antibusiness, and at times even anticapitalist slant of some reporting. Among the most imaginative solution was one circulated at a retreat of leading American industrialists: one executive suggested that twenty of them pool their company resources and simply acquire a controlling interest in the American Broadcasting Company so that "at least one network will present a balanced viewpoint."[34] The desire to control the power of the media is widespread within the American business community, according to a study of large-firm executives in 1979–80. Systematic interviews with managers reveal that they perceive the media to be the single most influential institution in America. And, if preferences could become reality, they would replace this media dominance with their own corporate dominance. Moreover, business perceptions that journalists are far more liberal on economic issues and critical of the social status quo are largely correct. Parallel interviews with several hundred leading journalists with the *The New York Times,* Columbia Broadcasting System and eight other top media organizations as part of this same study show that the journalists are significantly more favorably disposed toward income redistribution and the welfare state, and more critical of the legal system and other institutions, than are business executives.[35]

The business media are never short of room when it is time to report the successes, failures, acquisitions, and year-end reports of specific companies, at least for the leading thousand. Any edition of the *Wall Street Journal* or *Financial Times* is replete with the latest earnings statements and executive changes of the largest enterprises. Yet developments common to most firms also receive attention, and leading corporate figures are often called upon for comment and interpretation. Business journalists soon recognize where informed opinion on such matters can be obtained, and, if our suppositions are correct, members of the inner circle should be among their favored sources. Such a choice would be a productive one, for it is precisely these individuals who are most prepared, to use Mr. Butcher's terms again, to take a "visible role in communicating the private enterprise perspective on a variety of critical public issues."

For a systematic assessment of who comes to represent the voice of business in the media, we turn to *The New York Times,* a newspaper whose broad readership tends to favor general corporate coverage over specific company affairs. Quotation or citation in *The New York Times* can serve as a suitable sign of access to the media. The number of times the names of the 2,800 executives and directors in the U.S. set appeared during a three year period, 1975–77, averages 1.5, though two-thirds (68 percent) do not see their names reported at all.[36] Information shown in Table 4.6 indicates that the probability of entering the pages of *The New York Times* is, as predicted, a function of inner-circle status. The percentage of those appearing at least once in *The New York Times* increases from 27 percent among single directors to 51 percent among double directors and 62 percent among many-board directors.

Table 4.6 Frequency of appearance of U.S. corporate directors in *The New York Times*, 1975–77, by Inner-circle location

Number of large-company directorships	Appearance in *The New York Times*		(Number of directors on which column figures are based)
	Percentage with one or more appearances	Average number of appearances	
One	27.0%	1.14	(2306)
Two	50.6	2.52	(267)
Three or more	61.5	4.11	(226)
Ratio 3+/1 bd.	2.3	3.6	

SOURCE: Data compiled by author.

A fraction of this difference may be due to the more-senior corporate status of the many-board directors. A portion of the paper's reporting is purely concerned with individual company matters, and these directors' higher positions would more often lead to a role as official spokesperson for their firms. Further examination of the evidence, however, reveals that this accounts for only a modest fraction of the observed difference. The ratio of the average number of appearances, comparing the many-board and single-board groups, is 2.3. If we calculate our ratios separately for (1) those who are outside directors and (2) those who are the chairman, president and/or chief executive of one of the firms we have been tracking, thereby removing the possible effects of the aforementioned potentially confounding factor, we find that the ratio is reduced some but still exceeds unity. For the outside directors, the ratio is 2.1; for the seniormost managers, the ratio is 1.4. Thus, the inner circle seeks out, and is accorded, greater access than other business leaders to those broad publics served by the print media. Getting across the corporate point of view on matters of public controversy, sustaining the ideology of free enterprise, and struggling for control of the "idea marketplace"—all matters of considerable moment to most large companies—are causes whose leadership is assumed not by specific firms nor by individuals simply fond of media exposure, but by the same network that serves as the political arm of business in so many other areas.

The inner circle, then, forms enduring relations with the governing circuits through both formal and informal channels of access. The major business associations, with the Confederation of British Industry and Business Roundtable at the forefront, offer a decisive means of formal linkage. These associations screen those who would serve as spokespersons for business during meetings of government oversight and on advisory bodies of all kinds. Those company leaders who aspire to higher callings have their prospects for appointment radically improved if they also possess the qualities necessary to emerge as a luminary in the CBI or Roundtable. Multiple directors who have entered the association leadership circles are several times more likely than others to receive an invitation to assist the government, and, in the case of the U.S., even to run the government.

THE INFORMAL SCREENING OF BUSINESS CONTACT WITH THE GOVERNMENT

When the inner circle enters politics, its entry is structured in a fashion that favors the expression of classwide points of view and discourages parochial pleadings. We turn here to an examination of how this is achieved for one, perhaps the single most important, form of political outreach—advisory and administrative work for the national government. We have selected this area to permit a more detailed assessment of the "fine structure" through which inner-circle politics is expressed. Though the features vary, analogous screening systems are found to characterize the other areas of outreach as well. In what follows it is not suggested that the specific perspectives of individual firms do not find vigorous expression; obviously they do. Rather, alongside and partially competing with this "corporate" form of political expression is one that brings forward a far more general perspective. This classwide outlook is a direct product of both the economic and social foundation on which the inner circle resides.

The Time Burden of Contact with the Government

The economic foundation, that is, the factors directly related to company organization, can be seen in the apparent paradox of senior business executives, laboring under staggering time demands from their own company, still finding space on their calendars to attend government advisory meetings in London or Washington, to participate in the committee deliberations of various business associations, and to meet periodically with the governing board of their favorite hospital, university, or charity. Moreover, those who most often assume such time-consuming responsibilities are those already devoting considerable energy to overseeing the operations of several other corporations. Not surprisingly, in many instances, "Civic duties become a beastly burden for chief executives," in the lament of a *Wall Street Journal* headline.[37] Statistics support the *Journal*'s impressions. A 1975 survey of the chairmen and presidents of 380 large American corporations found that better than 90 percent were associated with at least one philanthropic foundation, and more than half served with five or more.[38] The weekly demand was, on average, three hours of company time and three hours of personal time, a total approaching 10 percent or more of the entire workweek (56 hours is the median workweek for chief executives of large U.S. corporations).[39]

Added to this is activity in Washington as well: two-thirds of the chief executives in another survey visited the capital at least every other week. Overall, chief executives devote from a quarter to half their time to external relations, according to several surveys of large companies, with government work the leading area of activity.[40] In one 1979 survey, for instance, the chief executives reported that on average 40 percent of their time was consumed by external matters.[41] Some executives reconcile these competing demands on their time only through radical extension of their already lengthy workweek. A query about the weary appearance of one British executive at the start of a mid-morning interview elicited the fact that he was serving as a special consultant to the prime minister, without diminishing any of his full-time managerial obligations, and he had arisen at four in the morning to prepare for an afternoon meeting with several senior civil servants.

Aside from the issue of time, even motivation should seem problematic. Much of the advisory work with government, for instance, is monetarily uncompensated and of little apparent immediate benefit to the firm whose managerial talents are being lent to the process. Shaping government policies in a fashion favorable to business is, of course, ultimately of value to the manager's corporation, but a favorable outcome benefits hundreds of other companies as well as the manager's own. Still, the involvement of senior managers in the work of government is so widespread that it is safe to infer the presence of powerful individual incentives drawing company directors into this promotion of a general "business good."

Divisible Company Benefits of Advisory Service to the Government

One obvious incentive is the possibility of securing a "company good" as a byproduct of contributing to the overall policy process. Indeed, some of this activity is quite narrowly construed, with company gains placed first; any benefits for business more broadly defined are fine but ancillary to the main thrust of the company lobbying. One public affairs director of a major British manufacturer under considerable attack from consumer groups, for example, oversaw an aggressive program for maintaining direct contact with virtually all principal members of government and Parliament. "Adequate contacts, including understanding of our viewpoint," he observed, "must be permanently maintained in advance of particular events with key Ministers, key officials at the right level, and MPs with an interest in the subject and our country." The director himself had even joined several clubs devoted to preserving antique cars and ships, not because he had any interest in the past (which he had not), but because several senior civil servants with whom he had been unable to cultivate a relationship were devotees. (In addition to making successful contact, he eventually acquired an authentic taste for preservationist activity.) He targets those he seeks to influence: "If you're looking for an individual, you just need to look him up in *Who's Who,* look up his interests, take a guess where he's likely to be, and go there." A number of Conservative members of Parliament maintain homes in the vicinity of where this director has chosen to reside, carrying on, in the director's words, "a sort of cross between the commuter and country-gentleman life which we all try to live." The local MP is a frequent dinner guest at the director's home; the MP from the neighboring constituency is his regular tennis partner; and he attends weekend "shoots" with one of the highest ranking officials of the ministry, an individual whose policies are potentially most costly to his company. The social ambiance facilitates ready intimacy with those in government whose decisions affect company livelihood and, the rules of sociability being what they are, if you know several of the MPs, you can meet any of the others. This manager expresses a lobbyist's precision that is beyond the calculating ken of most top managers. Still, more than a few other directors reported that they had accepted invitations to join certain government advisory boards largely because through their presence on these boards they acquired an opportunity for direct contact with a ministry department whose favor their companies sought.

In some instances, then, the company benefits are tangible, and companies readily encourage director involvement. If this is the main consideration, however, those who occupy the interface between business and government could not be expected to represent classwide business interests to government. The network of contacts would be structured according to the specific objectives of individual firms; the executives who participate would be the choice not of the business community but of their own primary employer; as advisors to government they would stress company as much as classwide interests; and the outcome would be little more than an inchoate aggregation of a thousand diverse attitudes. The organization of this informal network would be akin to that of the interlocking directorate not as it largely is, but as envisaged by those resource-exchange theorists who consider it to be a means for facilitating particularized relations between pairs of corporations.

Government Scan

There appears to be another consideration, according to those I interviewed, that is far more important in determining the type and extent of business contact with government. It is one that does enhance the expression of integrated interests by the inner circle. It is similar to business scan, the intracorporate dynamic that lent a diffuse structuring to the interlocking directorate. We will refer to it as *government scan,* and it has much the same consequence for the structure of ties between business and government.

Virtually all large corporations, of necessity, carefully monitor the political environment, one of the salient components of which is the evolving current of thought at the highest levels of government. As in monitoring the business environment, however, secondhand knowledge is no substitute for direct exposure. And for reasons parallel to those behind the decision to join other corporate boards as an outside director, senior managers find public boards a source of considerable "intelligence." When asked why he took the time to serve on several government bodies, the chairman of a British industrial company replied that the meetings were always of informational benefit: "There are none of these occasions when one doesn't benefit; you might think you understand some problem, but the world is changing so fast that there's always some new facet." Another British company director who sat on the boards of a merchant bank, three industrials, and several major government bodies, added that as part of his service to his companies, "I made it a point of maintaining contact with all the people who I judge to be in the key [government] positions. It doesn't require much conscious effort, because one tends to move in the same areas that these people move in. The job of a company director is to identify those who are the ruling few." Since this was achieved by "traveling in the same circles" with government officials, service on public boards was a required part of the itinerary. The information acquired in such circles proved at times to be of immediate, unique value for the company. But more often than not, it was of value for what it revealed of the concerns, political forces, decision making, and policy currents in the inner circles of state. It also is an invaluable source of information on the antibusiness pressures confronting the state. "Management time spent in community affairs," observes Reginald Jones, then chairman of General Electric Company, "or in learning what motivates the activists who have such powerful effect on public policy, is not time wasted. Unless we understand these powerful social forces, and learn to respond to changing public expectations, corporations are going to become an endangered species."[42]

Government Advisory Service as a Company Decision

As should be expected, then, government advisory service is a company, not individual, choice. Most major corporations encourage senior managers to accept appointment to government bodies, despite the loss of the executive's time. "It is an absolutely clear part of the top leadership of this company to be involved in the governmental and opinion-forming scene," asserted one senior manager. He had just returned from a private luncheon with a government minister. When asked if it was important for senior managers being considered for company promotion to have had government experience, a high-ranking executive of one of America's largest corporations offered this appraisal:

> We would not not consider somebody [without such experience], but our belief is that to operate a modern business enterprise, you need some familiarity with the processes of government. It is not so much the contacts that he might have made, but rather he can understand what the lobbyist is telling him, he can visualize in his mind's eye the intricate processes that have to take place [in Washington]. The whole apparatus of government and how it works—it's of great benefit to the senior manager to understand that.

Familiarity with the inner workings of government is not a decisive asset in executive promotion, but it can be consequential. The manager of a large British industrial firm described the criteria used in his company's evaluation of managerial performance:

> Knowledge of the political scene would be a bonus point, not a prime mover. We would require the man to be an effective executive, first and foremost. But then, given that we have enough effective executives, on balance a guy who was able to do this would get a leg up before the guy who wasn't.

Moreover, once promoted, the obligation to maintain contact with the highest circles of government further intensifies, particularly for a new chief executive. Several company chairmen reported that their government service increased considerably on accession to the chairmanship, a change both they and their company anticipated and encouraged. Most companies make such activity subject to at least informal review among senior management; invitations to join a government commission are generally discussed before the recipients would indicate their willingness to accept.

The specific public body that one joins is less important than its strategic location for contact with the highest circles of government. Thus, as in the case of outside corporate directorships, government service is not primarily structured around the parochial concerns of individual companies.

Rather, it is more diffusely spread across a range of positions so as to opti-
mize a company's awareness of the diverse workings of government. The
resulting network is formed in a way that downplays expression of specific
company concerns to government, while encouraging communication of
their integrated concerns. And, this is indeed what does transpire in many
settings, according to the directors' own reports. Special pleading, even
discreetly expressed, is discouraged by the informal mores that prevail. "A
frank exchange of views" on broad thematic issues of the moment, on the
other hand, is the norm.

THE INNER CIRCLE FAVORS ITS OWN

Parochial concerns are further screened out by an informal selection procedure favoring the inner circle whenever public board or government administrative openings are to be filled. Since the guardians of the selection
process are typically themselves drawn from the inner circle, there is a
powerful element of self-replication. Far more often than other business
leaders, members of the inner circle have established long-standing informal
working relations with various government officials. It is to these business
leaders, then, that officials first turn when seeking business nominees. They
may be recruiting candidates for new advisory panels, special commissions,
and even, on occasion, Cabinet-level appointments. The process involves a
highly discreet sounding out of select business leaders when new appointments are under actual consideration. This may take the form of a secretary's or minister's request to a company director for an off-the-record,
candid evaluation of a short list of business candidates. Or it may simply be
a request for the names of suitable nominees to form that list. One American executive described it this way:

> An incoming President has got to name a Secretary of Commerce, which,
> all other things being equal, should come out of the business world. The
> transition staff calls up Mr. CEO [chief executive officer] and says, "you
> got any ideas on who ought to be the Secretary of Commerce," and so you
> build a list. Then from that list you start testing it with a second array of
> phone calls. A third party calls up and says that "we have on our list some
> potential Secretaries of Commerce, there's Bill Simon, I know he was a
> director of your company at one time, or I know you serve on a board with
> him."

When asked to identify the criteria applied in evaluating such candidates, a typical response is that "character and integrity" are of paramount
importance. But when pressed to elaborate on the meaning of these traits
in this context, these are defined as the executive's ability to transcend the

immediate imperatives of his own company and to express a broader business vision. The ability to bring forward information about the common concerns of a range of large corporations is deemed essential. Thus, one American industrialist with a long and distinguished record of service to the government, including several years as a top-ranking civilian appointee in the Department of Defense, and who sat on the board of four major manufacturing firms at the time of the interview, named half-a-dozen prominent executives who exemplified the role of the business ambassador to the government as it ought to be played. These individuals are exemplary, in his view, because they

> are down in Washington undertaking responsibilities beyond the requirements of their own operation. They are heading the [Business] Roundtable and the Business Council, and you see them willing to step out and accept public responsibility even while they will carry out their private responsibility.

Similar themes emerge from a discussion with the chairman of a British company who also had a broad range of industrial and government experience. He described the rules implicit in his frequent consultation at the seniormost levels of the British government, including regular contact with a permanent secretary, the highest ranking civil servant in a ministry:

> Occasionally one of the Permanent Secretaries, particularly [in a ministry concerned with industry] would ask me to join him at a meeting he's having. The subject might be training, it might be university graduates, it might be engineering needs, or it might be the next budget and taxation. These are very useful meetings. But you cannot go with a narrow point of view, for it would be disastrous if you did. Some tend to push their company's interests, and that really is not helpful. You're much less likely to be sought after for advice if you do that.

Another company chairman who had been a civil servant for many years before entering business, and who remains close to many members of the government, offered a similar assessment: "If you're advising a Minister or senior Civil Servant on policy, you want the background of [your] judgment to be wide and experienced," and a valuable, if not indispensable element for gaining the necessary experience is close acquaintanceship with the operations of a range of large companies. A manager's political judgment receives first coloring by the demands of the executive office, but nonexecutive directorships add their own shading. "If I am being asked a question by either a politician or senior Civil Servant," remarked one British multiple director, "I would use the background data bank of knowledge from all three companies to temper my response."

Unspoken but well-defined rules of etiquette surround occasions in which the highest levels of business and government informally meet. The rules dictate exclusion of "backwoodsmen" and one-company ideas, and inclusion of the broadminded and classwide concerns. The most intimate and frequent occasions for such exchanges are company luncheons and dinner gatherings. They are more elaborated in code and occurrence in London than New York but are widespread practices in both cities.

The company luncheon—with a ranking government official frequently the guest of honor—yields yet another intimate forum for an off-the-record, two-way exchange of views. The government minister, secretary, or high civil servant is often joined in the directors' dining room by the company's four or five seniormost managers. So prevalent is the practice in London, where distance is no barrier, that some government officials must find rare occasion for lunch with any but corporate directors. The minister whom I had opportunity to interview confirmed as much as we concluded the interview. Grinning, he confessed that he was, in fact, on *his* way out to a noontime meeting with the top executives of a large multinational corporation. The discussion that would follow, would, typically, range over a broad terrain of contemporary economic and policy issues, but specific company matters and grievances would be avoided. One British merchant banker offered a description of his luncheon arrangement; it is one that most others in the inner circle would find familiar:

> We have a Minister, a Member of Parliament, or a senior member of the Civil Service in on average two or three times a month. Usually we're dealing with the general economic scene and general government programs. We don't use the occasions to pressurize anybody. It's very difficult to quantify the value, but it keeps lines of communication open should the need arise. You get to know the man and the man knows you. It gives us an idea of the background to general government thinking. It's just one of the factors that feed into your mind in arriving at your attitudes on the economic conditions facing the country. Obviously one can never abuse the occasion by asking direct questions.

Both parties obtain a better understanding of the other's broadest concerns:

> It has a two-way trade. They like being invited. They will ask us as many questions as we ask them. They will therefore get information as to what City opinion is.

The dinner setting is even less formal and more exclusive. In both London and New York, business dinner groups meet periodically to discuss matters of moment, usually with a well-placed member of the government as the guest of honor. With fewer than a dozen individuals, virtually all high in the inner circle, the setting offers such individuals an unparalleled opportunity to explore the broadest contours of government policy. A company chairman, who is also the director of a large industrial firm, is a regular participant in one such gathering in London. He and the chairmen of five other companies constitute "a little dinner group" meeting bi-weekly with an invited dignitary:

> We have everyone from the Prime Minister through five or six economic Ministers in the current Government, the Treasury, and some opposition people. It's highly confidential because it is on the basis that there is some very frank and honest speaking. It's two way: they get quizzed and then there is a platform for them to ask. It's all done over drinks and dinner.

American business leaders enjoy less geographic and social intimacy with federal officials, but informal discussions governed by similar codes of conduct are a common practice here as well. The chairman of a New York insurance company, for instance, was on intimate terms with the individuals who were then serving as the Treasury secretary and the chairman of the Federal Reserve. He had arranged on several occasions to see them in Washington to get his views across, but they had also called him from time to time for informal soundings. To further facilitate this exchange, he had invited them on several occasions to join him and other select leaders of the New York financial community for a private exchange of ideas over lunch and dinner. The code of conduct on all such occasions was strict on one point: "There is no discussion of any pet projects, it is not appropriate to raise your own company's affairs. Only the broadest issues, general trends in the economy, are raised."

TRANSCORPORATE EXPERIENCE AND BUSINESS-ASSOCIATION LEADERSHIP ARE PREREQUISITES

Both positional and personal criteria are utilized by members of the inner circle in determining which business leaders are capable of transcending parochial concerns and are worthy of nomination to a post in or around government. A candidate must have, first of all, a record of successful service as a senior executive of a large company. "What the government wants and needs on these boards," offered a British managing director and long-time political activist, "is the practical experience of senior businessmen who have actually been responsible for substantial companies and who can speak not from an academic point of view, but from the point of view of people who actually understand the economics of business." An American director expressed a similar viewpoint and one common to his own circle:

> You're looking for a mature judgment, independence, a person who can use counsel, whose counsel itself is valuable. And it's necessary that they have

some direct personal experience as a senior officer of something. Otherwise
you'll be spending a lot of time providing an education to a person who
should be providing a government role.

Yet the depth of experience one gets in running one corporation must be
supplemented with the breadth of experience that comes from directing
several companies. The political value of a mix of the two is underscored
by the observations of one British multiple-company director and veteran
participant in the world of government consultation:

> The wider a man's experience, the more he's likely to be able to contribute
> to this dialogue interface [between business and government]. I think I
> should qualify this by saying you can get cases of people whose interests
> are so widely scattered that they're not much good on depth. In my experi-
> ence, it's pretty important that a chap who gets into this area of interface
> has got real depth knowledge in at least one of his interests. Otherwise, he
> is likely to be skating about on the surface of all too many things. If a man
> has been chairman or chief executive of a company, if he has been doing
> that job for some years, that should at least give him the depth knowledge
> for one industry. But aside from this qualification, when a man in industry,
> for example, has also got some knowledge of the financial world, of a bank
> or insurance business, he is obviously likely to have a broader view than if
> he were just a manufacturer or banker.

A second means of determining an executive's ability to promulgate
acceptable business views is to see if he or she has done so in the past,
when given the opportunity. Projects and committee work of the Business
Roundtable, Confederation of British Industry, and the other peak business
associations offer nearly ideal settings for direct evaluation. Here, the skill
with which an individual identifies and champions the overall priorities of
business, rather than those of a single firm or sector, receives careful scru-
tiny from his or her peers. If a particular individual is reasonably successful
in these settings, a minor government appointment might be recommended,
and if the manager proves effective at that first level in expressing a broader
vision, a reputation is established and the person is moved toward the
front lines. In describing the political roles of three well-known chief executives, one senior manager of a major American utility suggested that the
three, all current or former members of the Business Roundtable and Business Council, had, as a result, become part of the first circle to which government officials frequently turn for a reliable test of corporate opinion: "If
you follow these guys who get around the network and who are authority
figures in the network and have currency in it—when you call them, first of
all you get a straight answer, and secondly you get a pretty good piece of
litmus paper."

The major business associations then provide a setting for sorting out those corporate executives who possess the classwide business focus and therefore those who deserve promotion as representatives of business as a whole. We have already seen that those who make up the inner circle are concomitantly those who rise to the top of these organizations. Once there, the leadership role they assume ensures that they will be continually exposed to a diverse range of business opinion—and a large number of government officials. A significant increase in the likelihood of public service thereupon follows. Key business associations serve as the stepping stones for inner-circle entry into the world of advisory boards and administrative appointments. They both groom and screen the select number of business leaders who are to act on behalf of all.

The funneling role of the associations can be seen in figures drawn from the U.S. and U.K. data sets. For clarity of presentation, we first create two groups—those holding a single, large-company directorship and those sitting on at least two major boards. These groups are then subdivided according to whether the directors are active with two key business associations, the Confederation of British Industry and the Business Roundtable. The rates of participation in government advisory service among the four resulting groups are compared, with an anticipation that the highest frequency of service is to be found among the multiple directors who are also in the leadership of the CBI or in the Roundtable. Evidence displayed in Table 4.7 shows this to be the case.

Only 3 percent of the British single directors not active in CBI governance have received appointment to a public board in 1978 or 1979. For single directors who have taken part in CBI governance, the chances are 5 percent, and for the opposite combination, the prospects are also only 5 percent. But for those with inner-circle position and CBI experience, the probability sharply increases to 31 percent. The percentage is 8 for American single directors, 18 and 30 percent for those who are either multiple directors or Business Roundtable members but not both, but 50 percent for those who are both. Further analysis reveals that the screening function is also performed, though with less precision, by the British Institute of Management, and, in the U.S., by the Business Council, Committee for Economic Development, Conference Board, and Council on Foreign Relations. The American organizations further serve to screen appointment to top government administrative posts. Multiple directors who have been active in one of the major associations are two-to-three times more likely to enter full-time government service than multiple directors without association experience, or single directors with experience.

It is evident that those with diverse corporate connections have their prospects for appointment to government service radically improved if they also possess the qualities necessary to emerge as a luminary in one of the

Table 4.7 Percentage of American and British directors who served on a government advisory committee or public board, by Inner-circle location and involvement in the Business Roundtable or Confederation of British Industry

Number of large-company directorships and involvement in business associations	Government advisory service[a]	(Number of directors on which figures are based)
One co. directorship	2.5%	(1461)
One co. directorship and CBI leadership	5.2	(93)
Two+ co. directorships	5.4	(367)
Two+ co. directorships and CBI leadership	31.4	(51)
One co. directorship	7.9%	(2236)
One co. directorship and BR leadership	30.0	(70)
Two+ directorships	17.5	(441)
Two+ directorships and BR leadership	50.0	(52)

SOURCE: Data compiled by author.

[a] Service on a national government major public board in 1978 or 1979 for the British directors; service on a federal government advisory committee in 1975 or 1976 for the American directors.

major business associations. Multiple directors who have entered the leadership ranks of the CBI, for instance, are six times more likely than other multiple directors or single directors in the CBI leadership to receive invitations to assist the government in the formulation of public policy, and the odds are ten times greater than for directors with neither attribute. From the standpoint of the individual corporate executive seeking to enter the inner sanctum of top-level contact with national policymakers, one of the surest paths is to join several other large companies as an outside director—and then to rise up the leadership hierarchy of the main business associations.

THE ROUTE TO THE INNER CIRCLE

Schools of business administration explicitly offer training in the science of corporate management and implicitly provide a course in the art of corporate ascent. Many graduates feel ready for both. Indeed, American corporate recruiters complain that far too many new MBA graduates seem certain that they are destined to become chairman of the board. What is not offered, however, is training in either the science or art of classwide leadership, which is left for on-the-job experience. For those few aspirants who do finally succeed in becoming chairman of the board, preparation for the broader leadership role will have been well learned along the way. The ability to mix adeptly in the highest circles, to comprehend the cross currents of complex political environments, and to serve as intermediary between the two frequently warring institutions—business and government—these are the requisite skills for which conventional schooling can offer little advanced preparation.

Classwide leadership abilities are acquired over a prolonged period of upward ascent in the company hierarchy and lateral movement into the affairs of other companies. Five stages of movement into the inner circle can be identified. These stages represent a codification of a complex career process—they oversimplify and underrepresent the career ladder—but they do describe the major discrete steps on it. The number of people who achieve each of these stages form a pyramid whose width is a rapidly diminishing function of height. Many are called up, but at each successively higher level far fewer are chosen. Prospective candidates are carefully reviewed at all steps, with increasing emphasis on informal criteria as the higher stages are reached. In the selection, training, and refining process, those few who pass through each stage are incrementally transformed from creatures of the corporation to representatives of the class.

(1) *Company ascent* Movement into senior management of a large company is the necessary first stage in this metamorphosis. Success in making this ascent is the product of an inconsistently weighted mix of individual educational credentials, social connections, sponsorship, managerial talents, divisional experience, personality, and even height, according to the considerable literature extant on the determinants of doing well.[43] The ideal combination is not the same in the U.S. and the U.K. Prestigious professional credentials, quintessentially an MBA degree from Harvard University, accelerate upward mobility in the U.S., while patrician origins and the proper secondary schooling, ideally at Eton, retain special cachet in Britain, most of all in the City. But whatever the route up to senior management of the large corporation, it must be traveled along the road that leads, for the select few, to the inner circle.

(2) *Outside directorships* Lateral movement onto the boards of several other large corporations, preferably diverse in operation and product, is the requisite second stage. The correlates of success here are less-well understood, but it is certain that it rarely happens to any but those at the most senior levels of large-company management. Among these managers,

descendents of established families have advantages over the purely self-made. For those who are chosen to help direct the affairs of other companies and display a flair for this new responsibility, two interacting consequences follow. The first is educational. Service on other corporate boards not only provides the manager an otherwise unattainable firsthand appreciation for the commonality of problems that tend to recur within diverse companies, but also introduces him to a wider range of solutions, and the circumstances under which each will tend to find success. The second consequence is an increased likelihood of movement up to the very top of his own employing firm, for chief stewardship is clearly bestowed on a preferential basis to those with demonstrated success in operating in the broader corporate environment.

(3) *Seniormost management* Though not absolutely essential, surmounting the third stage of ascent to the very top of the corporate hierarchy is a decisive asset for those aspiring to the inner circle. Occupying the post of chief executive, managing director, or one of several posts immediately below, offers the unique and invaluable experience, and the mark of having borne final responsibility for the success or failure of one's own operational theories.

(4) *Association leadership* The fourth stage, participation in the affairs of the leading associations of business, follows fast on the third. Indeed, those few gifted executives who have won advance over the vigorous competition at the earlier stages now experience a gratifying improvement in opportunities. The ratio of office seeking to unsolicited invitation for office tips decisively toward the latter. Acquiring a top corporate position and several outside directorships elicits a flood of new requests. The select executives who have arrived at this stage become certain targets for charities and universities seeking new board members. They become equally attractive candidates for invitation into the Business Roundtable, Business Council, and high posts in the Confederation of British Industry. There are exceptions of course. Mavericks find their way to the top of the corporate pyramid nearly as often as they find their way to the top elsewhere, perhaps most commonly because personal eccentricities prove no barrier to those with the entrepreneurial skills or ownership interests to place them on top of the large corporation. Though an endangered species in both countries, the owner-entrepreneur is far from extinct. Yet however indispensable the most *nouveau* of the *riches* may be to their own companies, they are often seen as liabilities to the business community if permitted to speak for it. Business associations ensure this does not occur. Only business leaders whose style and viewpoints are tested and true are moved to the

front ranks of association leadership. The few who are so advanced are now almost certain to reach the next and highest stage.

(5) *Government consultation*   The distinguished survivors become *the* business ambassadors to government, favored by the corporate community and political leaders alike. Those reaching this final stage often come to devote as much time to the pursuit of classwide missions as to the conduct of their own firm's business. Their counsel is widely sought and immensely respected. They are personally familiar with nearly all senior government officials involved in economic policy. In time they acquire long records of government assignments. They enjoy invitations to the White House or to 10 Downing Street. And some become public personalities, figures known to the informed public.

This is the standard route of ascent into the inner circle. The probability of reaching any one stage without having successfully passed through the lower stages is remote. Still, as in any system, the rules of career progression are at times unevenly applied. A business leader may lack all the seemingly necessary credentials and yet become an intimate of a Cabinet secretary or a minister. Such shortcircuiting is usually the result of some special personal connection between the two individuals, perhaps stemming from their university days or from old family ties. Relationships based on such narrowly idiosyncratic connections, however, are atypical and generally too few in number to serve as a model for an optional means of ascent. In Britain, however, though not in the U.S., there is one alternative route that is substantial enough to be examined as a separate, albeit still minor channel.

British circumstances are far more propitious than American for business contact with government. Britain's population is a quarter of that of the U.S. The headquarters of nearly all major financial institutions and more than half the 500 largest industrial companies are located in London, the nation's capital. To the geographic proximity of corporate and political leadership is added a social familiarity, catalyzed, if not created, by the upper-class presence at the highest levels of both.[44] One company manager comfortably operating in both milieus described it this way: "Inevitably, because members of Parliament and leaders of the press and so on come from a relatively small catchment area, we tend to have known them for a long time." The catchment is class, and the long time referred to frequently dates back to Eton or Harrow, Oxford or Cambridge days. Old contacts, reestablished and nurtured in the intimate world of London clubs and country weekends, can help one bypass the staging that would otherwise be required. Here corporate and intercorporate rationality gives way to upper-class rules.

The salience of the alternative route is revealed by analysis of the U.K. data set. Brook's, MCC, White's and the other renowned clubs are again used to provide a convenient index of who is traveling in the right London social circuits. If we examine only those who have achieved the fourth stage of the route to the inner circle—leadership of the premier business associations—entry into the club circuits adds virtually nothing to the likelihood of ascending into the fifth and final stage. But if we look at those who have not moved beyond the first stage, the London social networks do make a difference, and a considerable one. For business leaders who serve neither as nonexecutive directors of other large firms nor as luminaries in the CBI, participation in the club world doubles their probability of service on a public board. In the U.S., by contrast, similar analysis reveals that club life is largely ancillary, an attractive diversion but not an alternative means of advancement. Corporate and classwide principles control entry into the American and British inner circles, but in Britain upper-class principles retain a minor deciding power as well. Most entrants into the inner circle are selected through careful company and transcorporate screening. Yet in Britain a small, but not insignificant number of entrants circumvent the classwide screening altogether. They are, of course, screened, but by upper-class criteria instead. Those who are passed are exceptionally fine "old boys" but are thus also less attuned to the classwide concerns of large companies. The advice they render to the government is correspondingly different from the recommendations offered by those recruited through the more orthodox route to the inner circle.[45]

HOW TO IDENTIFY A MEMBER OF THE INNER CIRCLE

Social cues are an intelligence source that we continuously use to identify the station, wealth, and power of those we encounter, however personally reticent they may be to offer them. At one time, interviewers conducting home surveys could infer the occupants' income and education with fair accuracy as soon as they had entered their living room—and had a chance to observe whether an encyclopedia was present. No analogous artifact adorns the office walls of the inner circle and, alas, their subdued suits are indistinguishable from what everybody else is wearing on Wall Street and in the City. There are other indirect signs, however, clues that can reliably suggest inner-circle identity. Ask, for instance, whether the executive has taken an active part in programs designed to introduce business-oriented curricula into the schools. Most will profess that free enterprise receives short shrift in secondary schooling and certain denigration in higher education. Yet taking action is another matter. Improving youth's understanding of the importance of profits and free markets can serve all companies, but no divisible gain is apparent for those firms that actually do something to improve it, a classic free-rider problem. Despite widespread concern, it is not surprising, therefore, that few companies and executives find time to become involved.

Those business leaders who do become active consider the classwide problem too serious to ignore, despite their own company's preference that they make other use of their time. And more often than not this commitment is a product of traveling in the inner circle—or a sign of future ascent into it. Their action takes many organized forms; programs of the Confederation of British Industry and Business Roundtable are illustrative. The CBI has established a separate educational foundation to work with students, faculties, and school authorities to assist, in the words of its chairman and a quintessential representative of the British inner circle, Sir John Partridge, "the generation, throughout the educational system, of a better understanding of the national wealth-creating role of industry and commerce in our society."[46] Targeting secondary school youth aged thirteen to sixteen, the strategy has been to focus on their teachers—by introducing more discussion of business into their training program, establishing in-service courses on commerce and industry, and offering classroom materials with views and information more favorable to business.

The Business Roundtable has targeted a different constituency—those whose schooling is finished but whose learning is incomplete. With support from the Roundtable, the editors of *Reader's Digest* prepared a series of advertisements for publication in the *Digest* and reprinted in pamphlet form for further circulation. They address the issues on which public acceptance is most needed but least firm: how multinational corporations are helping "to create a peaceful and prosperous world," why government spending spurs inflation, what large companies offer that small ones cannot, and, the oldest adage of all, that corporate profits are the lifeblood of American capitalism. "Perhaps you've noticed that the case against the free market is seldom made on hard economic grounds, but rather on hard-to-pin-down philosophical issues," suggests one installment. "That's because the facts of performance are so overwhelmingly in its favor." Thus, readers are encouraged to be wary of the "economists, social reformers, 'con-advocates' and other self-proclaimed critics [who] are trying to convince us that our system is evil, that we should feel guilty about the way we live."[47]

Such campaigns are devoid of immediate, tangible payoffs for any given firm, but they help still opposition faced by all. Leading such campaigns, inevitably, are those who worry about the future of large corporations as a whole. If one is curious whether one's business associates are near the inner circle, one can thus inquire if they are concerned with the public's seemingly primitive knowledge about the economic facts of life—and if they have themselves taken actions to enhance public understanding.

There are circles within circles, and to further specify centrality it can be useful to make one further inquiry. Has the individual been personally approached by seniormost government officials with a request for reactions to a "short-list" of candidates for appointment to the major advisory bodies or even top administrative posts? Such requests are channeled toward the core of the inner circle, and the receipt of such a request is usually a reliable sign that the recipient is at the center. This very question was posed near the end of the interviews conducted for this study, at a point when the executive's inner-circle status had already become quite evident. Those at the center of the circle almost invariably said yes, they had been recently approached; those outside virtually always said no.

THE VIEW FROM THE INNER CIRCLE

The business activists who travel the classwide networks on behalf of the corporate community share views distinct from those of their fellow directors and managers. They differ in two respects. First, members of the inner circle have a better understanding of the aggregate opinion of large corporations on matters of contemporary economic policy. Second, they have a stronger understanding of the complexities and intricacies of the political environment in which business operates. As a result, those most active in the major policy associations and in representing business to government often share centrist opinions that transcend their own company's immediate welfare, and their perceptions reflect a deeper sense of how the political process works. Members of the inner circle are not necessarily cognizant of the policies that could ultimately best serve the collective welfare of large corporations. But they do hold views that reflect the broader thinking of the business community. They are the cosmopolitans, their single-company brethren the locals.

Consensus Building and Compromise

The differences of opinion on current economic questions can be seen in the distinct reaction of the American inner circle to the proposals of President Reagan's administration in 1982 to increased taxes and military spending. Firms divided deeply on both issues, most predictably according to their feelings about the obligations of government. Sector interests, not classwide concerns, seemed to determine responses. To reduce an anticipated federal budget deficit approaching a record $150 billion in 1983, the administration submitted a tax bill calling for an increase in government revenues, reversing its push for tax cuts in 1982. Some companies felt that the bill undermined the principles of supply-side economics, opened the way for more social spending, and placed heavier tax burdens on them. Others reasoned that an unchecked deficit could be adverse for businesses sensitive to a deficit-driven increase in inflation. Indicative of the breadth of division were the opposed stands of the sectoral associations: the National Association of Wholesaler-Distributors, the National Association of Independent Businesses (representing smaller companies), and the Chamber of Commerce lobbied in Congress against the measure; the American Business Conference (an association of growth firms), and the National Association of Manufacturers pushed *for* the tax increase. But the final stand of the Business Roundtable reflected the center of gravity. Led by chief executives involved in virtually all sectors of the American economy, the Roundtable belatedly and reluctantly endorsed the bill. A reconciliation of the views of bitterly opposed business sectors and groupings, the Roundtable's posture was ideal for none, but the least vexing for most.[48] The tax measure soon passed both the House and Senate and was signed into law by the president.

While the inner circle finally sided with the national administration on its proposals for tax increases, it was less supportive of its plans for record military increases. The Reagan administration called for the largest buildup in defense spending in U.S. history. Department of Defense contracting is highly concentrated among the largest U.S. firms, and many stood to profit handsomely. Still, firms in sectors such as retail and utilities saw virtually no direct benefits, and most worried that the arms expansion could slow economic recovery by sharply increasing the federal deficit. Here too the American business community was in disarray, with executive opinion often reflecting the firm's own immediate calculus of loss and gain, as it has often done on military spending in the past.[49]

By late 1982, the elite network within the business community, reflecting on these competing considerations, moved toward cautious but open opposition. The tentative consensus for slower military growth appeared, for instance, in the annual meeting of the Business Council as it convened with government officials in the fall of 1982. The one hundred chairmen and former chairmen of large companies who attended the gathering generally favored less-rapid expansion and a tightening of control over defense spending. This attitude extended even to those who managed companies deeply involved in defense contracting. The chairman and chief executive of United Technologies, Harry J. Gray, whose company's production of helicopters and jet engines makes it the nation's second largest military equipment supplier, said, "I don't think there's a part of the United States budget that should be sacrosanct, and I would say, yes, look at defense." Reginald H. Jones, recently retired chairman of the nation's fourth largest military equipment contractor, General Electric, similarly observed, "I just question whether we can spend the projected increase wisely. You don't solve problems by throwing money at them." Representatives of other sectors expressed nearly identical opinions. Philip Caldwell, chairman of Ford Motor Company; Donald V. Siebert, chairman of J. C. Penney Company, the nation's second largest retailer; and David Rockefeller, recently retired chairman of the third largest bank, Chase Manhattan, joined in the view that without constraint in military spending, the prosperity of most could be in doubt.[50]

The closing of ranks around compromise positions, one of the inner circle's main goals, can also be seen in the policies of the Business Roundtable. Its task forces study and develop positions on topics of general interest to large business, ranging from antitrust policy to corporate governance. Sectoral concerns are officially eschewed. Yet at times, when particular sectoral concerns threaten to be deeply divisive, the Roundtable's ability to bring about a reconciliation of these competing interests is crucial. Exxon and other energy producers participate in the Roundtable, but so also do many of the nation's largest energy consumers. When energy policy is under active congressional debate, the Roundtable works hard to accommodate its members' opposing stakes. To learn of their stakes, the Roundtable may directly survey its members, as it did in late 1979 concerning measures the nation might best adopt should the oil supply from abroad be disrupted (the emergent consensus was for more consumer conservation, expanded nuclear energy, and less-stringent coal-emission standards). More potentially divisive was 1977 legislation introducing phased decontrol of oil, a measure sought by producers but potentially costly to users. The Roundtable's task force on energy, despite the higher energy costs many of its members were certain to face, sided with petroleum and pushed for decontrol and related changes sought by the industry. Other companies fell behind the policy as well, viewing it as a necessity in the long run even if their own incomes were to suffer as an immediate consequence.[51]

A similar accommodation of divergent interests is evident in the Roundtable's successful role in developing legislation limiting U.S. company compliance with the Arab boycott of those doing business with Israel. The Roundtable worked closely with the B'nai Briths's Anti-Defamation League to draft and finally secure passage of an anti-boycott bill in 1977. Some Roundtable members—General Motors, General Electric, Exxon, and Bechtel—had major investments in the Middle East, and others had acceded to the boycott stipulations. But faced with intense pressures from the Jewish community, Congress, and the Carter administration, the Roundtable was able to rally its members, even those certain to lose, around a measure that would sharply limit compliance with the boycott. "The Roundtable stood in a key position to negotiate the inevitable compromise by virtue of its ties to all parties concerned with the issue," conclude two analysts who had carefully tracked the Roundtable's role in this legislation.[52] A special group of attorneys established by the Roundtable and the Anti-Defamation League developed not only the principles underlying the legislation, but even the final compromise language adopted by the Senate and signed into law by President Carter.

Understanding the Political Environment

The inner circle also shares a more developed and nuanced understanding of the political environment and how it is most productively influenced. Here the aggregated opinion of the corporate community is both relied upon and transcended at the same time. Those who lead the Business Council, the Business Roundtable, and the Confederation of British Industry have acquired an appreciation for the give and take of political life to which more isolated company managers are less tolerant. They are more accepting of compromise and reform, less taken by intransigent defense of corporate interests. The unalloyed exercise of raw corporate power, they recognize, can generate more problems than it is intended to solve. They are thus more prepared to accept the permanency of labor unions and government regulation, not in principle, but as a necessary compromise whose alternative could generate adversarial turmoil far more threatening to the future of free enterprise.

The difference in attitudes between those at the center and on the periphery of the inner circle might be made clearer by examining George Lodge's characterization of what he describes as the two opposing systems of thought prevalent in managerial circles. The first, labeled Ideology I, stresses "individualism, private property, free competition in an open marketplace, and limited government." The second, Ideology II, "defines the individual as an inseparable part of a community in which his rights and duties are determined by the needs of the common good. Government plays an important role as the planner and implementer of community needs." More than two-thirds of the corporate managers that Lodge surveyed in the mid-1970s identified with the first, individualistic ideology, but a significant minority were drawn to the "communitarianism" of the second.[53] It is this sense of partial detachment from the narrow concerns of the individual firm and partial attachment to the broader concerns of the classwide business community that centrally characterizes the inner circle's outlook.

Collective engagement implies collective responsibility, and business leaders who travel the inner circle are also more drawn to what S. Prakash Sethi has termed social *responsiveness*. He distinguishes this stage of corporate behavior from the earlier stages of social *obligation* and social *responsibilities*. In the obligation stage, a company is narrowly oriented toward its stockholders and goes little beyond meeting its legal and economic requirements. In the socially responsible stage, a company incorporates concern for other constituencies into its decisions. In the social responsiveness stage, however, a corporation recognizes that the consequences of its actions ramify throughout society, and such a corporation will take steps to ensure that management anticipates these consequences and their less clear ramifications before it acts.

Companies that are obligation oriented resist government intervention and avoid contact with government other than for their own lobbying purposes; responsible companies are more open to outside involvement in the policy process; and responsive corporations become actively engaged in the formulation of policies that go far beyond the protection of special interests. Obligatory behavior is akin to what we have described as the *corporate* principle in company action; responsive behavior is similar to guidance by *classwide* principles.[54] Sethi and other analysts who have developed similar distinctions, such as James Post, suggest that large companies are evolving, albeit at varying rates, from the isolated, obligatory stage to the engaged, responsive stage.[55] The motor behind the movement to this more advanced stage, according to our analysis here, is the rise of the classwide system of organization within the corporate community.

The inner circle's greater appreciation for the complexities of the political environment can be seen in the British network's tolerance for unions and acceptance of legislation protective of employees. The tolerance is premised on the belief that working with the unions, rather than attempting at every turn to destroy their power, offers the business world greater political stability in the long run, prevents the growth of anti-capitalist ideology and militancy within the labor force, and rationalizes labor-management relations. Illustrative of the distinctive stance here is the inner circle's reaction to a new labor bill introduced by the Conservative government at the very moment I was interviewing British company directors in 1980. The "Employment Bill" called for a reduction in union power in several ways, including a ban on secondary picketing, facilitation of secret balloting in union elections, and limitation on the closed shop. Though clearly an attack on labor prerogatives, this bill was generally recognized by political commentators and company directors alike to be a relatively mild measure, and certainly one that stopped far short of what Conservative-party philosophy might have dictated. In point of fact, CBI leaders had consulted extensively with the minister of Employment, James Prior, as he prepared the bill, and it was they who were responsible for many of its key provisions. Inner-circle members with whom I held interviews around this time generally backed the bill's language as well. Their line of reasoning was that a frontal attack on labor, given the ambivalent political climate of the moment, could achieve some immediate gains for employers, but at the same time drive new segments of labor into the hands of a then-growing activist minority bent on socialist transformation of industry. Thus, stronger medicine than that of the bill would be likely to infuriate labor, increase militancy, and in the long run, create more instability for British business than any short-run achievements could justify. Directors of single companies, far more concerned with their immediate labor negotiations and falling productivity than any grand defense of business, were, by contrast, disappointed by the limited scope of the bill. Soon after the bill's introduction in the House of Commons, they spearheaded a successful effort to reverse the CBI's stand against the need for any additional anti-labor legislation, especially on the question of the closed shop.

Corporate Liberalism

Analogous differences characterize American business opinion, focused here more on the role of government than the power of labor. Reform, regulation, and state intervention are less onerous to those central to the transcorporate network than to those on its margins. Interviewing 130 business leaders in the early 1970s, for instance, Allen Barton found that those most active in the major business associations, such as the Committee for Economic Development and the Council on Foreign Relations, and those most identified by other leaders as key figures in the inner world of national policy formulation, hold distinct political outlooks: Keynesian economic policies and reformist social policies are seen far more favorably. For example, those most active in the business associations and most identified as opinion leaders were more opposed than other business managers to the position, "In times of recession, government spending should be held down to avoid a deficit." They were more favorable toward such positions as "The federal government should support the creation of jobs in the public sector for those to whom the private sector does not provide employment," and a plan then being promoted by the White House to rationalize the welfare system.[56] In my own interviews, similar elements of moderation were evident on the single, most-pressing issue then, the rise of government regulation. The one-company managers were adamant in their opposition to the actions and policies of the cross-industry regulatory agencies. Those traveling the inner circle were no less opposed, for they too were cognizant of the costs to their firms. Yet they were less certain that wholesale dismantling was the proper solution. Public opinion could be inflamed, they feared, and they were aware that environmental, consumer, women's, and labor groups had sufficient power to require a compromising attitude in any case, not the issuance of non-negotiable demands.[57]

Historians of American business have often noted that large corporation leaders, or some fraction of them, have frequently adopted a more "progressive" attitude toward unions, labor legislation, and social reform.[58] Sometimes termed "corporate liberalism," this attitude is rooted not in a commitment to reform, nor in an enlightened acceptance of labor and government opponents, but rather in the recognition that the entire business community and the future of the private economy will best prosper if it assumes a posture of compromise. It is this rejection of a rigid opposition to everything that organized labor and government programs represent, an embracing of that complex of attitudes perhaps best termed "corporate liberalism," that distinguishes the inner circle's views.

THE LEADING EDGE

We have seen that the representatives of business to the government and the third sector emerge from that section of the corporate community most capable of acquiring a systemwide awareness of the long-range concerns of big business and most willing to promote public policies serving these needs. Core members of the inner circle are, depending on the precise measure, two-to-six times more likely than other corporate leaders to be invited by government to render advice on new employment legislation, operation of the BBC and Voice of America, and much else in between. Cultural organizations, universities, foundations, and trusts utilize strikingly similar criteria when issuing their invitations for outside business counsel. The inner circle of the corporate community is overselected by ratios of up to six-fold when nonprofit organizations form their governing boards. They are comparably overrepresented among business supporters of political candidates and business personages in the media. It is this core, then, "with simultaneous contacts in industry, finance and government," which can, in the words of one observer, "provide some element of planning and control in an otherwise unplanned economy."[59] Thus, in the succinct phrasing of another analyst, "the device of interlocking directorships succeeds in creating a form of unity in a situation of diversity, without going all the way to a monopoly in a single organization."[60]

Less formalized business access to government, then, emerges out of widespread corporate interest in monitoring the political environment. Though a product of individual level corporate rationality, government scan generates a spanning network whose structure favors classwide rationality. Corporate managers who are not capable of transcending a narrow point of view are not invited in, or at least not invited back. Those who remain learn to concern themselves with the broadest worries of both finance and industry. The informal consultative network acquires an autonomy from the corporate base out of which it arises. While constituted to promote narrow interests, the unanticipated consequence is an orientation toward the more general. It then becomes self-policing according to a new logic of its own. Insiders protect the portals, favoring only their own kind when business nominations are sought for government service and shortlists are shortened. The power of this autonomy is evident in its reactive effect on corporate leadership itself. Managers aspiring to reach the corporate summit must prove themselves in the world of government consultation. Those not well received on the outside are also less well received on the inside. Yet once granted a favorable reception on the outside, the corporate manager tends to look far beyond the firm's immediate needs. Thus, those who ultimately reach the highest executive suites are selected in part by their success in serving the firm, but also in part by their success in serving the entire corporate community.

The inner circle has thus become the leading edge of business political activity, a special leadership cadre. Its strategic location and internal organization propels its members into a unique role on behalf of all large corporations. Business leadership is something far more than an unorchestrated expression of opinion by the executives of a thousand large corporations. In arguing, for instance, as Lindblom does in his influential analysis of business and politics, that in matters of "public affairs . . . government leadership must often defer to business leadership," it must be kept in mind that such leadership is organized in a complex, specific fashion that contains crucial implications for the kinds of policies to which government leadership is compelled to listen, if not defer.[61]

FIVE

Classwide Politics and Corporate Decision-Making

The inner circle's classwide influence is not exercised solely outside the executive suite. It acts through the corporate office as well. Members of the inner circle are virtually all senior managers of large companies, and they are positioned to move corporate resources in ways beneficial to the broader corporate community even when there is no divisible benefit to the individual company whose resources are moved. They can impose a classwide logic on corporate decisions, and they often do. Thus, corporate behavior cannot be fully understood without reference to the extracorporate concerns of the inner circle. It has the ability to move companies to do what they otherwise would never do. The consequences are nowhere more evident than in the area of "corporate responsibility"—whether manifest in philanthropic giving, issue advertising, or political subvention. All such programs help shape the national political culture, the ideas and leaders that prosper, the ideologies and candidates that fail. And all are partly the result of classwide, not corporate considerations. The inner circle thus enters politics not only through personal participation, but also through the corporate actions of the companies it commands. This subordination of corporate rationality to classwide logic is indicative of the autonomous power that the inner circle has now acquired to mobilize corporate resources on behalf of its own transcorporate political ends.

NONCORPORATE CRITERIA IN CORPORATE DECISION-MAKING

Traditional economic theory, organizational analysis, and conventional wisdom adhere to a rationalist, individualist image of the modern business firm. The corporate principle rules supreme. In the final analysis, according to these perspectives, each corporation must be—and indeed is—oriented toward rational decision-making, rational, that is, from the individual firm's own standpoint. True, the process is highly imperfect and the outcome equally so. Still, the fundamental guiding principle is effective advancement of the firm's individual interests. The operational measure of the corporate principle in both the U.S. and U.K., according to academic analysis and business belief alike, is quite simply business company profits. Government policies, business competitors, and other institutions impose constraints on how profit growth is best achieved, but they should not, and indeed do not, reduce the central importance of profitability in firm decision-making. Ulterior criteria—protecting the environment, reducing racial disparities, or restoring public confidence in capitalism—are not only not proper, from this viewpoint, but not in fact salient either. Good managers necessarily concern themselves with the broader "good," but only insofar as it affects the firm's potential for profitable growth.[1] And indeed, an extensive research literature, discussed in Chapter 2, readily confirms that large corporations do discipline their decision-making around this criterion. Though social theory often displays woefully scant resemblance to reality, here they are happily coincident.

Yet this is not the whole story. To the large corporation's guiding internal logic is added another logic not of its own making. This extracorporate rationality derives from the autonomous power, distinct interests, and strategic location of the inner circle. The power is autonomous in that while it arises from the nation's large corporations, it is far more than a sum of its parts; the interests are distinct in that they reflect concrete corporate concerns yet transcend their more mundane components; and the location is strategic in that its members occupy high position within a firm and yet are responsive to a constituency far beyond it.

In most areas of top decision making, the corporation's inertial guidance is far too fixed to permit intrusion of any extracorporate considerations, even if the inner circle were disposed to impose them. Yet in certain select areas inroads have occurred. This most often happens when three conditions prevail: First, the decisions have no immediate bearing on company profits. Whatever the policy adopted, no threat is posed to the firm's first law of financial welfare. Second, the decisions do bear on classwide questions. If properly fashioned, the policies can enhance the welfare of the broader corporate community. Third, there are arguable though usually intangible benefits accruing to the individual company itself. These conditions obviously characterize only a small fraction of a company's major decisions. But the areas to which they most clearly do apply are precisely those where corporate decisions leave economics and enter politics, where actions have tangible consequences for government policies and nonprofit programs: the underwriting of political candidates, the shaping of ideas, or the financing of cultural organizations.

Wearing two hats, inner-circle managers welcome an opportunity to honor both. The large corporation unwittingly becomes another instrument for promoting a better political climate for all big business. This can be most clearly seen in three types of corporate actions, each of which will be considered in turn: philanthropy, issue advertising, and political finance. We will show that when many companies make decisions affecting these areas, both corporate and classwide considerations are taken into account. The decisions to make a financial contribution to an arts organization, to devote advertising space to contemporary issues rather than company products, and to give money to a congressional campaign are partly made as a product of company logic, but also, the evidence indicates, as a result of classwide considerations. The network of the inner circle is the channel through which these classwide considerations are transmitted, and in the final section of this chapter we describe ways in which the network is used to influence and at times pressure companies to take actions they would not otherwise consider.

CORPORATE PHILANTHROPY

A visitor to virtually any performance of the Metropolitan Opera at Lincoln Center or the Royal Opera House at Covent Garden knows from the evening's program that large companies are now at the forefront of arts subvention. And even those not so fortunate to attend are still reminded by frequent, offtimes lavish announcements in up-scale periodicals. "The top executives of American Can, Atlantic Richfield, AT&T, Exxon, GE, GM, IBM, Mobil, Prudential and U.S. Steel invite you to perform with them at Kennedy Center," proclaimed one widely circulated advertisement. These business leaders have committed their companies to underwriting the center, it is stated, and thus, "of all the stars who've ever performed at Kennedy Center, these executives are certainly among the brightest."[2] Statistics confirm the trend. Support for the arts in the U.S. still constitutes little more than 10 percent of total corporate philanthropic contributions, but the fraction is up sharply over earlier years and the practice has become so widespread that 95 percent of all large companies now provide at least some backing for the arts.[3] The aggregate level of annual arts support, according to one survey, reached more than $430 million in 1979, up from $220 million in 1976 and only $22 million as recently as 1967.[4]

Relative to the U.S., company sponsorship in the U.K. is still in its infancy, but the trends are on the same upward slope. Approximately 7 percent of all company donations are now directed at the arts, suggests one survey of large companies in 1979, and three-quarters of the corporations give at least some money to the arts.[5] The total level of business support is estimated to not yet exceed more than £10 million annually, but even this amount is far above what it was only a few years earlier.[6] Leading business advocates of expanded funding have sharpened the trends by establishing organizations expressly devoted to that very purpose. The Business Committee for the Arts, founded in the U.S. in 1967, and the Association for Business Sponsorship of the Arts, created in the U.K. in 1976, aggressively encourage companies to underwrite more culture on the simple principle that, in the words of the British association, "sponsorship is good for the arts and it is good for business."[7]

Corporate sponsorship of education, health, and human services also makes good business. Universities, hospitals, and community welfare organizations benefit from the generous *oblige* of much corporate *noblesse*. Of an estimated $2 billion in U.S. corporate contributions in 1978, education received a third, and health and welfare obtained another third.[8] Though impressive in the aggregate, company philanthropy has never constituted a major item in a company's budget. The typical large U.S. corporation allocates less than 1 percent of its pretax net income to such causes.[9] Nonetheless, it is substantial in the total, and corporate philanthropy does add distinctive influence to programs in the nonprofit sector.

Such investments, however, do not originate entirely in company self-interest, despite management claims to the contrary when annual justification is offered to the shareholders. Extracorporate criteria in corporate giving are best illustrated by concentrated examination of a single type of corporate philanthropy, and for this I have selected subvention of culture and the arts. Corporate criteria in company decision-making are described first, and then we turn to the intrusion of classwide criteria into such decisions.

Corporate Criteria in Company Donations to the Arts

Identification of a company's name with a revered museum or performing-arts organization yields divisible advantage to the sponsor. Indeed, this is always the starting justification. Sometimes the gain is in company image, other times corporate access. "Arts sponsorship," reports a public affairs manager of the British manufacturer Imperial Group is good for "developing corporate image by demonstrating a company's social responsibility. It's the opinion-formers we try to appeal to, through helping the arts."[10] Such appeals do generally reach opinion leaders. America's single largest producer, the Exxon Corporation, finds evidence from its own surveys that its generous support of cultural programs improves its image among those who count.[11] Similarly, a national survey reveals that the public regards some industries to be high in social responsibility, others low; and that these public perceptions correlate with the actual level of industry contributions.[12] Not coincidentally, Exxon and other companies in the politically sensitive petroleum industry are among the most active supporters of the arts on public television and elsewhere.[13]

In addition to national opinion leaders and the public, image improvement is aimed as well at employees and communities in which branch offices and plants are located. Corporate sponsorship, accordingly, is often directed at areas of the country where operations are most concentrated. This also partly explains why company contributions are so slanted toward the most prestigious arts organizations in a region.[14] Dollar for dollar, few better investments in corporate reputation can be found than identification with the community's premier arts. It can even be more effective than explicit promotion of corporate reputation. One large U.S. manufacturer invested extensively in the visual arts, for instance, contributing especially large amounts to major New York museums. That culture cultivates more than aesthetic ideals is a working axiom of the company's chief executive, whom I interviewed:

> There's an indirect editorial kind of credibility to arts giving. You can take ads and say, "Look at how good we are," but if you *do* things, you get editorial attribution, which I think is more believable. The payoff is not readily discernible, but I do think it is incremental, and I do believe that over time you get a larger and larger audience that has a better opinion of you.

Transnational companies carry the logic to wherever their operations may be located. In 1980 IBM United Kingdom underwrote new productions of the Royal Ballet, Royal Opera, and the Royal Academy. An IBM spokesperson offered a simple explanation for the regal association: "IBM as a major multinational obviously has an interest in making sure that its corporate image is associated with something both creative and culturally laudable."[15] Corporate patronage of the arts is undertaken with discretion, but it is a discretion exceedingly well placed.

Image aside, sponsorship also begets access. Art museums, opera houses, and theaters receiving company support become privileged places, according to the interviews, for company entertainment as well. Receptions, backstage parties, and hard-to-obtain tickets are extended to customers, government officials, and others whose favor might be sought. Subscriptions to Covent Garden, home of the Royal Opera and Royal Ballet, are especially favored by London companies. Civil servants, always fastidious about even the hint of improper contact with special interests, are known to waver, said several of the directors interviewed, in response to an invitation to enjoy the international stars of opera or dance in the company of an equally illustrious audience.

Finally, participation in the world of art collecting and giving constitutes one further strategy for managerial scan of the environment. Peter G. Scotese, the chief executive of Springs Mills, a major textile company, serves on advisory committees with the Metropolitan Museum of Art and Museum of Modern Art in New York and the American Federation of Art in Chicago. He is an avid collector of art himself, and his company makes generous donations to the Fashion Institute of Technology and other cultural organizations. "Art hones our perceptions and our sensitivities so that we have a keener awareness of our business environment," he says in defense of his company's involvement. "We become adept at spotting change, using a kind of cultural early-warning system. We become attuned to the tastes and feelings and unexpressed desires of the public." So important is this form of sensitization that managers at Spring Mills are expected, as is the case in many companies, to be personally involved in the arts. "Familiarity with the arts," Scotese concludes, "is considered job-related education in our business."[16]

Classwide Criteria in Company Donations to the Arts

True, "it takes art to make a company great," is the blunt justification of one American company for underwriting an exhibit of German expressionism.[17] Yet for many corporate contributions, neither image nor access determines the beneficiaries. Indeed, no certain benefits of any kind accrue. During my interviews, I asked senior managers what their own company gained from specific charitable programs in education and the arts. For a majority of the programs, they could cite no single, divisible advantage. They were quite prepared, nonetheless, to defend program propriety. In describing why they considered this philanthropy so important, and how they selected suitable recipients, classwide criteria often proved to be far more significant than any company calculus. The influence of classwide criteria can be seen in (1) the loose fit between company considerations and gift decisions, (2) the importance of intercorporate consultation in reaching these decisions, (3) the use of corporate positions to raise funds for arts organizations, and (4) the rationale offered to justify arts donations when there is no apparent company benefit. Drawing on the interviews, we briefly consider each of these features of corporate giving in turn, and then turn to systematic evidence corroborating the importance of classwide influence: companies that are more tied to the classwide network of the inner circle are found to be, regardless of size and other organizational factors associated with purely corporate logic, far more generous toward the arts and other areas than are firms less subject to the influence of the inner circle.

Consider, first, the process of choosing recipients from a very large field of deserving supplicants. If company criteria are paramount, selection of one arts organization over another should have been based on considerations related to company operations. Frequently, however, especially in Britain, the choice is almost purely a matter of personal preference of senior management. Fewer than a third of the companies questioned in one survey had a written policy concerning their sponsorship programs.[18] Some British companies, by custom, simply divide their annual funds among the dozen or so executive directors and allow each to underwrite his own favorite orchestra or museum.[19] Other British companies, committed to more ambitious programs, assign the decision to special committees or even the full board. But even here individual executive taste often carries the day. On occasion, not knowing where to allocate the funds, companies have asked the national Arts Council to make the decision for them.

Large American corporations typically rely upon more bureaucratized systems. Among the very largest firms, special offices with full-time staffs follow highly rationalized procedures in finding suitable recipients, though they still operate with close guidance from the company's senior managers. Under the supervision of an executive-filled, sixteen-member "Corporate Responsibility Committee," Chase Manhattan Bank channeled nearly a quarter of a million dollars in 1979 into some seventy-five separate arts organizations.[20] But systematizing the procedure does not necessarily diminish the influence of classwide over corporate factors. Executives of American firms still report that their personal preferences play an important role in both establishing budget levels and selecting grant recipients. The aesthetic values underlying their decisions are sometimes longstanding, other times only weeks in germination. Yet in either case the origins are idiosyncratic, a product of private taste and personal connections little related to the company upon which they are imposed. Chance events can thus often determine which arts are favored, and at what level. One American company, for instance, abruptly entered the leading ranks of corporate supporters of the visual arts. The origin of its precipitous start in a field for which the firm had exhibited no prior interest is described by the chief executive of another company:

> You couldn't get [the chief executive] to look at a picture, period. Then somebody persuaded him to sponsor something at the Whitney Museum, and suddenly everybody in his company was interested. They went to a formal cocktail party and dinner at this [exhibit] they had sponsored. He

got very excited about the whole scene, being invited to the Whitney and having the company sponsor it. And now, the next thing I know, Christ he's calling up people including myself: "Say, would you host a little party of artists that are coming together." . . . It's catapulted him as a person into an interest in the arts.

Corporate funding decisions are further shaped by intercorporate consultation. Contribution officers frequently advise one another on which organizations are deserving of corporate largess. Informal groups of those most central to company philanthropy meet periodically in both New York and London to pool their experience and construct guidelines for corporate giving. Such interfirm collaboration is indicative of the absence of suitable internal company criteria for structuring the contribution decisions. Classwide cultural tastes and definitions of proper arts activity determine corporate decisions where corporate criteria alone cannot. One consequence is "contribution setting." Analogous to price setting but obviously devoid of any anti-trust implications, company officials of the leading firms establish a uniform level of support in response to solicitations that none feel can be ignored but all conclude deserve only modest support. An appeal for restoration of Westminster Abbey, for instance, was received by a number of City firms; the managing directors consulted one another and quickly fixed a common-donation level of £500.

Corporate contributions are also determined by extracompany demands arising from widespread executive participation in fund-raising committees and governing boards of nonprofit organizations. New York's Metropolitan Museum of Art, for instance, solicits assistance through an "Arts Business Committee," whose membership is a blue chip roster of city executives: among others, R. Manning Brown, chairman of New York Life Insurance; Donald B. Smiley, chairman of Macy's; and Arthur Ochs Sulzberger, chairman of *The New York Times*. On the principle that "it's good business for business to support the nation's preeminent museum of art," committee members vigorously solicit donations through their extensive business contracts. Discussions with managers in both America and Britain reveal that the decision to serve on such bodies is typically a private one, unlike the decision to join other company boards or government advisory groups. This is true despite the frequent intrusion of outside fund raising into company time, and despite association of the company's name with the executive's efforts.[21] Though a private involvement, business leaders are not reluctant to rely on corporate connections to solicit funds. Indeed, they are expected to do precisely that, for they were selected in the first place because of such connections.

Other executives who are targets of the campaigns report that it is virtually impossible to reject the personal appeal of another corporate manager, despite the irrelevance of the contribution from the standpoint of the company's operations. The president of a Wall Street firm offered one example:

> I got a letter from a chairman of a major corporate client of ours, a *major* client. He's personally heading a drive here in New York, and he wrote me a follow-up personal long-hand note. I call him back, and I say, "Pete, is this important to you." And he said, "Fred, I'd really appreciate your help." Well, $5,000 is going to this very worthwhile cause.

Thus, senior managers allocate both company money and their own time to arts organizations whose activity is unrelated to any tangible company benefit. And they do so according to considerations largely unrelated to any company logic. The managing director of a British merchant bank even elevated extra corporate criteria to the level of ethical stricture. For appeals other than a few renowned charities and special causes, it would be presumptuous in his view for a company to make its own decision:

> I have a frank approach to charity here. There are a limited number of charitable causes which probably commend themselves to any group of citizens, like the Red Cross. . . . But there are only a very limited number of such causes. Then there are a certain number of causes that commend themselves to any business organization because they are so attached to it, viz. an appeal for St. Paul's, the Cathedral of the City. The City institutions must put up money. But most of the things—the starving children of Biafra, boat people, poor broken down old horses in Cairo, historic churches, "please save the Bellini Madonna for Birmingham"—I believe in regard to those that it is impertinent for a businessman to say that it is better to give to starving children in Biafra than to save the Bellini Madonna for Birmingham. It's not in a businessman's judgment. So you look to see who signed [the appeal]. If Francis Sandilands[22] sends you an appeal for Covent Garden, you jolly well chip some money in. But if Joe Block sends you an appeal for the starving children, you don't.

The logic that does prevail, however, is not devoid of business reference. It is cast instead at the level of overarching corporate purpose. The arts are viewed as enhancing the quality of urban life, reducing alienation, and promoting a culture conducive to the prosperity of free enterprise. The arts are one of "our most effective tools in the effort to rid our society of its most basic ills—voicelessness, isolation, depersonalization," argues one of the leading American advocates of more corporate sponsorship; company backing can also be justified, contends another, because a privately sponsored art sector can "limit the power of government" and "enlarge the definition of freedom in art and commerce."[23] Ultimately, the arts are to politics as preventive care is to good health: "It's in our best interests to postpone the revolution," is the diagnosis of an official of Equitable Life Assurance.

"The arts are essential to the healthy flourishing of society."[24] A survey of more than 400 chairmen and presidents of large U.S. corporations revealed why their firms supported the arts. "Corporate citizenship" and the "business environment" are identified as the two most important reasons, far ahead of public relations.[25] Such themes consistently emerged during my interviews, though, not unexpectedly, far more often during discussions with those executives who are involved in the affairs of business far beyond the confines of their own company.

WHICH COMPANIES GIVE?

The inner circle's special interest in the prosperity of the third sector is carried into company decisions. Corporations managed by charter members of the inner circle, whatever their size and other organizational dimensions, find more reason to give than do companies whose management is little connected to the transcorporate network. Purely corporate logic is of course still important. This can be seen in standard statistics on U.S. corporate philanthropy. But it coexists with a classwide logic, evident in figures specially compiled for this study.

Size is strongly correlated with the amount of money a company is prepared to dispose; it is, in fact, a commonly used baseline for calculating the appropriate level of company philanthropy. Thus, firms with assets in the $50- to $100-million range contributed a little over $100,000 in 1976 on average, while companies with assets exceeding $2 billion gave nearly $1.7 million. As a percentage of pretax income, however, the contributions are an inverse function of size, ranging from 1.2 percent for the smaller firms to 0.5 percent for the largest.[26] Sector too is determining. Paper companies contributed an average 0.7 percent of their pretax net income, while banks contributed at twice this rate (1.4 percent). High technology companies invested more in education than did retail firms; petroleum firms favored art and culture far more than did utility companies.[27] Much of the sectoral variation can be traced to firm-level factors: the largest contributions are offered by companies in sectors whose profits are high, whose products are directed at consumers, and whose competition is low.[28] And profit growth is influential as well. The Public Broadcasting Service, for instance, is more favored by firms whose profits are on the upslope than by companies with similar profit levels but whose profit trends are flat or declining.[29] A final indicator of the importance of philanthropy for purely company advance is its association with advertising. Comparison of interindustry variations in expenditures for advertising and philanthropy finds a high correlation between the two, implying that philanthropy is treated in part as an extension of marketing.[30] Similarly, a study of America's 55 largest electric utilities in 1976 reveals that the level of their charitable contributions is closely tied to their spending on customer services and advertising.[31]

Classwide considerations add, however, to this purely corporate logic. To see this, we divide the 212 American firms and 196 British companies selected for special study into three groups with similar numbers of firms in each: those whose senior management and directors maintain many, some, or few ties to the inner circle. The number of ties is defined as the total number of outside, large-company directorships held in the aggregate by the managers and directors.[32] Firms managed by those integrally a part of the inner circle are expected to be more forthcoming than firms whose management is relatively isolated. The latter are more insulated from the collective pressures of the inner circle to devote company resources to classwide ends.

The absence of systematically available firm-level data on contributions for American companies dictated use of several related indices: (1) company membership in the Business Committee for the Arts (BCA); (2) identification of the company as a major arts contributor by a standard guide to the field; (3) selection of the firm to receive an annual award for outstanding corporate contributions to the arts by the Business Committee for the Arts during the 1966–78 period; (4) company membership in the Council for Financial Aid to Education, an organization devoted to expanding corporate sponsorship of education; and (5) identification of the company as an exemplary sponsor of educational programs by a leading reference source.[33] British firms fortunately report their total charitable contributions in their annual report, and their level of commitment is assessed by taking the average of the annual contributions in 1977, 1978, and 1979.[34] British firm activity on behalf of high culture is also gauged for U.S. firms by two additional indices: membership in the Association for Business Sponsorship of the Arts (ABSA), and receipt of an annual award for "Business Sponsors of the Arts" bestowed by the ABSA and the *Daily Telegraph*.[35]

The relationship between a company's connection with the inner circle and its commitment to philanthropy is shown in Table 5.1.

By many measures, corporations more integrated into the inner circle display a greater commitment to culture. Among American firms with few ties to the inner circle, only 13 percent are members of the Business Committee for the Arts; but of firms with many ties, 28 percent have joined. Similar differences appear for four other indicators of company philanthropy, with ratios of the percentages ranging from 1.3 for receipt of an award for arts contribution to 4.2 for membership in the Council for Finan-

Table 5.1 Company commitment to corporate philanthropy, by number of major outside directorships held by senior managers and directors

Type of company commitment	Total number of outside directorships[a]			
	Few	Some	Many	Ratio[b]
U.S. Corporations				
Member of Business Committee for the Arts	12.7%	8.1%	28.2%	2.2
Featured in guide to corporate giving in the arts	28.2	33.9	54.1	1.9
Recipient of award for arts contribution	25.4	24.2	33.8	1.3
Member of Council for Financial Aid to Education	4.2	11.3	17.6	4.2
Featured in guide to education programs of leading businesses	22.5	17.7	44.6	2.0
U.K. Corporations				
Average annual charitable contributions, 1976–78 (£1,000)	6.7	42.9	98.6	14.7
Member of Association for Business Sponsorship of the Arts	4.4%	12.1%	33.9%	7.7
Recipient of award for sponsorship of the arts	2.9%	1.5%	9.7%	3.3

Source: Data compiled by author.

[a] The number of corporations upon which the figures are based are 71, 62, and 74 for the three American columns, respectively, and are 68, 66, and 62 for the three British columns.

[b] Ratio of percentage or figure for companies with many outside directorships to those with few outside directorships.

cial Aid to Education. Similarly, the average annual charitable contribution of British firms with few ties to the inner circle is £6,700; of those with some ties, £42,900; and of those with many ties, £96,800. Four percent of the companies with few outside ties are members of the Association for Business Sponsorship of the Arts, while 34 percent of those with many ties are members; 3 percent of the peripheral firms have been recognized for their sponsorship of the arts, but 10 percent of the central firms have been so honored. Some part of these differences is due to the fact that larger firms give more, whatever their attachment to the classwide network. Yet, when firm size is taken into account, the observed differences are only modestly diminished.[36] Through the agency of the inner circle, classwide imperatives are translated into individual corporate practices.

SOLICITING CORPORATE CONTRIBUTIONS

For nonprofit organizations seeking business favor, the present analysis contains implications not ordinarily found in guides to securing corporate sponsorship. The inner circle can be viewed as a kind of corporate fault line through which external appeals are transmitted with particular speed. Whether constituting a governing board or soliciting corporate contributions, this autonomous power of the inner circle can be used to special advantage.

Implicit in the nomination of business executives to nonprofit governing boards is an expectation that their corporations will be generously forthcoming. If company contributions were purely a product of corporate logic, the optimum strategy in constituting a board would be to appoint top executives whose companies are flush with comfortable earnings. The intrusion of classwide logic into company contribution policies, however, implies an additional selection strategy. Regardless of earnings, companies whose officers are well connected into transcorporate networks are considered a better source of trustees than companies less-well connected. Other things being equal, the officers of well-connected companies are more likely to find value in an opera, university, or medical center. It is these executives cum trustees who will be most sympathetic to special appeals for company money. Thus, in considering alternative business candidates for a nonprofit governing board, the income of the candidate's firm is important, but so too is his or her firm's ties into the broader corporate community.

Prospective business candidates for boards of trustees vary themselves in their fund-raising potential. Regardless of the specific corporate post, business leaders in the inner circle will prove far better fund raisers than business leaders on the outside. Indeed, inner-circle status is the best single indicator of a corporate officers' potential for securing business contributions. High corporate position is important; multiple corporate positions are indispensable. This principle is well understood by the participants. David M. Roderick, chief executive of the United States Steel Corporation and trustee of several educational, arts, and community organizations, describes the principle: "Every person who comes to a board has connections of one kind or another, and this may be the chief criterion for selecting most board members. . . . The network of sources that provides funds, services, and goods, not to mention the channels to other people with parallel and interlocking networks of their own, are what really oils the board activity of every group."[37]

Companies also vary in the mix of corporate and classwide logics underlying their contribution decisions. For more-isolated companies, appeals must promise special benefit to the company if they are to find any responsiveness. But for well-connected firms, appeals with arguable payoff for both company image *and* general business climate will find more success.[38] With two distinct sets of concerns, inner-circle managers will have double reason to respond favorably. When soliciting contributions from well-connected firms, better that the program offer both individual-firm and general business benefits.

Identifying which corporate leaders and firms are well connected with the transcorporate network can be done through judicious combination of public and nonpublic information. Profiles of the top executives and directors of major firms can be readily compiled from a variety of standard reference sources. The most important single strand of information contained therein is the number and identity of the directorships held jointly with major corporations other than the executive's own. These individual profiles may be aggregated to create an overall measure of a firm's ties to the inner circle. A more precise pinpointing of the individuals and companies most sympathetic to classwide causes can then be achieved through informal inquiry. Members of the inner circle carry a refined social map of their own network. If presented with a short-list of candidates for a nonprofit governing board or fund-raising campaign, most would be able, provided they are willing, to identify the most suitable prospects.

ISSUE ADVERTISING

A second area of corporate activity encouraged by classwide politics is issue advertising. Nonproduct advertising increased sharply during the 1970s. By one estimate, such spending by large U.S. companies and trade associations reached nearly $500 million in 1977, up from less than half that in 1971, though the growth rate may have slowed in more recent years.[39] Most nonproduct advertising is designed to promote company recognition or reputation. But one in five of the major American companies devote resources to the advocacy of neither product nor image but of company views on contemporary political and social issues.[40] Newspapers and magazines with wide and influential readerships are the favored vehicle for such corporate "aditorials."

"Forsaking our religious heritage, not only in our schools, but everywhere," is a root cause of America's critical problems, according to Tiffany & Co. It is this one factor, not inflation, recession, or overburdened social programs, that is responsible for our "accentuating crime, immorality, greed and selfishness." Renowned for its jewelry but less for its social analysis, Tiffany nonetheless devoted costly space it had purchased in *The New York*

Times to a diagnosis of the U.S. "national calamity" rather than to the virtues of its fine giftware.[41] The range of subjects addressed in the corporate aditorial is as diverse as contemporary politics. SmithKline Corporation, a major pharmaceutical company standing midway on the *Fortune* 500 list of top manufacturers, allocates a generous share of its national media budget to promoting neither Contac pills nor Sineoff, nor even to expressing company philosophy on the proper role of government. Instead, it buys space to permit featured intellectuals to express themselves on issues of moment. The title of one advertisement appearing in *Newsweek* and elsewhere is indicative: " 'To afford lasting gains in quality of life, we must renew America's aging industrial base,' concludes distinguished sociologist Amitai Etzioni." Professor Etzioni's views on reindustrialization occupy more than two full pages of prime advertising space.[42] Dresser Industries reproduced an interview with a black South African woman opposed to withdrawal of U.S. corporate investments, requiring two pages in the *Wall Street Journal*.[43] W. R. Grace & Co. extensively advertises its view of proposals to alter the U.S. personal income tax rates.[44] Union Carbide uses its space to report the results of a national survey it commissioned on public attitudes toward government and the economy.[45] And of course Mobil Oil Corporation has long played a leading role in this field, devoting its regular place in a number of periodicals to its views on a nearly limitless range of topics, some with exceedingly faint bearing on Mobil operations. Under the banner of "A modest proposal," one Mobil advertisement appearing in the *Wall Street Journal* and *The New York Times* chided the *Washington Post* for its handling of a report that President Carter may have electronically eavesdropped on President-elect Reagan just before the 1981 inauguration. The *Post* later conceded the report was based on no more than rumor, a rumor it found in any case "impossible to believe." Yet for Mobil the apology was not a sufficient act of contrition. It chose to render the unfriendly advice through its aditorial space in the national media that the *Post* create a new rating system for its stories, akin to those in use for motion pictures: the letters CST would designate articles that "contain some truth," while BR would be applied to articles based on "believable rumor"; AFST would indicate "absolutely for sure true," and, at the other end of the veracity scale, TUBI would be reserved for articles that are "totally untrue but interesting."[46]

Though there often is no discernible connection between the content of these aditorials and the product for sale by their corporate sponsor, such efforts to persuade the public are not without tangible reward. Officials of several American companies found that giving space to issue advertising brought them the discreetly expressed approval of fellow business leaders and government officials alike. One firm with extensive operations in Britain had just placed an advertisement in several dozen British newspapers and magazines commenting on a vexing policy question of the day. The executive responsible for the firm's U.K. operations discovered gratifying response in the highest places:

> Twice I was in Hamish Gray's office [the minister of State for Energy], and he referred directly to an ad that occurred in the last day or two that we had put in the paper. . . . He complimented me and asked me to pass his compliments to [our] headquarters in New York, or, as he put it, to my shareholder, for that sort of quality advertising.

Issue advertising thus promises dual payoffs. Public opinion may become more sympathetic to the firm's position on the policy issue addressed—and to the firm itself for its "public service" in bringing the issue to their attention. The opinion of opinion-making circles is considered vitally important here, and most aditorials are so targeted. The same American executive described the overall thrust of his British issue-advertising campaign:

> We've taken opinion surveys from opinion leaders—Civil Servants, Members of Parliament, newspaper editors, professors, and professionals. . . . We try to find out what opinion leaders think of us and we try to direct our corporate advertising to the opinion leaders. And if you would look at the list here or the U.K. or anywhere of the publications where we print our ads, you will see it. For example, in the U.K., we put it in the *Times,* we put it in the *Observer,* we put it in the *Telegraph,* we put it in the *Guardian,* we put it in the *Economist,* but we would not put it in the *Evening Standard* or the *Daily Mail* or the *Star* or the *Sun.*

Public opinion in the U.K. of business has never been high; opinion in the U.S. as well has turned negative in recent years. National surveys in the U.S. reveal that the 1970s was marked by a precipitous decline of confidence in all major institutions, corporations included.[47] The unfavorable climate reduces companies' room for maneuver and enhances the likelihood of anti-business legislation. If deepened, an antagonistic public mood could evolve into a legitimacy crisis not only for business but for capitalism itself.[48] Elements of American business mobilized during the mid-1970s to counter the negative public image. Placing much of the blame on the print and electronic media, business leaders initiated a range of programs to improve news coverage.[49] These included the establishment of policy institutes to supply the media with pro-business interpretations, special awards to honor favorable reporting on business, conferences in which members of the media and corporate executives meet, and advertising campaigns on contemporary political questions. Trade associations initiated many of these campaigns, but so too did individual firms. Companies in industries bearing the brunt of public criticism were of course in the first ranks of the advocacy advertisers. Yet, as in the case of corporate contributions, purely private motives did not fully account for all who entered the fray. Again, firms most sensitized to the broader political climate by virtue of their ties to the inner circle are found at the forefront of this campaign. Their senior managers moved company resources into advertising that may ultimately generate greater yield for the business climate than for the firm footing the bill.

POLITICAL CONTRIBUTIONS AND POLITICAL ACTION COMMITTEES

The third area of corporate activity especially sensitive to classwide pressures is political contributions. Financial backing of parties, candidates, and other political organizations holds out the same dual payoffs as are evident in corporate philanthropy and issue advertising. Though originating in decisions of individual firms, here too the benefits are not only individual but collective as well.

The divisible benefit to a contributing company is the special access to a successful candidate's office such activity may provide. Corporations especially affected by government decisions are correspondingly more often disposed to create and preserve such access. In the U.S., executives with defense contractors and firms in highly regulated industries are found among the largest federal campaign contributors.[50] In the U.K., companies most fearful of nationalization by a Labour government, such as large insurers, are among the most generous supporters of the Conservative Party.[51] The nondivisible benefit, on the other hand, is a more favorably oriented political climate. The election of probusiness candidates and the success of the Conservative and Republican parties can be a windfall for all large companies, including both those who give and those who refrain from giving. The free-rider disincentive will thus tend to discourage contributions by firms narrowly fixed on their own welfare. But such a disincentive will prove less a barrier for firms whose managements are not given to such narrowly focused goals. Consequently, companies with managements attached to the transcorporate network and its overarching political interests are more often found at the forefront of political contributors than firms whose management is less broadminded. Corporate political logic generates political outlays; but so too does classwide logic.

Corporate political contributions in Britain are direct, while in America they are necessarily indirect. U.K. corporations are permitted to donate company money to parties and candidates they favor; U.S. corporations by law cannot. Managers of American companies may give limited amounts of their own funds, however, both directly to a candidate and also through a new social invention—the political action committee. Whatever the channel, in both countries money generated by corporations is increasingly flowing into politics. Indeed, the flow has been transformed in the 1970s from a trickle to a torrent. The scale of increase is so great that corporate money has now become a fundamental force in both British and American politics.

The rise of company financing of British politics can be seen in trend figures for the 196 large companies receiving special attention in this study. The Companies Act of 1967 requires limited companies to report political contributions of more than £50 in their annual report, making British donations far more easily tracked than American funds. The bulk of the disclosed donations went, of course, to the Conservative Party, but four other business-oriented organizations received significant backing as well. These were British United Industrialists (largely a Tory conduit, with 80 percent of its collected funds going to the Conservative Party[52]); the Economic League, an antilabor organization; Aims, an ardent defender of the principle that "freedom means free enterprise"; and the Centre for Policy Studies, established by Margaret Thatcher and Sir Keith Joseph in 1974 to provide research services to the Conservative Party reflective of their own special brand of monetarism.[53]

Total company political contributions have grown strongly in recent years, especially those going directly to the Conservative Party (Table 5.2). The average company donation more than doubled during this period, from £1,761 in 1974 to £3,320 in 1975, £3,707 in 1978 and £4,551 in 1979. The composition has changed as well, with the share going to the Conservative Party rising from 52 percent in 1975 to 60 percent in 1979.

Table 5.2 Annual average political donations of 196 large British companies, 1974–79 in pounds

Recipient of company donation	Year of donation					
	1974	1975	1976	1977	1978	1979
Conservative Party	11	1724	1420	1715	1867	2748
British Industrialists United	855	1063	1180	1132	1330	1378
Economic League	302	370	349	386	382	353
Aims[a]	327	119	24	91	62	41
Centre for Policy Studies	266	44	33	49	66	31
Total political contributions	1761	3320	3006	3373	3707	4551

SOURCE: Data compiled by author.
[a] Formerly Aims of Industry.

British Industrialists United has become a more favored recipient, while funds for the Economic League held constant and the other advocates of free enterprise lost ground.

The U.S. ban on direct corporate financing of political campaigns has generated two alternative avenues of support. Officers of large firms generously give of their personal funds, on occasion with the understanding both within the firm and the receiving organization that the contributions are, in effect, company, not private. In addition, a substantial number of large corporations have established political action committees that collect funds from management and channel them to candidates deemed friendly to business or to the company. Business-related funds flowing through the latter conduit exhibited explosive growth during the 1970s. Fewer than 100 corporate PACs were in operation during the 1972 election; by 1980 the number exceeded 1,100 (Table 5.3). By contrast, the number of labor political action committees exhibited sluggish growth, rising from 200 to under 300 by the end of the decade.

The divergent growth curves for corporate and labor PACs are evident as well in the aggregate level of their funding. In 1968, corporate and business-related committees are estimated to have spent $1.4 million on candidates for national office, while national labor committees distributed $7.6 million to House and Senate candidates. A decade later, business committees contributed more than $17 million to federal candidates (another $20 million went to other campaigns); but labor spending on federal campaigns had risen to only $10 million (an additional $8 million was spent on other candidates). While political action committee underwriting of Democratic candidates rose two-fold between 1972 and 1979, support of Republican candidates more than tripled. Since the parties themselves decreasingly financed the campaigns of their own candidates during this same period, PACs acquired special significance for aspiring politicians. During the 1978 campaign, for instance, the two parties directly and indirectly provided $11 million to candidates for national office, while PACs gave $35 million. In

Table 5.3 Number of American corporate and labor political action committees, 1972–80.

Type of political action committee	Years[a]				
	1972	1974	1976	1978	1980
Corporate	87	89	294	784	1153
Labor		201	224	218	290

SOURCE: Epstein (1979, 1980a, 1980b).

[a] The 1972 figure is for November; the 1974, 1976, and 1978 figures are December; and the 1980 figures are for June.

1980, the PAC contribution to House and Senate campaigns rose to $55 million, approaching a quarter of the total congressional campaign receipts of $252 million. In 1982, PAC contributions to congressional races are estimated to have reached $80 million, a jump of nearly two-thirds over 1980.[54]

The importance of corporate PACs relative to labor committees can be seen in the findings of a study of the leadership of the 97th Congress. Using data compiled by Common Cause, Tracey Boyce examined the contributions received from PACs by the majority and minority leaders, whips, and committee chairs in 1981–82. The House leaders were elected or re-elected in 1980, and the Senate leaders in 1976, 1978, or 1980. Of the 24 Senate leaders, the median percentage of PAC contributions relative to all contributions stood near 23; for the 29 House leaders, the median percentage was near 49. In other words, half of the Senate leaders obtained more than a fifth of their campaign-contribution income from PACs, and half of the House leaders received nearly half their campaign funds from such committees.[55]

In Senator Dole's (R, Kansas) successful bid for reelection in 1980, for instance, $324,000 was raised from PACs, an amount that was 27 percent of the total amount contributed to his campaign, $1.2 million. Of this, 97 percent came from PACs affiliated with corporations. When the Republican Party took majority control of the Senate in 1981, Dole assumed the chairmanship of the Senate Finance Committee. Representative Jim Wright (D, Texas), Majority Leader of the House, received a third of his 1980 campaign contributions of $807,000 from PACs, of which three-quarters came from corporate PACs (slightly under one-quarter came from labor PACs). The chairman of the House Budget Committee, Jim Jones (D, Oklahoma), raised 42 percent of his total campaign contributions of $286,-000 from PACs, of which 20 percent was contributed by labor PACs and 78 percent by company committees.[56]

Overall, 82 percent of the total political action committee contributions received by Senate leaders derived from corporate PACs, while only 12 percent was given by labor PACs (the remaining 6 percent came from independent PACs). For the House leaders, 67 percent of their campaign income came from company PACs, and 30 percent from labor committees. Thus, over two-thirds of the PAC income for the leaders of the 97th Congress was supplied by company committees. The corporate support was highly concentrated on the more conservative congressional leaders, with the most conservative nineteen receiving nearly three times as much as the most liberal twenty House and Senate leaders. Yet even among the leaders who are most liberal (as rated by the Americans for Constitutional Action and Americans for Democratic Action), corporate PAC contributions exceeded labor PAC support by a ratio of 4 to 3.[57]

The potential influence of PAC support is suggested by the shifting voting record of U.S. Representative Thomas A. Luken, who went to Washington in 1974 as a "labor democrat" and by 1978 had become a "business democrat." In 1974, the Ohio Congressman received a rating by the Americans for Democratic Action of 78; in 1981 his rating had dropped to 40. His AFL-CIO rating declined from a "perfect" 100 in 1974 to 65 in 1978. A former civil-rights marcher in Selma in 1965, and campaign worker for John F. Kennedy in 1960, Luken had in recent years become the favored recipient of PAC support from U.S. Steel, Kennecott Corporation, Dow Chemical, and Exxon, receiving nearly three-fifths of his total re-election campaign contributions in 1980—some $175,000—from political action committees. Coincidentally, or not, he had also increasingly sided with industry on key legislative fights in recent years, backing, for instance, an industry-sought amendment that would have significantly weakened the Clean Air Act. "Tom Luken decided early in his congressional career to become a PAC-man," concluded an official of Common Cause. "He got there before Atari did."[58]

Corporate PAC activity is highly concentrated among the nation's largest companies. Nearly half (45 percent) of the 821 corporate committees active in the 1978 election campaign were of firms among *Fortune*'s list of the 1,300 largest enterprises. And it is among the very largest that the committees are most often found: of the manufacturing firms ranked in size between 501 and 1000, 7 percent had formed a PAC, but of the 500 top manufacturers, 40 percent had. And of the 100 largest, 70 percent sponsored a PAC. Moreover, PAC expenditures were far greater at the top of the *Fortune* list: the committees of firms among those ranked 501 to 1,000 disbursed under $2,000 on average; those right above, the bottom of the top 500, contributed a mean $6,000 each; the PACs of the ten largest industrials provided $70,000 on average.[59] By 1982, corporate PAC expenditures for congressional candidates reached in some cases well into six figures. Citicorp spent $223,000, Grumman Corporation distributed $225,000, and Tenneco Inc. gave $425,000.

Not surprisingly, the rise of company financing of electoral candidates is most apparent in those companies most central to the classwide network. We again examine the 196 British firms under study and correlate their degree of integration into the inner circle, and their average levels of political contributions in 1978 and 1979 (Table 5.4). The level of contribution to both the Conservative Party and the four political organizations devoted to defending British enterprise are observed to be a direct function of each firm's connections to the network. Firms with few ties gave an average of £1,207 per year to the Tories; with some ties, £2,407; and with many links, £4,521. The ratio of Tory contributions by central to peripheral firms

Table 5.4 Average level of political contributions (in pounds) of British companies, 1978–79, by number of major outside directorships held by company directors

Recipient of political contributions	Average contribution by number of outside directorships[b]			Ratio[c]
	Few	Some	Many	
Conservative Party	1207	2407	4521	3.7
Other political organizations[a]	459	588	5019	10.9

Source: Data compiled by author.
  [a] British Industrialists United, Economic League, Aims, and Centre for Policy Studies.
  [b] The number of companies upon which the figures are based are 68, 66, and 62 for the three columns, respectively.
  [c] Ratio of contributions by companies with many outside directorships to those with few directorships.

is 3.7. Company giving to four organizations more immediately concerned with the political climate of business is even more closely correlated to inner-circle orientation. Firms little connected to the inner circle contributed an average £459 annually, while those strongly linked gave £5,019, a contribution ratio of nearly 11 to 1. Again, the gaps remain even when differences in the firm's size and other economic characteristics are taken into account.

Highly connected corporations are also at the forefront of U.S. campaign contributions. This applies both to indirect support provided by company officers and directors, and to direct subvention by political action committees. The first pattern is revealed in a study, by Richard Ratcliff and associates, of banking in St. Louis.[60] They examined the contributions of nearly 900 directors of all seventy-eight commercial St. Louis banks to local and national electoral candidates in 1976 and 1978. They found that regardless of the size of the bank, the level of the personal contributions by the bank's directors was strongly affected by the bank's ties with other large corporations. The tighter the bank's integration into the top of the corporate community, the more its directors gave.[61] The same pattern prevails on the national level, according to a study of corporate contributions to the 1972 reelection campaign of Richard Nixon. In this analysis, Thomas Koenig divided the *Fortune* 800 firms—the 500 largest industrials and 50 largest companies in banking, insurance, and four other sectors—into three groups according to the number of shared directorships each had with the other top 800 firms. The average contribution of the directors of 543 relatively isolated companies was approximately $13,000; for peripheral firms, the average was $14,000; while for the best connected, the average reached nearly $20,000.[62]

Table 5.5 Percentage of American corporations with political action committees and average level of expenditures, 1978

Corporate PAC activity	Total number of outside directorships[a]			
	Few	Some	Many	Ratio[b]
Percentage of corporations with a PAC	32.4%	27.4%	41.9%	1.3
Average expenditure of the PACs	$9,430	$10,658	$16,157	1.7

SOURCE: Data compiled by author.

[a] The number of corporations upon which the figures are based are 71, 62, and 74, respectively.

[b] Ratio of corporations with many outside directorships to those with few.

Centrality to the inner circle affects corporate PAC activity as well. Dividing our 212 American corporations into three levels of connectedness as we have before, and focusing on the 1978 election, centrality is found to be a good determinant of which firms have a PAC and of how much they distribute (Table 5.5). The percentage of isolated, peripheral, and central companies with PACs is 32, 27, and 42; and the corresponding average expenditures of those that do have a PAC is $9,430, $10,658, and $16,157.[63]

With the new U.S. restrictions on individual campaign contributions wrought by the Watergate scandals of the early 1970s, private wealth is giving way to corporate money as the high octane of electoral politics. Under the Federal Election Campaign Act, individual gifts to a political party are limited to $20,000 annually, $5,000 per year to a political committee, and $1,000 per election to an individual candidate. The costs to a candidate of soliciting contributions are inversely related to the cap on individual donations, and the relatively low limits have consequently enhanced the attractiveness of corporate PACs to aspiring candidates. At the same time, the special value of a PAC is also being recognized by large firms eager to enhance and systematize the political donations of their managers. The institutionalization of the contribution process can now be made at company expense. Under federal law, company monies may be used to establish and operate a political action committee. Thus, with administrative costs borne entirely by the firm, all solicited donations can be fully passed through to selected candidates.

Political action committees solicit from stockholders and managers, though usually only the latter. The PAC itself decides on whether its contributors are permitted to earmark their gifts for specific candidates. In practice, two out of three corporate PACs do not allow such restrictions on the funds they receive, and thus decisions on how to allocate monies are usually made by the PAC itself.[64] With time and the resources to render careful evaluation of potential recipients, PACs add precision and coherence to political contribution decisions that corporate managers acting individually could never achieve. In surveying the impact of the rise of corporate PACs in American politics, a leading analyst, Edwin Epstein, describes the corporate rationalization: "PACs allow corporations and business-related associations to organize and *institutionalize* their electoral activities in a highly efficient way."[65]

The political action committee of a major New York bank illustrates the special effectiveness that collective mobilization of corporate money can have. Created in 1979, this PAC solicits all managers with the title of vice-president or above, about 300 individuals. By law, nobody can be pressured to give, and names of contributors are considered confidential and known only to the committee's treasurer. In common with some other firms, the procedure here is for the donor to send his contribution to an outside agency, in this case a leading accounting firm. Still, the PAC is in business to raise money, and it is not shy about its purpose. Upon its founding, the company's chairman announced his strong support for the committee and urged his fellow managers to give generously. The expected amount is left unspecified, but the committee's literature suggests one-fourth to one-half of a percent of the manager's gross income. The committee's literature also makes clear the special value of its orchestrating role: "We all work for the same company and we all have a stake in seeing that our business . . . is understood by politicians. By pooling our resources, we will be able to give meaningful contributions to candidates who are willing to listen to our problems."

Within six months of its founding, this bank PAC had received contributions from 100 of its senior managers, totaling about $10,000. Since the "purpose of the Committee is to make the most of our resources through the pooling of our contributions," donors may not specify their preferred recipients. This decision is reserved for a seven-person steering committee composed of top-ranking company officers. Since this PAC (along with all other corporate PACs) is publicly registered with the Federal Election Commission, it routinely receives solicitations from dozens of candidates during an election year. An appeal in the 1980 election from Ronald Reagan's campaign committee was not honored, nor were those of most others. The committee instead concentrated its funds on only three candidates. On the principle that money should go to political figures "willing to listen and to understand the problems faced by a company such as ours," the committee chose Congressman John J. LaFalce, Democrat of New York, a member of the House Banking Committee; Senator Robert H. Morgan, Democrat of North Carolina, a member of the Senate Banking Committee; and Senator Daniel Patrick Moynihan, Democrat of New York.

LaFalce was favored because he has a "good understanding of banks," Morgan because he listens if he doesn't always respond on banking matters, and Moynihan because he is an effective advocate for the state in which the bank does its business. As is generally the case, incumbents were preferred over challengers by the committee; Morgan was not reelected, but Moynihan and LaFalce were.

Corporate PACs add company rationality to business giving, but they add an element of classwide rationality as well. Just as in decisions on corporate philanthropy, the criteria for recipient selection are not set by company standards alone. By purely company logic, money should be channeled to candidates friendly to the firm or industry. But by classwide logic, money should be directed at candidates who are known defenders of free enterprise, regardless of their record on more specific matters. A New York banker describes the joint mix of particular and universal criteria in the work of his own PAC:

> We would have a special interest in people who are on the [U.S. House and Senate] banking committees. . . . But generally we would try to support people that in a very broad sense we feel would make a positive contribution to the development of the country in general—and free enterprise.

The chairman of another corporate PAC, run by a major utility company, directed his committee's contributions in the 1978 election to some 150 candidates. Their selection over others depended in part on their attitude toward the company: enemies of the utility were not rewarded. But among the nonenemies, attitudes toward big business in general were highly salient considerations. A slavish defense of capitalism was not required, but at least an openmindedness and a willingness to hear the PAC's argument was. In the words of the PAC chairman:

> The crucial criteria are two. One, by their actions it is evident that they are somewhat supportive of the private enterprise system, are a friend of business. Two, even though they may be very anti-business in most of the things they do, we know from our legislative contacts that they will listen on a serious issue even though they can't be out front and will react when we have a good solid case.

To determine who meets these criteria corporate PACs rely on several measures of the candidates' records on business. The utility, for instance, examined incumbents' voting profiles on key barometric issues—tax legislation, occupational safety, a labor picketing bill. Only one of the legislative measures was of special interest to the utility's own welfare. In addition, ratings of the voting records of U.S. representatives and senators prepared by several conservative political organizations were used to identify the candidates' overall attitude toward business. Finally, information was exchanged with other corporate PAC officials on the worthiness of those soliciting business money. Here intercorporate consultation, as in the case of philanthropy, provided guidance for decisions that company considerations alone could not fully resolve. Thus, factors far beyond a company's immediate welfare can come to figure prominently in the final funding decision. The aggregate welfare of all large business is frequently prominent among these when the firm's management is attuned to the more generic concerns of the broader corporate community.

PRESSURING THE CORPORATION

The intercorporate network inadvertently influences corporate behavior by sensitizing management to classwide political concerns. The influence can be said to be inadvertent in that the network was not created to do this. Yet once in place, the network serves as an effective transmitter of such concerns. That there are often important though unintended consequences of purposive social action has few clearer illustrations.

Transcorporate directorships in Britain and America are the product of company strategy to ensure that its officers are well informed about the affairs of other large companies. The strategy is intended to enhance a company's mastery of its environment, not environmental mastery of the corporation. Yet once established, the network can reactively constrain and move the firm caught within it. The intercorporate network can serve as a vehicle for the imposition of classwide discipline on the firm. Since government regulation of business practices is of relatively limited scope in both societies, especially Britain, self-policing has become a particularly important form of social control within the large corporate communities.

The impetus for self-regulation originates both within and outside the corporate communities. An internal discipline is at times imposed to control deviant behavior of single firms, behavior threatening to other large companies. It is also imposed to elicit desired behavior, actions benefitting other companies. But classwide self-regulation is also occasionally more a reactive response to external pressures than to the direct concerns of corporations. Externally originated (though internally imposed) discipline is most common when the public reputation of all large enterprises is being damaged by the egregious actions of a few. It also occurs when other corporations fear reprisals against themselves if they fail to take actions against allied firms whose behavior has become the center of public controversy. This kind of self-regulation is more effective in Britain than America, though in both countries instances are yet more scattered than systematic. Still, the formation of classwide networks has increased the intensity with which the informal norms of proper behavior are felt.

Internal business discipline appears in the occasional use of threats to isolate a corporation whose action are considered unacceptable. Readers of the business press in both countries are well familiar with the threatened or actual withdrawal of credit lines, shareholdings, or outside directorships from firms whose behavior is deemed dangerously deviant. Woefully ineffective management, hostile takeover bids, and flagrantly illegal actions are among the deeds that can invite punitive action by the business community against its constituent members.

The intercorporate network provides a convenient channel for disciplining maverick firms, but there is also a positive side to this. Good behavior can be rewarded as well, and companies encouraged to take actions that serve the broader corporate community—even when there are no special advantages for their own earnings. The induction of favorable actions is illustrated by the study of St. Louis banks by Richard Ratcliff and several associates. They examined the lending behavior of all seventy-eight commercial banks in the metropolitan region. Of special interest was the proportion of the loan portfolio that each bank placed in two forms of investment—loans to other corporations, primarily commercial, industrial, and other financial firms; and loans to private home owners, mainly for single-family dwellings. For all banks combined, 46 percent of their total loan value was placed in business, and 16 percent in home mortgages. However, the specific portfolio varied widely from bank to bank. Furthermore, the composition did not correlate with bank profitability: banks with high percentages of business loans did no better than those with lower percentages. Since the banks' profits were not at stake, banks had considerable latitude in allocating their investments. The question then is why some favor businesses, others private borrowers. Ratcliff and associates reasoned that those banks most closely tied to other large companies in the region through intercorporate networks tended to devote more of their loan portfolios to business investments, less to home mortgages. Well-connected banks, they expected, would be encouraged to be more responsive to the special needs of area companies and less responsive to demands from outside the corporate community.

In Ratcliff's study, a bank's shared directorships with other St. Louis companies served as a measure of its connectedness to the local corporate community.[66] With a high degree of accuracy, this connectedness factor predicted the composition of the bank's loan portfolio. Banks central to the St. Louis inner circle strongly favored corporate loans over home investments, while the converse held for banks peripheral to the inner circle.

Taking the bank's size and a range of other potentially predictive factors into account reduced the explanatory power of centrality some, but the basic differences nonetheless largely remain. Moreover, a bank's connectedness to the corporate community is a better predictor of its loan portfolio than any other single factor examined.[67] The transcorporate network can thus both help constrain deviant behavior and induce preferred actions among firms enmeshed in the classwide lattice.

Intracorporate control is occasionally exerted with some explicit pressure, but this is the exception, not the rule. As is common to most systems of influence, changes are normally achieved through purely voluntary compliance. Companies and managers within the network recognize the importance of mutual accommodation. They are prepared to respond to special appeals originating in the transcorporate network of which they are part. This is evident, for instance, in the influence of the Business Roundtable. Its impact on member firms is often as important as its direct lobbying in Washington. By informing and marshalling company resources, it moves corporate lobbying in directions that the companies themselves would not likely embark upon as a consequence of internally generated initiatives.

Through its meetings, committee projects, and position papers, the Business Roundtable enhances the political awareness of the nearly 200 chief executive officers who are its members. The Roundtable also helps sensitize its members to the interdependent political consequences of the actions taken by each of their firms. The second-ranking manager of an American manufacturer, whose top officer is a key figure in the Roundtable, described this effect on himself and his company. The Roundtable helps his company, he said, "to recognize that the implications of what you do reverberate way beyond your company and may have unforeseen impact on people whose situation is different from yours."

Having heightened company awareness of how their actions may impinge on the political welfare of others, the Business Roundtable is then able to bring member firms to support public policies they would not otherwise do, or at least not with the same degree of vigor. Corporations jealously retain great independence on these matters, of course. But when an issue is of no great moment to a company but of overriding importance to the business community, a chief executive may lead his company to take a public posture in support of the Roundtable's position. The willingness of the executive to do this depends on the possible negative effect on his own company—if small, he may be willing; if large, probably not. A senior manager of a major American petroleum firm reports, for instance, that his company lobbies in Washington at times on behalf of positions on which it has no strong opinion but for which its support is nonetheless expected. At other times it demurs:

We have to make judgments as to whether or not we have to pay our dues on a particular issue even though it's not of primary importance to us, because of its supreme importance to other Roundtable members. You have to take it case by case. We do it both ways—do fully participate with the Roundtable and do our share on some issues that aren't of primary importance to us, but we do sometimes sit one out.

It is understood that group discipline has its limits. "Sometimes we fell in line, sometimes we didn't," remarked a former officer of a company whose chief executive had been active in the Roundtable. "We usually argued pretty strongly for our own position" within the Roundtable. And if it did not prevail "and we felt strongly enough about it, we made clear we were not going along with the Roundtable." In small but significant ways, then, members of the Business Roundtable move to act in ways cognizant of their mutual interests, even when their own immediate interests would not so dictate. This can even lead companies to lobby for positions contrary to their own welfare. In a few instances, chief executives instructed their Washington offices to reverse company stands after the Roundtable had taken a position opposed to that of the company. But this is rare. More commonly, the Roundtable stance leads to a strengthening or weakening of a firm's own lobbying position, rather than as a determinant of it.

Still, it is evident that the network of which the Roundtable is a moving force can influence corporations to enter politics in ways not entirely a product of their own private calculus. The network can also transmit pressure originating not within the business community—but outside it altogether. Again, there are sanctions for both negative and positive actions. Undesired company behavior can be discouraged, favored actions encouraged.

Firms whose policies on labor, the environment, and other areas of special public interest sharply diverge from accepted practices may add tarnish to the reputation of all business. Labor, environmental, consumer, civil rights, feminist, and religious organizations have effectively used this concern to press for change in individual company policies.[68] In both America and Britain, for instance, a range of groups have lobbied for reduction of bank and insurance investments in South Africa. Public education campaigns have been launched to create a climate hostile to those firms that continue to invest. And campaigns against "worst offenders" have brought even more direct pressure to bear. Threats to boycott company products, introduction of anti-investment resolutions at shareholders meetings, and personal visits to corporate headquarters are among the tactics.

Corporate and classwide logics that would guide a firm's response often divide on South African investments, just as on other controversial practices. Though unpopular company policies can be lucrative for some firms, by eroding corporate credibility, they impose costs on all. Vigorous anti-business lobbying around such issues can significantly heighten the collective cost. In this circumstance, firms well connected into the corporate community may be pressed to retreat by their brethren, whether withdrawal is desirable from a company standpoint or not. Or, in more positive framing, they may be encouraged to adopt higher standards of social responsibility.

Officers and directors who travel in the inner circle will be more open to arguments that their policies may be damaging for business as a whole. And even if they are not more responsive personally, their firms will find it harder to resist the entreaties of other companies. By contrast, when such pressures are directed against companies on the periphery of the corporate community, their unfortunate isolation can in this instance prove a defense indeed.

Public pressuring of the corporation can be made even more forceful when classwide and corporate welfare are jointly threatened. If a company refuses to alter its practices in response to direct lobbying, indirect pressures can be brought to bear through its corporate allies—providing of course the offending firm has allies. The company that can resist strikes, boycotts, and propaganda campaigns by its employees or consumer groups may be incapable of withstanding the secondary pressures stemming from actions taken against its corporate friends. Successful application of this tactic is evident in labor's organizing drive against the large American textile firm, J. P. Stevens & Co.

After years of successfully resisting unionization, Stevens finally agreed to a settlement with the Amalgamated Clothing and Textile Workers Union in 1980. Contributing to Stevens's final capitulation was the union campaign to break Stevens's links to the national transcorporate network. The campaign, according to its chief architect, was intended to engender "an alienation of the corporate and Wall Street community away from J. P. Stevens."[69] This was achieved by pressing other companies sharing directorships with Stevens to sever them. The chairman of Stevens, James D. Finley, served as an outside director of Manufacturers Hanover Trust Co., the nation's fourth largest bank, but he declined to stand for reelection in 1978 after a union threat to withdraw $1 billion in pension funds from the bank. Finley also sat on the board of New York Life, the fifth largest insurer, and its chairman, R. Manning Brown, Jr., in turn served on the Stevens board. Both of these ties were broken when the union announced an insurgent slate of candidates for the board of New York Life. The chairman of Avon Products Inc., David W. Mitchell, then also an outside director of Stevens, resigned when his own company was threatened with anti-Stevens agitation. E. Virgil Conway, chairman of Seaman's Bank for Savings in New York City, successfully resisted efforts to force him off the Stevens board. But he was thus inspired to push Stevens actively toward early settlement.[70] "No institution like J. P. Stevens," observed the organizer of the union campaign, "can exist in a vacuum."[71]

Connected corporations abhor a vacuum nearly as fiercely as does nature. The specter of ostracism is thus a potent weapon. Threatened or actual withdrawal of intercorporate ties can affect not just peripheral corporate practices such as philanthropy, but the core of company operations as well, labor relations included. Of course finding access to the inner circle is no easy task for an outside lobby group. But once a leverage point is uncovered, the network can be used to help move companies to do what they would otherwise never be prepared to do.

THE DUAL LOGIC OF CORPORATE AND CLASSWIDE DECISION CRITERIA

Most corporate decisions are, of course, still largely a product of the internal logic of the firm. The influence of a classwide logic is still modest in most corporate decisions. Still, the influence is increasingly felt, though its effect varies by policy area, type of company, and the era.

Company decisions most subject to the dual effect of the two logics are those in which earnings are unaffected and the aggregate welfare of business is affected. Most major policy areas have much to do with the former and little with the latter, and for them classwide pressures are usually inconsequential. But for several policy areas the reverse prevails, and these are precisely the domains most defining of the corporation's public face: issue advertising, political underwriting, and charitable giving. Classwide influence is felt in the subjects selected for aditorials, the candidates picked for political subvention, and the organizations chosen for company philanthropy. Classwide criteria are often as important as company considerations in decisions on what to support and how much to give.

Companies themselves vary in their responsiveness to extracompany criteria. Corporations central to the transcorporate network tend to be more responsive, others less so. Individual leadership still remains important. A chief executive or managing director embued with the value of the arts can move a company into this field without regard to the presence or absence of extracorporate pressures. But the probability that a given company is led by such an individual is affected by the firm's ties to the corporate community. The more extensive the intercorporate links, the more likely is the company to be guided by those who believe they must play a leadership role larger than that required by the firm's quest for profits—and that their role must begin at home. This translates into directing their own firms to underwrite charitable causes, start political action committees, and act in ways the corporate community would define as socially responsible.

Socially responsible corporate behavior is defined as behavior that, if not by intention, at least by effect reflects well on the reputation and legitimacy of business. The payoff for the firm is less significant than the contribution to the community. Thus, while we have seen that a company's integration into the corporate community is a strong predictor of its charitable contributions and other socially responsible activities, other investigations reveal that a company's profitability is a poor predictor at best. Some studies have compared companies whose overall records on social responsibility vary across the spectrum; others have examined specific areas of company policies, such as charitable donations, environmental protection, and affirmative action. The research has not yielded entirely consistent conclusions. One study, for instance, focused on 28 firms in four industries, and found that companies better rated in social responsibility reported stronger growth in earnings.[72] Yet other studies find no association between profits and socially responsible behavior. In a study of forty-seven companies rated for their overall social responsibility, no correlation is found between the rating and the market performance of the companies' stock.[73] Another study of thirty commercial banks in Texas focused on separate measures of social performance, such as minority hiring, investment in low-income housing, and charitable contributions, and found little systematic relation between the performance measures and level of bank income.[74] Analysts who have reviewed the studies examining the linkage between corporate social behavior and financial performance generally side with Lee Preston's assessment "that there is practically no evidence of any strong association among socially relevant behaviors, whether desirable or undesirable, and any of the usual indicators of economic success." Highly profitable enterprises are as diverse in social performance as product. "For every Xerox there seems to be a J. P. Stevens," Preston concludes, "and low-profit firms can be cited at both ends of the spectrum as well."[75] If not company profits, what it is that does count, according to the present analysis, is the extent to which a firm is responsive to classwide considerations in reaching its decisions on matters of public concern.

The significance of classwide forces on company decisions also changes with the era. When transcorporate networks are strong, transmission of interfirm influence is effective; when feeble, much less so. A final case cannot be made that the networks are now stronger than ever before. But a range of indicators of network structure, described earlier,[76] indicate that they are more diffuse and inclusive at present than at any moment during recent decades. The House of Morgan may have lent a structure to American business at the turn of the century that will never again be achieved; and the seamless web within British finance may never be quite so perfect as it was at the height of the Empire. Yet for all the fissures of the present, the network is more evenly spread, more reinforced, more extensive than at any time in the past. The growth of intercorporate ownership, diversification of product lines, and spread of diffusely structured shared directorships across old divides have given the corporate communities a degree of transcendent organization without precedent. Intercorporate influence is, consequently, at a peak. This is partly why calls for large companies to become socially and politically involved in the life of the nation have so intensified during the past decade. Yet this is only part of it. A second and equally crucial ingredient has been a series of citizen-group-articulated and government-managed challenges to the power, position, and prerogatives of business. These challenges assumed special potency during the 1970s, and the rise of classwide business politics cannot be understood apart from this movement, the subject of the following chapter.

The presence of classwide criteria in the decision making of some large firms should lead us to rethink our traditional conception of the firm. The firm is conventionally viewed as *the* unit of action, individually striving to maintain and enhance its own profitability. True, there are many impediments to realizing this objective. Management often accepts satisfactory profits if the search for maximum returns is too risky. And management frequently seeks short-term gains at the expenses of long-term growth. Such corporate shortsightedness is even viewed by two analysts as a root cause of America's sluggish economic growth. "Maximum short-term financial returns have become the overriding criteria for many companies," assert Robert Hayes and William Abernathy, and U.S. competitiveness and product innovation have suffered as a result.[77] But whatever the revisionist view of corporate behavior, including that of the managerial-revolution thesis itself, the firm is viewed as the basic entity acting to sustain itself. The success of other firms is of concern only as the health and survival of these other firms constrain a firm's own ability to survive and succeed.

The present analysis does not reject this view of the firm. Nor does it challenge the view that profit growth is the overriding objective of corporate action. But it does suggest that there is a second, distinct calculus that guides some corporate decisions. It is the rationality of classwide profit growth. This calculus must deal with the same problems attending company-profit calculus—the substitution of satisfactory results for optimal performance, the displacement of long-term growth objectives by the drive for immediate return. But whatever the complexities, classwide rationality represents a fundamentally new determinant of corporate behavior. Its import still remains modest compared to the power of the autonomously, internally determined objectives of the individual firm. Trend figures, however, suggest that the influence of classwide criteria has increased in recent decades, and this influence is most felt in managerial decisions critical to the shaping of the political environment in which business must operate.

SIX

The Challenge of
Profits, Labor, and Government

Only a handful of large American corporations maintained a public affairs office in 1970. Ten years later, 80 percent of the 500 largest manufacturers ran a public affairs operation.[1] Few large British companies gave money to the Conservative Party in the early 1970s, but most did by the end of the decade. It was a period of intensifying corporate activism, and it was expressed on many fronts. More than coincidentally, the decade ended with conservative, probusiness governments firmly in power. Radical reductions in spending on social programs and ardent support of free enterprise were the dual banners of both the Reagan administration and the Thatcher government. Indeed, the reinvigoration of private capitalism, according to the philosophy of both governments, required nothing less than the dismantling of state welfarism. "Higher public expenditure," stated the Conservative government, "cannot any longer be allowed to precede, and thus prevent, growth in the private sector."[2]

The political mobilization of business is partly the result of growing social and economic interdependencies among large corporations. Yet the willingness and capability of the corporate community to act has been affected by external events as well. These critical challenges to the power and position of business have added new elements of classwide unity. As a consequence the inner circle has acquired an autonomy and political strength it had been incapable of achieving on its own.

The new powers of the transcorporate network are, ironically, the indirect consequence of the declining powers of individual companies. Increasingly unable to cope separately with worsening economic and political environments, firms increasingly recognized the need for joint action. The challenges confronting American and British business were perceived to be universally shared and too profound to permit individual solution.

The challenges of the 1970s and early 1980s came from two fundamentally different directions. One was economic, the other political. The economic challenge was the decline of company profitability, a problem endemic to most business sectors. While the economic threat was common to both countries, the political challenge could not have been more different. In Britain, it was the rise of labor socialism; in America, the spread of government interventionism. Trade union and Labour Party threats became the rallying cry of British business, while consumer activism and federal regulation became the hostile forces around which the ranks of American business closed.

DECLINING COMPANY PROFITS

Few events discipline the corporate mind as fast as a drop in earnings. Workforce and administrative changes inevitably follow: officers are replaced, staffing pared, divisions reorganized, unprofitable units sold. Corners are cut as well, as Marshall Clinard and Peter Yeager found in a study of 582 of the largest U.S. companies in 1975 and 1976. To answer the question of why some firms violate environmental, labor, antitrust and other federal laws and regulations, while others do not, they compiled records of legal actions taken by 24 U.S. agencies against these companies. They discovered that declining financial performance was among the best predictors of illegal corporate behavior.[3] When the profit line is threatened, strategic action follows, not always within the law.

But individual solutions necessarily had their limits in the 1970s, for the problem was too widespread and fundamental for anything short of collective response. In both countries, profit margins were in decline across the board. Virtually all sectors were affected, and exceptions were notable for their infrequency. The profit eclipse was not necessarily an extension of some longer cycle or trend. The evidence is yet equivocal on whether British and American capitalism are subject to some law of falling profit rates.[4] But what is certain is that the 1970s were years of shrinking returns for most major business.

The declining profitability of U.K. industry had been apparent since the mid-1960s, reaching extremely low levels by the late 1970s. This assessment stands whether profit is measured before or after taxes, as a rate of return on investments or as a share of income. And it accurately describes both aggregate trends and the profit pictures of major industrial sectors taken separately.[5] The decline of pretax, inflation-corrected rates of return on U.K. industrial and commercial assets is shown in Table 6.1. In 1963 and 1964, the profit rate averaged 11.7 percent; during the last half of the 1960s,

Table 6.1 Annual rates of return on assets of U.K. industrial and commercial companies, 1963–80[a]

Year	Pretax real rate of return (%)	
	Annual	Period average
1963	11.4%	
1964	11.9	11.7%
1965	11.2	
1966	9.9	
1967	10.0	10.2
1968	10.1	
1969	9.9	
1970	8.6	
1971	8.8	
1972	9.3	8.2
1973	9.1	
1974	5.2	
1975	5.3	
1976	5.4	
1977	6.2	5.5
1978	6.2	
1979	4.3	
1980	2.9	2.9

SOURCE: Bank of England 1981.
  [a] Excludes North Sea activity.

it dropped to 10.2; for the first five years of the 1970s, it further declined to an average 8.2; and for the 1975–79 period, it stood at only 5.5 percent. By 1980, it had sunk below 3 percent.

Trends in U.S. industrial profits in the postwar period are on a less precipitous downward slope, but the 1970s were sluggish years for American business as well.[6] Martin Feldstein and Lawrence Summers, for example, examined pretax rates of return for nonfinancial U.S. companies, examining the ratios of domestic profits to assets, adjusted for trends in depreciation, interest payments, and other factors. The annual corporate profit rate averaged 12.5 percent at the end of the 1940s, 11.8 percent in the early 1950s, and 10.4 percent in the late 1950s. The movement in the 1960s was modestly upward, peaking in the middle of the decade at nearly 14 percent, as can be seen in Table 6.2. Thereafter it declined, however, reaching unusually low levels in the mid-1970s. Indeed, lower profit rates

Table 6.2 Annual rates of return on U.S.
nonfinancial corporations, 1948–76[a]

| | Pretax net rate of return (%) | |
Year	Annual	Period average
1948–49	11.6 to 13.3%	12.5%
1950–54	10.3 to 13.2	11.8
1955–59	8.5 to 12.4	10.4
1960	9.9	
1961	9.8	
1962	11.2	11.2
1963	11.9	
1964	12.8	
1965	13.7	
1966	13.4	
1967	11.9	12.2
1968	11.7	
1969	10.2	
1970	8.1	
1971	8.4	
1972	9.2	8.1
1973	8.6	
1974	6.4	
1975	6.9	
1976	7.9	7.4

SOURCE: Feldstein and Summers 1977.
  [a] Excludes earnings and assets abroad.

were recorded in the 1970s than in any period of comparable length since
the Second World War. The average annual rate for the first half of the
1960s was 11.2 percent; the second half, 12.2 percent. But performance for
the first five years of the 1970s declined to 8.1 percent, and for the next two
years to an average 7.4 percent.[7] Extending the estimates to 1979, Feldstein
and two colleagues found the profit rate in 1979 to be lowest in two decades, save the recession years of 1974–75.[8]

Similar trends appear even when other measures of profit levels are
used. Aftertax returns on capital, for instance, have been gauged by David
Holland and Stuart Myers since 1947, and they too find that compared
with the 1960s, the 1970s were years of very poor performance (Table 6.3).[9]
Aftertax profits averaged 7.5 percent in the early 1960s, up from the 6.1

Table 6.3 Annual rates of after-tax return
on U.S. nonfinancial corporations, 1947–78

| Year | Aftertax rate of return (%) | |
	Annual	Period average
1947–49	7.0 to 9.0%	8.1%
1950–54	5.2 to 7.2	6.1
1955–59	5.0 to 7.3	6.1
1960	6.1	
1961	6.0	
1962	7.7	7.5
1963	8.2	
1964	9.3	
1965	10.3	
1966	10.2	
1967	9.1	9.0
1968	8.3	
1969	7.2	
1970	5.9	
1971	6.2	
1972	7.1	6.0
1973	6.5	
1974	4.3	
1975	5.5	
1976	5.8	
1977	6.1	5.9
1978	6.0	

SOURCE: Holland and Myers 1980.

percent of the 1950s, and reached 9 percent in the late sixties. But after that
they declined considerably, dropping to 6 percent in the early 1970s and
5.9 percent between 1975 and 1978.

The plunge in corporate profits continued into the early 1980s according to other studies. A survey of the profits of 279 large corporations in the
second quarter of 1982 by *The New York Times,* for instance, reveals a
significant overall decline from the previous year's profits. A similar survey
of 558 companies by Data Resources, an economic analysis firm, finds a
better than 20 percent drop in quarterly profits compared with the previous
year. Data Resources estimates that the inflation-adjusted profit rate in 1982
had reached its lowest level since the early 1970s. "This had better be temporary," said Otto Eckstein, chairman of Data Resources. If the 1982 profit

rates continued "for the next three years, the American economy would be devastated."[10]

THE CHALLENGE TO BRITISH LABOR

To the bleakness of this profit pictures was added political challenge. British business came under increasing pressure from labor, while American business suffered under the growing encroachment of government. The challenges confronted all businesses; few corporations did not experience some dislocation. But here too, equally few could effect individual solutions, and of necessity the response became one of collective reaction. From common adversity emerged new strength and purpose.

Relations between labor and management have long been more strained in Britain than America. Large companies in Great Britain are confronted by a labor movement that is better organized and more able to affect public policy than has ever been the case in the United States. British unionization has been on the rise during the past decade, while American union membership has been in decline. Half of the British workforce but less than a quarter of the American workforce is now organized. Moreover, among the largest British enterprises, the rate of unionization is even higher, exceeding 70 percent.[11] And in recent years, union membership is increasingly concentrated in a diminishing number of unions of larger and larger size, themselves united under the single umbrella of the Trades Union Congress (TUC). At the turn of the century, over 1,300 trade unions were officially recognized; by 1960, the number had dropped below 700, and by 1974 to under 500. Only a quarter of these unions are now affiliated with the TUC, yet this quarter represents over 90 percent of the organized workforce.[12] In the late 1970s, three British unions alone raised more political funds for the Labour Party than did the largest 800 companies for the Conservative Party.[13]

British shop stewards are given to greater militancy than their American counterparts, though strike rates are no higher. National bargaining is conducted on a more centralized basis and traditional socialist programs, such as public ownership of key industries, are important in the British labor agenda but find only weakest expression in the American labor movement.[14] Moreover, though the importance of American unions to the Democratic Party should not be underestimated, the attachment of British unions to the Labour Party is far more extensive and organic.[15] At the time of the 1974 election, for example, trade union members numbered 5.7 million of the Labour Party's 6.5 million members, and trade unions supplied 80 percent of the party's total income (only somewhat more than half of the Conservative Party's central income derives from company contributions).[16] The difference in the levels of union support in the U.S. and the U.K. is explained by the varying success of Democratic administrations versus Labour governments in reducing unemployment: while both have records superior to those of their Republican and Conservative Party counterparts, Labour governments have been significantly more effective in alleviating unemployment than have Democratic administrations.[17]

Further exacerbating the division between labor and management in Britain is the persistence of class disparities that manifest themselves not only as differences of wealth but of language, demeanor, and sensibilities. Compared with the U.S., movement into the higher strata is more restricted; class-based party attachments are stronger, and the social distance between labor and management is greater.[18] The differences are reinforced by distinctive educational systems. The British system emphasizes more selective enrollment and elite attitudes, the American system more open admission and democratic values. The outcome carries over into the workplace. British schooling has been especially prone, observed one business analyst, to "foster negative attitudes in work-management relationships characterized by a 'them' and 'us' dichotomy."[19] While such distinctions mask numerous exceptions and run the danger of being overdrawn, there is an enduring antagonism between labor and management in the U.K. that finds but faint parallel in the U.S.

The specter of the labor challenge and the "socialist threat" pervaded many of my personal interviews with company executives in London; rarely did either emerge in the parallel discussions in Boston and New York. There was simply nothing analogous in the American interviews, for instance, to the repeated expression of concern in the British financial community about eventual government takeover of the major institutions of the City. Much of this anxiety stemmed most immediately from a Labour Party proposal to nationalize the major clearing banks and insurance houses. A study group of the National Executive Committee of the Labour Party had issued a programmatic statement on banking and insurance in 1972 calling for public takeover of the largest financial companies. Its task was "not whether but how" to bring about the change. The insurance companies and the banks should be nationalized, the Labour study group concluded, because of inefficiencies in financial services. But nationalization was also dictated by "the political questions of wealth and power," questions "crucial to a socialist party, as the current financial system perpetuates, and increases, the unequal distribution of wealth."[20] To achieve this change, a single, publicly owned British Bank would be melded from the assets of the clearing banks, and it would be empowered to acquire still other banks, including the accepting houses. Similarly, when "Vesting Day" arrived for insurance, the twenty-nine largest insurers would be folded in a British Insurance Corporation, a state-owned agency with power to acquire the remainder of the insurance industry. Building societies, suppliers of most home mortgage funds, would be transformed into a single public institution as well.

The proposals could not have posed a more fundamental threat, for the City would simply have ceased to exist. The leading business associations of the companies singled out for nationalization—the Committee of London Clearing Banks (CLCB) and the British Insurance Association (BIA)—sounded the alarm and mounted vigorous counter campaigns. Union employees of the threatened firms were encouraged to issue statements opposing appropriation, Labour members of Parliament were aggressively lobbied, and advertising space was purchased to defend the merits of private banking and insurance.

The mobilization and consolidation of the British Insurance Association were, ironically, among the few final legacies of the Labour proposal. Differences of opinion among the BIA membership on other issues paled before the perceived attack on private enterprise, and consensus was more readily achieved on these and other matters as well. Moreover, BIA members came to recognize more strongly than ever that despite their competitive differences, on fundamentals they were and must remain united. And, with the experience of resisting a proposal for nationalization, the BIA felt better prepared to tackle new issues of lesser import. The impact on the Committee of London Clearing Banks was less profound, yet similar in effect. Moreover, since both the clearing banks and insurance companies were under simultaneous attack, loose coordination developed between the two organizations during their campaigns against the Labour proposal. The linkage so established between the two principal associations of the City far outlived the threat itself. The Labour proposal was swiftly defeated.

The City's victory was soon overshadowed, however, by a new labor assault on all large corporations, banking and industry alike. Under the Labour government, the Department of Trade established a "Committee of Inquiry on Industrial Democracy," and its final report in 1977 called for the restructuring of large companies to include worker participation in corporate governance. The document, commonly known as the "Bullock report" after its chairman—Lord Bullock—urged that company boards be radically reorganized to include "employee" directors on a numerical par with "stockholder" directors.

The proposal struck at the heart of managerial control of production. It was vigorously resisted at many levels, but especially by the inner circle and the organization it leads, the Confederation of British Industry. The

CBI assumed an uncompromising stand, one of "total opposition to any legislation which sought to impose directors on company boards irrespective of the wishes of shareholders."[21]

The opposition was especially animated by management's deep suspicions of labor's ultimate objectives. "For industrial democracy to be effective, you have to have a common philosophy between unions and management," observed one director, "but it isn't there." Unlike organized labor in the U.S., he continued, "even right-wing unions in Britain are suspicious of profits. They regard profit as a dirty word. Instead of saying, 'let us produce the maximum profit in order to share the cake,' they prefer to say, 'if there are big profits, let's get at them.' " Opening the board room to labor was thus perceived to be handing managerial power to those not only without the requisite talent, but to those without commitment to private enterprise. In arranging for the foxes to guard the chickens, it was feared the Bullock proposals could unintentionally bring the beginning of the end. However appealing worker participation might be in principle, the unions' entirely different conception of how to govern a company left most managers feeling that industrial democratization could as surely as nationalization spell the demise of free enterprise.

The perception of a life-threatening attack on all engendered new trust and common purpose among the major companies. The chief executive of a manufacturing company, holder of several outside directorships, and a member of a special CBI group established to defeat the recommendations of the Bullock report, described it this way:

> It was a major threat to the government of a company, and it was recognized as such. The terms of reference of the report were fixed. We knew we were under challenge right from the start. We did a vast amount of consultation (with members of the CBI), and we really did know what the membership felt. And we backed this up with a lot of documentation of what they were personally doing. I remember [a high official of the CBI] saying to Jim Callahan, then the Labour Prime Minister, "Jim, I feel like the General Secretary of the TUC (Trades Union Congress): I can say no, and I say no with full support." And we won. CBI members woke up to the fact that they have greater strength than they realized, and that has stayed with them.

Another director of several companies and a central figure in the CBI's leadership during this period offered a similar assessment:

> There is no doubt that the Bullock report was a considerable catalyst in uniting companies in this country in fierce opposition to a report that the then-Labour government was very seriously considering. It certainly helped the president and director-general (of the CBI) to mobilize the troops in a way that nothing else might have done. I would say that the cohesion as a

whole has been well sustained since then, although Bullock has been put on a shelf. It gave a sense to the membership of the CBI of what can be done by a very determined and united stand.

Like most crises followed by lasting change, the threat of codetermination was more a precipitant than a true determinant. The specter of worker-directors moved to action many who were on the verge of action anyway. Grievances had already accumulated, and the Bullock report became the one too many. The director of a large consumer products company with a third of a million employees saw the plan to have worker representatives join him and his colleagues on the board as the breaking point:

> If you had to pick out the one single issue that really galvanized and united the CBI, it was the Bullock report. That, however, would be misleading if one just said that, because already the influences had started and in a sense this was a touchstone . . . There have been other issues—government sanctions on government contracts in order to try to force a government incomes policy. And there the CBI pretty well stood solid and said, "Sorry, we won't sign those contracts if you insist on those terms." Before that the planning agreements were a very similar issue. Although Bullock is probably the most famous, there are in fact a number of these.

The director concurred with others in concluding that although the Bullock proposals were not the only cause, they were the most proximate cause of the CBI's enhanced power. "Now even the leading Labour politicians," he concluded, "would themselves say that the CBI is a much more meaningful body than it was before and one that they have to take much more seriously."

As in the case of the Labour proposal for the nationalization of banks and insurance companies, none of the major recommendations of the Bullock committee were ever implemented. The challenge, however, did lead to an unintended change in the organizational and attitudinal preparedness of the CBI, and more generally the transcorporate network of which the CBI is a part. New strength was added to the rolls, resolve, and administrative apparatus of the CBI. Some companies that had been loath to join finally enlisted. The CBI, as a result, acquired an even stronger standing as the undisputed leader of British business. John Methven, then the Director-General of the CBI, "always said the Bullock proposals were a turning point in his organization," observed one manufacturing director and former member of Parliament. "It brought the membership together," he said. "Before that, many people thought it was too cooperative and compliant with government. Now, after the Bullock proposals, the picture has changed, and there's much greater feeling that the CBI is the genuine voice of business—and an effective voice." The participants' remembrance of Bullock's seminal impact is corroborated by the historian's appraisal. "The Bullock proposals antagonized management on political grounds," writes Keith Middlemas, "and stimulated their most cogent collective activity for thirty years."[22]

THE CHALLENGE OF REGULATION IN THE UNITED STATES

The most important challenge to American business in the 1970s was of very different origin. "England starts with a two-class society," offered one partner of a large American investment bank during an interview, and there "the adversaries of business are very closely associated with labor. The case here is strictly over involvement of government in business." The manager of an American petroleum company had reached an identical conclusion from his own extensive experience in both countries. He had run his firm's U.K. operations for some years and had just assumed a senior post in the New York headquarters at the time of the interview. "Out of necessity," he commented, the CBI is a product of "the them-versus-us approach in the U.K. born of Fabian socialism. . . . There has always been a class distinction, the worker versus management, and they do not view it as a common effort where they can mutually benefit, but as an intrinsic conflict. The CBI's strength and [its] having a composite organization is born of that. Business owners and managers *must* have as united a voice as they can have against the trade union movement." But in the United States, he observed, the "foremost problem is government regulation." The difference is evident in the central thrusts of two countries' major business associations. While the CBI and British trade associations devote great attention to labor questions, American associations are far more concerned with regulatory issues, according to a study by Udo Staber.[23] Government, not labor, is the preoccupying concern.

A qualitative shift in the nature of U.S. government involvement during the past decade has given new coherence to the business circle most actively opposed to it. While industry-specific regulation has often served to fragment business, regulatory agencies and programs created in the 1970s achieved much the opposite effect because their impact was universally shared. Managers of companies in diverse industries found little common cause in dealing with industry-specific regulatory agencies, but they did find much to share in their unhappy experiences with the newer, functional agencies. Moreover, industry-specific regulation was usually developed with some degree of industry cooperation, while general regulation has been far more adversarial in origin and implementation.[24] At the forefront of this new, overarching regulation are the Occupational Safety and

Health Administration (OSHA), the Equal Employment Opportunity Commission (EEOC), and, above all, the Environmental Protection Agency (EPA). One utility executive's appraisal of EPA's attitude is characteristic, if somewhat overdrawn, of many. He was bitter over the EPA's "unscrupulous methods," the self-serving actions of its bureaucrats, but most of all its lack of balance. "Did you ever see an important official in EPA," he concluded rhetorically, "who wasn't a rabid environmentalist?"

The disparate growth rates of the specific and general regulatory programs are reflected in the expenditures trends of the key agencies. Between 1974 and 1979, the annual outlays of the Environmental Protection Agency more than doubled, rising from $232 million to $552 million (Table 6.4). Similar growth rates of near or more than 100 percent are observed for four other cross-industry agencies—Occupational Safety and Health Administration, Equal Employment Opportunity Commission, National Labor Relations Board, and the Securities and Exchange Commission. The aggregate expenditures for these five agencies increased more than two fold during

Table 6.4 Expenditures of U.S. government regulatory agencies, 1974–79, in millions of dollars

Agency	Fiscal year					
	1974	1975	1976	1977	1978	1979
General industry regulation						
Environmental Protection Agency	232	317	363	436	473	522
Occupational Safety and Health Administration	69	90	109	127	129	150
Equal Employment Opportunity Commission	42	56	59	72	88	108
National Labor Relations Board	55	61	67	81	92	100
Securities and Exchange Commission	34	44	51	54	66	65
Total	432	568	649	770	848	945
Industry-specific regulation						
Civil Aeronautics Board	89	81	91	103	101	96
Federal Trade Commission	32	39	44	52	62	64
Federal Communications Commission	38	48	53	56	70	66
Interstate Commerce Commission	38	44	47	59	64	69
Total	197	212	235	270	297	295

SOURCE: Budget of the United States.

this six-year period, from $432 million in 1974 to $945 million in 1979. For the industry-specific regulatory agencies, however, the 1970s were a period of less-bullish growth. The total expenditures for the four largest agencies—the Civil Aeronautics Board, Federal Trade Commission, Federal Communications Commission, and Interstate Commerce Commission—grew by only 50 percent, climbing from near $200 million to just under $300 million. Moreover, the outlays of the general regulatory agencies rose substantially faster than did overall government spending or business itself. By the end of the decade, the great majority of federal regulatory expenditures were devoted to general rather than industry-specific agencies.[25]

The cost to large companies is widely believed to be massive, though few of the interviewed executives could cite a specific cost figure for their own firm. An overall estimate comes from a study by an accounting firm of the direct impact in 1977 of six general regulatory agencies and programs, including OSHA, EEOC, and EPA, on forty-eight large companies, all members of the Business Roundtable. Using company-supplied data, this evaluation found a total annual cost of $2.6 billion, of which three-quarters stemmed from EPA regulations alone.[26] By another estimate, OSHA regulations caused companies in 1975 to spend $4 billion just on equipment required to bring the company into compliance with new rules on workplace safety.[27] The total annual burden of both industry-specific and general cross-industry government regulation has been estimated for all companies to run as high as $58 billion to $73 billion by one study, and even $100 billion or more by another, though the necessarily tenuous assumptions underlying any aggregate calculations dictate cautious interpretation.[28] There is some evidence that industries most subject to health and safety regulation have suffered somewhat lower rates of return, indicating that some fraction of the cost has been absorbed by the affected companies, not all being passed on to the consumer.[29]

Executives of large corporations reported that the business community became aware that each was experiencing increasingly burdensome federal demands and that a joint counteroffensive was long overdue. One senior manager of a large metals producer observed that across the business community "there is a better understanding of common objectives now, certainly on the tax situation, on OSHA, on pollution, and on regulation in general. Everybody finds that the costs escalate." The collectively shared impact of these government policies was a major impetus for the rise of the Business Roundtable. Dating from 1973, the Roundtable has enlisted the chief executives of the 196 largest corporations to carry the holy war to Washington. The guiding idea was expressed by one bank chief executive and member of the Roundtable:

For a long period of time there was really a gap in communication among businesses themselves and, of course, particularly between the corporate leaders of business and the government. Most of the communication took place through professional trade associations such as the National Association of Manufacturers and the American Bankers Association, and their professional lobbyists would then deal with more specific issues. The purpose of the Roundtable was to be much more catholic, not representing the banking industry nor the oil industry nor the steel industry, but representing the very fundamental business climate in the United States and, in effect, the survival of the free enterprise system.

To the burdensome economic costs of the new regulation has been added political irritation. To empower an agency to regulate is also to empower it to decide when to enforce and who to constrain. The formal criteria for making regulatory decisions are, of course, framed in largely technical terms—plants can be fined or closed if workers are overexposed to the carcinogen vinyl chloride. Yet limited agency resources in the face of perceived widespread violations necessarily opens all decisions to agency discretion. There is ample room for political considerations to appear.

Regulatory agencies are believed by many business leaders to act as much to promote political interests as to reduce real industry abuses. Corporations fortunate to have supported the winning candidate for the White House, it is felt by some of the interviewed executives, can expect favor; others less so. The agencies themselves are also believed to exercise their discretionary powers to protect their own mission and advance agency interests. The Environmental Protection Agency may more aggressively cite violators that have attacked the agency's role than violators with lower political profiles. A major utility company, for example, mounted a vigorous and highly visible advertising campaign against what it viewed as government blindness to many of the problems of the energy crisis. As soon as the advertising appeared, the chief executive of the utility received a number of calls from officers of other companies. All expressed support for the media statements, but none were willing to openly endorse or join the campaign. Their reluctance was lamented by the utility chief, but it was unsurprising:

> The federal government is so pervasive and it has such enormous power that there are few people who are willing to speak out against an agency. They feel that they can expect retaliation and not necessarily from the agency about which they were talking. It's a big club down there and the next thing you know you have some regulatory body or Internal Revenue or some other agency beginning to harass you. Of course they deny that there is any connection but having been around the horn a few times, I disbelieve most of these denials. When you speak out against the government generally or against an agency you can just count on retaliation.

His own campaign, targeted largely against the Environmental Protection Agency, elicited such a response, though it was one he anticipated and whose price he was prepared to absorb. Among the incidents of intimidation he chronicled was a speech by the Deputy Head of the EPA before a trade association audience: "He adverted to our advertising and how critical it was of the EPA and suggested that unless we bowed out he would find a way to put me in the clink." The utility did not bend, nor was the chief put away. Yet even if idle and a rare threat at that, the message was clear for the many to whom it was recounted.

The economic costs of regulation are the crux of the corporate critique, but the potential for political misuse of regulation, fueled by real, if infrequent incidents, added special irritation. Dissident political movements in America have often been angrily animated by even the hint of government reprisal or repression, and the bitter lament of corporate officials exhibits a striking, if ironic, parallel. The belief in corporate circles that there is occasional departure from technical criteria in regulatory decision making creates an indignation far more widespread and intense than any adverse consequences for the affected firms might ordinarily justify.

As some British managers saw industrial democratization as leading to de facto nationalization, some American managers feared that regulation pointed down the same path. Reversing the rise of state regulation thus acquired transcendent purpose. If the new regulation cut into corporate profits, it also threatened an end to profits. Whether well founded or not, fear of final defeat can transform a tactical attack into a holy crusade. "You can polish the brass on the Titanic," offered the chief executive of a New York bank, "but if in the environment we hit icebergs we are going to sink. . . . Why spend the money to nationalize," the banker continued, "when you can absolutely control through regulation. . . . We have tended to go the route of—'don't buy them, just control them.'" Regulation is perceived to be only the leading edge of a far more profound and ominous trend in American society. "If one looks back at the last 20 or 30 years . . . the basic political consensus in this country has been increasingly socialistic, increasingly turning to government for answers to socioeconomic-political questions. And as a consequence it has been increasingly turning away from the private sector with obvious antipathy." He described the present as a watershed, a moment in which concerted business attacks on regulation could achieve an historic reversal of mounting state interventionism. Regulation had become the battleground for a far broader struggle. The struggle, in *Fortune* editor Paul Weaver's view, has been nothing short of an authentic "class conflict," a clash arising from the intensifying hostility of the "new class" toward "corporate capitalism."[30]

Such challenges threatening an end to free enterprise are never laid at the door of U.S. labor, organized or otherwise. Indeed, American corporate opinion at the highest levels, in stark contrast to the outlook in similar British circles, considers organized labor to be one of capitalism's staunchest allies. In the arithmetic of one executive, American business and labor may go to battle with each other over 20 percent of the issues, but on the remaining 80 percent they are united. While observing informal discussions among U.S. industrialists organized by the Conference Board, Leonard Silk and David Vogel also reported on the widespread perception among members that labor is more ally than adversary.[31] I asked the second-ranking executive of a large diversified manufacturer what benefit his company derived from the chief executive's active role in the Business Roundtable. No reference was made to gains against trade unions, strikes, or the cost of labor. The corporation gained instead "from whatever the Roundtable can do to keep the private business sector performing its mission rather than [being]—pounded out of business is a strong word—inhibited by government regulation with well-meaning objectives that don't take into account the cost to the economic system." Furthermore, labor is not perceived to be the shadowy force behind the rise of regulation. According to a survey of large company executives, consumerism and related movements are viewed as the number one problem for business, not labor activism.[32]

If labor action has inspired more cooperative attitudes within the Confederation of British Industry, government action has animated the spirit of joint effort within the Business Roundtable. The Roundtable has consequently assumed an integrative role that no other association has had or could achieve. Its blue chip membership roster, compact size, and sense of mission combine to yield a unique forum for internal adjudication and external action. The Roundtable "has been an effective means of developing what is the position on these areas" of government regulation, observed one senior manager, "and then having developed that consensus, it is an effective means of presenting it to our friends in government who must act on it." The fewer than 200 chief executives in the Roundtable gives it consensus building powers impossible in other business organizations. "There is no way we could have got there," this manager added, "through broader things like the Chamber of Commerce or the National Association of Manufacturers because they are so big and diffuse that they can't come to agreement on anything." Rather than shared labor problems, then, it is common regulatory problems that have encouraged business leaders to overcome their tendency to speak in a "babble of tongues," as one analyst characterized it, and to be "more willing to evolve collective means" of addressing the government.[33]

In the U.S., important spheres of policy making that affect business are in the hands of state and local authorities, and analogous organizational developments have appeared at these levels as well. In New York City, for instance, some twenty principal officers of major firms, including the chief executives of Chase Manhattan Bank, Citibank, Metropolitan Life Insurance, and American Telephone and Telegraph, have formed a partnership similar in intent and structure to the national Business Roundtable. Its goal at the time of its 1979 inception was to "increase the influence of the fragmented business community by giving its many groups one voice on economic and civic affairs."[34] Boston's leading firms have congregated since 1958 as the Coordinating Committee, or "The Vault," an appellation deriving from its dominance by banking interests. The membership is limited to the chief executives of the city's twenty-two main financial institutions and largest employers (and a few others), but the agenda is unlimited. In recent years it has concentrated much of its energies on the tax structure and fiscal health of the city of Boston.[35]

At the state level, sixty chief executives have formed the Massachusetts Business Roundtable, and eighty have constituted the California Roundtable. The mission of both is self-consciously modeled after the national Roundtable. The California association asserts that its main purpose is "to encourage chief executive officers to look beyond the limits of their own industry and self-interest, and to aid in the support of basic principles important to preserving the free enterprise system."[36] A bank official who was instrumental in the founding of the Massachusetts body described its main goals similarly as an effort to overcome business fragmentation. Before the formation of the Massachusetts Roundtable, he said,

> industry self-interest would come to bear. The insurance companies would fight for their interests, the banks would fight for theirs, and the energy companies would be left to fight their battles all by themselves. That's not right. . . . Take the subject of hazardous waste. It's terribly important for the manufacturing companies that function in Massachusetts, but it's not terribly of concern to us—the banks, or insurance companies, or the financial community. But when you stop to think about it, by god if we have no policy, there is no way for people to dispose of the hazardous waste, and then Massachusetts gets a black eye and is unattractive for the kind of industry that might locate here, chemical companies or whatever, and we get an indirect loss as a result of that. If that's one of the major problems facing the manufacturing business in Massachusetts, it should be of concern to the banks, the insurance companies, and certainly to the manufacturers.

The Massachusetts Business Roundtable was formed to ensure that such mutual concerns are understood and embodied in policy initiatives. It is, according to the state's major newspaper, the *Boston Globe*, "the UN of the business view."[37] One of the first orders of business upon the organization's founding in 1979 was the formation of a task force on the environment, hazardous wastes at the top of the agenda. Other task forces were appointed to develop business policy toward higher education (state plans to reorganize public higher education were backed), employment (new training programs for high technology personnel were urged), and fiscal policy (the ballot initiative for tax limitation, "Proposition 2–½," was neither endorsed nor opposed).[38]

Specification of a shared policy, no simple task itself, is, however, only half the state Roundtable's reason for being. Implementation is the complementary second half. Viewing other statewide business associations as too sandbagged by their mass and thus passive membership, the state roundtables adopted the national's blueprint for fast action. "We wanted to make it like a club, a very exclusive arrangement," confided one of the Massachusetts roundtable's founding figures. Like the national Roundtable, the state Roundtables are constituted of the principal offices of the state's largest corporations. Regional balance is sought, as is sectoral representation. Banks, insurers, retailers, utilities, and manufacturers are all present. The chairman and three vice-chairmen of the California Roundtable, for example, are the chief executives of Southern Pacific Co., Carter Hawley Hale Stores, Dart Industries, and Hewlett-Packard. The Massachusetts Business Roundtable is led by the senior executives of The First National Bank of Boston, Boston Edison Company, John Hancock Mutual Life Insurance Company, and the Gillette Company. The stature, power, and drive of the state inner circles ensure maximum impact once the state Roundtable plans are in place. The bank executive who was an early organizer of the Massachusetts association identified the membership as its unique asset:

> When the work is completed, when the "white paper" is written, that message is communicated by the chief executives. One of the problems of a lot of these other business organizations is that they have good staff, have done great work, have come up with great studies and recommendations, but that's where they stop. A report sits on a shelf and gathers dust. If it doesn't have political constituency, it dies on the vine. Part of the objective of the Roundtable is to meet quarterly with the leadership—the Governor, Senate President, House Speaker, and say, "as far as business is concerned, here are the following five items—an energy plan, hazardous waste disposal plan, a tax restructuring plan, a pension plan. These are important Mr. Governor, Mr. President, Mr. Speaker, and we make the following recommendations."

The factors most immediately precipitating the formation of the state and metropolitan counterparts to the national Business Roundtable varied considerably. While federal regulation was at the forefront of the national organization's concerns, energy, employment, educational and fiscal policies led the state and local associations' concerns. However, though varying challenges have motivated the formation of the various roundtable-type organizations, these challenges had common elements. The reduced equation is: business is faring poorly, policies of state and local government are a root cause, and the problems of both are worsening.

The formations of the state Roundtables followed a process that was much the same as for the national Roundtable. A few individuals, typically long-time activists in the space between business and government, identify the need for a more forcefully integrated, regional voice for large corporations. From experience, they perceive that state and local policies are increasingly important to business, that the stakes had grown, and that the proper vehicle for response did not exist. In the case of Massachusetts, the Coordinating Committee in Boston initially attempted to act on behalf of business statewide, and ad hoc efforts were made to intervene in state political issues. Yet the Vault's regional limitation both compromised the legitimacy and hampered the success of such efforts. Believing state legislation increasingly vital to the business climate and that the climate had become more chilly, several figures central to the Coordinating Committee initiated a series of steps to found the statewide Roundtable. One individual, already a member of the national Roundtable and impressed with its streamlined power, had become alarmed at the deteriorating political climate at home:

> We had a total lack of understanding of business and of the linkage between the health of business and employment in the state. We had a state which was perceived by business in other states to be very hostile. So it was felt that we had to do something to turn around this attitude so that legislators and the public would understand that a healthy business climate was necessary for the maintenance of jobs. The national Roundtable was a good model.

The already extant California Roundtable also proved to be a good model. A small Massachusetts delegation visited the California organization and were convinced that the concept of an exclusive club of CEOs was the way to proceed. Symbolic of the organizational replication was the presence of an official of the California Roundtable at the founding meeting of the Massachusetts organization. The problems facing California businesses were far from identical to those before Massachusetts companies. In 1978, for example, the California organization devoted resources to study the electrical energy supply; programs for improving contact with universities and public officials; promotion of pro-business curricular materials for the classroom; and the problems created by the tax limitation measure, "Proposition 13."[39] Yet the organizational design and the programmatic thrust of the two roundtables are in essence very similar. The formation of a more formal apparatus for the promotion of classwide politics on the national scale is thus being closely paralleled by the creation of generically similar systems at the state and local levels.

THE MOBILIZATION OF BUSINESS

In both countries top managers have increasingly embraced the inverted exhortation, "Businessmen Unite." A further irony is that just as the adamant antipathy of certain businesses to the union movement made the success of unionism inevitable, labor and government challenges have brought about a unity and resolve the corporate community could not have imposed on its own. The principle that cohesion comes through conflict is upheld once again. As Louis Coser and other analysts have identified as a near universal of group life, there are few more unifying experiences than struggle against a common foe.[40] Commenting on the consequences of the new regulation, David Vogel writes that American "business has the political effectiveness of its adversaries to thank for enabling it to adopt a more cohesive political outlook."[41] In Britain, the labor adversary has had the same impact. The capacity of large corporations to promote their aggregate political interests through such organizations as the Confederation of British Industry and the Business Roundtable has been irreversibly strengthened. The focus of this new strength, however, has not been entirely the same in both countries. At the head of the British business agenda has been a determination to reduce the influence of big labor; first on the American agenda has been an equally strong commitment to constrain the power of big government.

Fueling the political mobilization of large corporations and the evolution of classwide organizations has been a decade of poor profit performance. Whether returns on investment in the 1970s could be considered adequate by some fixed standard, by any dynamic yardstick they were far weaker than what management had been accustomed to expect. Compared with those of the 1960s, the profits for most large companies were significantly lower. Just as trends in labor wages can be as powerful a determinant of strike activity as wage levels themselves,[42] so too may profit trends be a powerful determinant of business political agitation. The 1970s were marked in both countries by profit rates lower than for any other period since the Second World War.

Corporations in extremis will press for better internal performance. Among the responses of the early 1980s was a search for the secret of Japanese management success, reported in such works as William Ouchi's *Theory Z*.[43] But corporations in a profit crisis will also seek improved external conditions. In the name of "reindustrialization" or "recapitalizing capitalism," government spending was also singled out as a chief impediment to such prosperity. Named in addition were U.S. government intrusion into business decision making and U.K. labor intention to join the decision making. Business organized itself politically to reduce state spending, dismantle government regulation, and constrain labor.

The general political thrust, electoral success, and continued commitment to economic policies that were buffeted by events of both the Conservative government of Prime Minister Margaret Thatcher and the Republican administration of President Ronald Reagan were in no small part a product of this business mobilization. Corporate ranks were disciplined, resolve heightened. Both the Business Roundtable and the Confederation of British Industry increased their level of political activity and became better at it. And at the urging of these organizations and the inner circle, firms increasingly devoted company resources to political ends. Company advertising was given to public education and the promotion of new government policies; managers more often sought and accepted invitations to defend business in the electronic and print media; corporations set out to cultivate better relations with journalists, civil servants, academics and other influential opinion shapers. Business money also increasingly flowed directly into political campaigns and organizations devoted to fostering a political climate more favorable to business.

The early 1980s were a period of extraordinary political transformation in the United States and Great Britain, and a critical factor, though only one of several, was the heightened level of business political action instigated by the developments of the preceding decade. The dominant national political cultures became decidedly more sympathetic to private enterprise, less toward government and labor. Both the Reagan administration and Thatcher government entered office and once in office remained firmly and unabashedly pro-business, though neither always heard precisely what business was saying. Still, they ruled under the flag of reinvigorating private capitalism.

In both countries wherever possible government spending for human services and social programs went into decline, a reversal of historic significance. In the U.K. government attitudes toward labor and in the U.S. toward regulation became more hostile as well. The Conservative government proposed legislation to reduce the power of organized labor by imposing a ban on secondary picketing, facilitating secret balloting in union elections, and limiting the closed shop. The Republican administration acted through executive order to reduce the activism of the general regulatory agencies, by appointing so oriented top administrators, by slashing budgets, cutting staffs, and easing rules. The ensuing erosion of agency power was further evidenced in the continuous declarations of new regulatory policies during the first years of the Reagan administration: "The EPA announced it would temporarily allow companies to resume dumping hazardous liquid waters"; "Worker access to health, safety records would be narrowed under OSHA plan"; "SEC enforcement chief to ease pressure for disclosure if charges are unproven."[44]

The simultaneous rise of corporate enemies and fall of company profits suggest the immediate genesis of the rising corporate activism. The rise would not have been as rapid, however, nor its thrust as effective were it not for the presence of the transcorporate networks of the inner circle, the classwide social organization that had gradually developed over the years, largely for reasons unrelated to political mobilization but highly facilitating of it. The preexistence of this transcorporate organization, itself strengthened by the forces threatening business during the 1970s, allowed for more rapid mobilization, quicker identification of the common cause, and stronger expression of the right policies.

Greater overall planning initiative was, as a result, assumed more by business, less by government. Rather than having to sift through the often-competing demands of a thousand chief executives, government officials were increasingly presented with a more integrated vision, a vision already developed by that circle of senior managers and directors best positioned to reconcile the competing demands. Government decision makers are, of course, subjected to numerous constraints and the pressures of other constituencies, and business preferences were only partly and always imperfectly expressed in policies ultimately adopted. Still, the organization and articulation of a classwide voice has made the business outlook more authoritative and less easily ignored.

SEVEN

Family, Managerial, and Institutional Capitalism

Classwide principles of organization in the business community are ascendent. Along with corporate principles of organization, they now guide business political activity. The third type of logic shaping corporate behavior, upper-class principles, are largely descendent. The change has been nearly imperceptible; the strands of organization are almost invisible, but as powerful transcorporate networks have been formed, they have been transformative. Born of individual corporate strategy, the networks have become the avenue for collective political action. Barring a depression or severe political crisis, the progressive strengthening of the transcorporate linkages seems certain to continue. The inexorable movement of recent years has been toward more cohesion, less fragmentation.

It does not follow that big business is therefore more powerful in public affairs; we have seen that the rise of classwide organization is, in part, a response to collective adversity. While the corporate community is thus more capable of collective action than had it not responded, it is not necessarily more influential than in earlier decades when there was neither stimulus (organized adversity), nor response (transcorporate political expression). It is, however, organized in a different fashion than it once was, one that leads to new forms of political behavior. Central to the emergent classwide organization has been the inner circle that has come to play a critical role in the expression of classwide political concerns. The diverse corporate ties of the senior managers and directors who constitute the circle have engendered a broader vision of the evolving political priorities of the nation's largest corporations. And these managers and directors are better positioned than other members of the corporate community to define and promote that vision.

The appearance of classwide forms of social organization within the American and British corporate communities requires revision of our thinking, a new way of seeing business politics. Business leadership on matters of public moment must be seen as something far more than the unorchestrated action of the principal officers of the thousand largest companies. It must be kept in mind that business leadership is organized in a specific, complex fashion. It is a fashion that is generative of policy initiatives, and it has different effects than if the leadership represented little more the cacophonous policy suggestions of their respective firms. The separate company views certainly are heard, but now so too is the filtered, refined view of large companies as a bloc.

Business relationships with nonprofit institutions must also be understood for their full complexity, a complexity reducible neither to a thousand separate relationships nor to a single, predictable relationship. Consider the frequent university practice of inviting business leaders to serve on boards of trustees. Prestigious private universities are particularly fond of this practice, in part because they are so heavily reliant on private gifts. Often half or more of their trustees are drawn from the most senior ranks of the nation's largest companies. On first glance, it might appear that this reflects little more than a logical means of drawing generous corporate largess, and senior managers are, in fact, highly successful at bringing it in. Yet closer inspection reveals a more subtle principle behind the selection of the business trustees. What generates the flush of corporate beneficence is not the appointment of a board laden with business leaders, not even big business leaders, but rather a board of leaders with impeccable inner-circle credentials. Major private universities most effectively elicit private business donations not when they forge ties with specific firms, but when they cultivate relationships with the transcorporate network linking the firms. Other universities and nonprofit institutions attempting to emulate the fund-raising success of the private universities could find their aggregate level of corporate support very disappointing—unless the business leaders invited to join their governing board were selected with the same discerning care. To invite leading business figures is not enough; to invite the core of the leadership circle is the idea.

The surge of business political activism may prove a passing phenomenon. The mobilization of both British and American business in the 1970s and early 1980s could be a largely transient response to a challenge of the time. The decline of corporate profits, and labor and government successes in making free enterprise feel less secure put large corporations on the defensive. But the downward slope of corporate profits may have been more cyclical than permanent. And the increased intensity of the demands of British labor and American consumer and environmental regulation may also have represented more a temporary condition than a new stage of industrial confrontation from which there is no turning back.

Yet while the triggers of the political mobilization of business may prove transitory, the organizational foundation on which the mobilization was mounted and through which it achieved focus has been growing progressively stronger, to a point where the change seems to have established itself as irreversible. The central pillars of the foundation are the increasingly inclusive and diffuse networks of intercorporate ownership and directorship, and the formation and deepening consolidation of the explicitly classwide business associations, most notably the Confederation of British Industry and the Business Roundtable. These elements of classwide organization are certain to remain, and they represent a new stage of capitalist development, not economically but organizationally. The triple challenges of lowered corporate profits, greater labor power, and aggressive government intervention may subside, and the fires of business political activism may be banked. But as business-government relations return to normalcy, the corporate side of the equation, while possibly adopting a lower profile, will not revert to its precrisis form. Classwide principles are irrevocably stronger, corporate and upper-class principles forever weaker. As business encounters its next crisis, whether economic or political, it will be better prepared to meet the challenge, to offer classwide answers. And, if recent experience is any guide, one effect again would be to consolidate further the classwide system of organization.

This is not to suggest that business will necessarily emerge as more powerful than other interest groups, nor that its influence on public policies will be any greater than before. Indeed, it is arguable that the new corporate activism is in fact a product of greater weakness, not strength. But it is to suggest that the way the business community expresses its views on matters of public importance will be different.

The difference in the way the voice of business is expressed is a product of a broader transformation in the internal social organization of the American and British business communities. Organizational features associated with family capitalism have largely given way to those of managerial capitalism, and both are being now eclipsed by the rise of the classwide organization of what can be termed institutional capitalism. All three forms of organization still simultaneously structure the ways in which business attempts to shape its political environment. The salience of the first two, however, is a product of earlier stages of business development, the traditions and conventions of which remain powerfully with us but whose generative powers are lessening compared to those of institutional capitalism.

While America and Britain share these developments in common, and their business communities display remarkably similar classwide organizational properties, the process of arriving there has not been the same. Different paths have been followed, with distinctive consequences for the specific configuration of business politics. The most significant is the contrasting degree of informal intimacy between government and business officials in each country: in Britain there is a mutual respect and friendly contact, while in America the relationship is more distant. The political outcomes within each system may be similar, but the social texture could hardly be more dissimilar.

THREE STAGES OF DEVELOPMENT IN THE UNITED STATES

The upper-class, corporate, and classwide principles of organization remain in uneasy coexistence in the American business community today. All three simultaneously structure the ways in which business attempts to shape its environment. The lingering importance of the first two, however, is a product of the earlier eras of family and managerial capitalism in the U.S. The growing salience of the third is a product of an entry into the era of institutional capitalism.

Family Capitalism

The rise of the upper-class principle corresponds to the foundation of the great family enterprises during the latter half of the nineteenth century. It was the era of family capitalism, an era in which entrepreneurs managed their firms as an extension of themselves, when kinship, ownership, and control were synonymous, and where dynastic marriage was a means of corporate merger. Swift ascent in the company hierarchy was assured those of proper descent.[1]

As family fortunes compounded, and kinship multiplied within the enterprise and crossed into others, the American business aristocracy came of age. This business-based upper class in time evolved the many institutions necessary to lend a distinct collective identity, define its perimeters, preserve its culture, and socialize its young. Metropolitan clubs were established to acquaint its members, symphony orchestras sponsored to exhibit its tastes, preparatory schools formed to educate its heirs, and Social Registers published to demarcate its membership. But above all, the interests of the founding families occupied a primacy in company decision making, overriding even company interests.

Managerial Capitalism

But the real power of family capitalism has long since given way to corporate rule, as Daniel Bell has detailed.[2] The slow but irreversible displacement in business politics of upper-class dominance by corporate interests is a product of the historic transformation of the firm from an extension of the founding family to a distinct entity with an internal logic entirely of its own. This transformation at times allowed the growth of very large firms, and at other times was made inevitable by the continuing drive of most firms toward even greater size. A corresponding creation of multidivisional structures demanded new forms of administrative coordination, the formation of a professional management and complex career hierarchy within the firm, and the movement of both daily and final decision-making power from the founding family to trained managers.

The divorce of ownership from control, the "managerial revolution" of Adolph Berle and Gardiner Means, was a leading feature of this transformation, but only one feature. The nature of the business corporation was undergoing change with far more profound implications for business politics than just the emergence of control without appreciable ownership. Family capitalism was giving way to the "visible hand," the economy of the modern business enterprise in which administrative coordination displaced market power as a guiding mechanism of resource allocation. Market exchanges among the nation's many small, family-run firms became internally incorporated within a greatly diminished set of large, management-guided firms. Administrative calculus replaced the invisible hand of the market, as Alfred Chandler has described it, though, of course, the market still determined the allocation of resources among the larger firms. At the top of the new enterprise appeared a "new subspecies of economic man," observes Chandler—the salaried manager. His appearance was a signpost of a far broader transformation in American capitalism. This was the replacement of family rule of the company by the supremacy of the company itself. "In many industries and sectors of the American economy," concludes Chandler, "managerial capitalism soon replaced family or financial capitalism."[3] By the 1970s, many had become most, with the managerial revolution virtually complete among the largest companies in all industries and sectors. Evidence compiled by Edward Herman on this point is compelling.[4]

Yet as equally compelling data gathered by Herman and others have also shown,[5] the rise of managerial capitalism was still a rise of capitalism, only now even more efficiently pursued by a professional cadre of managers whose organizational role has left them no choice but to place growth in profits at the top of the corporate agenda. The transition from family capitalism to managerial capitalism is thus not one in which the fundamental guiding principle of free enterprise is altered or watered down. Rather, it is a transition in which the priorities of the firm come to take precedence over the priorities of the founding family. As the principal officers of large corporations enter the political process and direct company resources into politics, the guiding concern is no longer preservation of the fortunes of the upper-class families who once built and controlled the firms, but preservation of the profits of the enterprises that now control the families' economic destinies. Rather than the firm serving as an instrument for the accumulation of family wealth, the manager has come to be the instrument for the accumulation of company wealth. Class was replaced by organization as the lever of decision making.

The transition from family to managerial capitalism is evident in the alteration of the rules of succession for top management. In family-controlled firms, the owning family exercised the major voice in deciding both who became the chief executive, often a member of the family itself, and how long he or she remained in office. In the large firm managed by professional executives, however, control of this decision was assumed by management itself. Control of executive appointment and dismissal slipped from the owning family into management hands. This difference can be seen in the longevity of chief executives of more than two hundred large industrial firms studied by Michael Allen. The average tenure of the principal officers of management-controlled firms was near nine years, while the tenure for those running family-controlled firms was over seventeen years. Thus, when companies are in the hands of professional managers, they are quicker to replace faltering leadership than when the companies are still controlled by an owning family. The firm's interests take precedence in the first instance, the owner's interests in the latter. When companies begin to show poor profits, finds Allen, family-controlled firms do not move to replace their chief executive, but management-controlled corporations are swift to do so.[6]

The peak moment of the transition from family to managerial capitalism was near the turn of the century, but the process has been prolonged and continues to this day. Still, by the 1950s its consequences had become widely recognized. So striking and socially traumatic was the subordination of the individual to the objectives of the organization that it became a favored target of social commentary. William Whyte's "organization man"—the manager whose personality is reduced to those elements that are required for corporate success—and David Riesman's "other-directed" person—the individual who looks to the surrounding organization and culture for what should be thought and done—captured the extreme and problematic consequences of the rise of corporate rule.[7] The continuing power of the corporation to so completely shape the lives of its managers is apparent in more recent commentary as well. New strains of personalities specially adapted to achieving corporate success, above all the "gamesman," are a product of the era, according to Michael Maccoby.[8] Features of American life as far afield as the sexual division of labor have been traced by Rosabeth Kanter in part to corporate organization; gender stereotypes, she finds in her intensive study of one large firm, are partly a product of the struggle of men and women managers up an extremely steep and rapidly constricting career pyramid.[9] And a corporate "invading of all spheres of its managers' lives" is a phenomenon frequently described in study and fiction alike.[10] Though labeled an era in which management control of the firm had emerged ascendent, it would be more accurate to say that corporate control of management had become complete. "Many businessmen made the goals of their firm the ultimate values," finds a study of American enterprise near the turn of the century, and "the firm was able to command the all but ultimate loyalty of businessmen."[11]

The displacement of upper-class by corporate principles thus corresponds to, and indeed is a product of, the replacement of family capitalism by managerial capitalism. The transfer of power required many decades to complete but had largely run its course by the 1970s. Yet just as organization overpowered family in the conduct of company business, in recent years the dominance of the company itself has been giving way to the power of classwide social organization. Although family rule has been largely replaced by corporate dominance, the rise of classwide organization has not yet, and ultimately probably never will, eclipse the autonomous power of the individual business firm. Yet a classwide logic has come to coexist alongside a corporate logic in the making of many company decisions, and it adds a fundamentally new dimension to the way in which business political activities are orchestrated.

Institutional Capitalism

If the professionalization of corporate management is the driving force in the rise of corporate over upper-class politics, it is the formation of an intercorporate management network that is the engine behind the rise of the classwide principles associated with institutional capitalism. In both instances, the transition to the new stage is the unintended byproduct of other forces. For the managerial revolution, the dispersion of ownership and the superior capacities of managerial hierarchies in large organizations propelled the transformation. For the emergence of classwide organization, the creation of transcorporate networks of ownership and directorships as extensions of individual corporate strategies generated the transformation. Both transitions were thus rooted in changes in corporate organization necessitated by evolving market and bureaucratic conditions. But the consequences of these transitions have extended far beyond market and administrative questions into the many ways that large firms enter and affect the political process. The guiding organizational principles of family and managerial capitalism are now joined by, and in part displaced by, the principles of institutional capitalism.

The Governance of Nonprofit Organizations

Changing business relations with nonprofit organizations illustrate one consequence of the rise of institutional capitalism. At the end of the nineteenth century, for instance, the upper class had forged intimate ties with the nation's premier cultural institutions. Boston's patricians created and then enveloped the two arts organizations which to this day remain the city's premier institutions—the Museum of Fine Arts and the Boston Symphony Orchestra. This "alliance between class and culture," as Paul DiMaggio has described it,[12] still retains much of its original force, but in recent decades the alliance has increasingly become one between business and culture, with corporations replacing the upper class as high culture's prime benefactor.

Similarly, from the foundation of Harvard University during the seventeenth century until the Second World War, it was overseen, as E. Digby Baltzell's study of the Boston aristocracy has shown, "by a unified ruling class of Bostonians," with the relationship reaching an apogee during the mid-nineteenth century.[13] Governance of the university was long considered a special calling for the Brahmins of greater Boston. Indeed, service on the Board of Overseers, the institution's ruling body, was held to be a singular mark of achievement within the city's upper class.[14] Harvard, for its part, well understood the distribution of power and resources in Boston on which its fortunes depended. On its governing board was always ample if not dominant representation of Boston's aristocracy. By the middle of the nineteenth century, at the height of Brahmin influence, the upper-class trustees were there because they were of proper descent, not because they may have coincidentally prospered commercially.

The formation of modern enterprise at the conclusion of the nineteenth century, however, and the corresponding rise of corporate over upper-class power subtly changed the composition of the governing boards of the nation's premier nonprofit organizations. Increasingly what counted for appointment was corporate position rather than family heritage. Systematic analysis of the governing boards of fifteen prestigious private colleges and universities, including Dartmouth, Yale, and Princeton, from 1860 to 1930 documents the magnitude of the transformation. Manufacturers and financiers constituted just over a quarter of the typical board in 1860, but over half by 1930.[15]

Since the Second World War, what has become increasingly important for invitation onto a board of trustees is neither lineage nor company position, though the former still helps and the latter is essential for what does count: membership in the classwide network of top corporate executives. Those who travel the inner circle are far preferred over others for appointment to governing bodies. Leaving the circle is grounds for non-reappointment. In the past, the fact that a patrician company president retired would not mean the end of his usefulness to a nonprofit board. His lifelong status as a leading figure of the local upper class would leave him a valuable asset to the board. But it carries less weight today. Once he no longer runs his own operation, other company boards will quietly pass over his name at renomination time. And once both the corporate position and multiple corporate connections are lost, nonprofit boards will tend to pass over him as well. Despite impeccable class credentials, the retired president, shorn of his outside directorships, will not be able to pull his full weight on the nonprofit boards. Thus, just as inner-circle status has come to be the best single predictor of who is chosen to represent business on the governing boards of the nation's preeminent nonprofit institutions, it is also the strongest determinant of who will be kept on the boards as the trustees' professional circumstances change.

Managerial Succession

To assert that managers control executive succession is to say that the corporation itself has assumed power over its own actions, for professional executives are ultimately creatures of the organization, not the converse. But just as the company managers took power from the owners in this area of decision making, the classwide network of select managers is now taking some power from the individual organizations. Decisions on senior management are still largely a product of purely internal deliberation, but increasingly influential is the external voice of the inner circle. Its influence was earlier apparent in the description of the route to the top of the large corporation. Senior managers consistently insisted that decision-making and leadership abilities, as demonstrated *within* the firm, were the prerequisites for promotion of top officers. But they were equally consistent in their stress on demonstrated leadership *outside* the firm as the final prerequisite for accession to the chief executive's office. Only if an aspirant plays a recognized leadership role in major business associations; serves effectively on other company boards; and achieves a reputation for access to the highest circles of government are his or her prospects for promotion brightened;

if not, they are dimmed. Firms vary of course in the extent to which outside validation of managerial potential is taken into account. But the fact remains that in large companies purely internal criteria are no longer the only basis for appointing managers to the very top. Indeed, a committee of the Business Roundtable urges its chief executives to place even greater emphasis on managerial outreach in considering promotion. The Roundtable's Resource and Review Committee suggests that CEOs ask themselves: "To what extent are our top executives effective in dealing with the public policy aspects of our company's business?" and, "To what extent are our candidates for succession to [top] executive positions qualified to perform effectively in the public policy aspects of those positions?"[16]

The three stages of capitalist development are thus marked by decisive shifts in control over seniormost executive selection and retention. Owner influence yielded to executive sovereignty with the shift from family to managerial capitalism. Executive sovereignty is now itself giving way in part to intercorporate control with the rise of institutional capitalism.

TWO AND ONE-HALF STAGES OF DEVELOPMENT IN THE UNITED KINGDOM

The organization of business in the U.K. has reached much the same stage as in the U.S. The route, however, has been shorter. Rather than managerial capitalism supplanting family capitalism only to be challenged itself by institutional capitalism, upper-class social organization rooted in land ownership and early commercial formations, especially finance, was more directly harnessed to the service of classwide ends. The middle stage of corporate hegemony never achieved the same absolute rule as it did in the U.S. If the family hand gave way to the visible hand and this now to the collective hand in America, in Britain the stage of the visible hand was never quite so complete.

The Professionalization of British Management

Despite the rise of the large, multidivisional firm in Britain, the professionalization of management has proceeded at a far slower pace than in America.[17] While a university degree has long been a required credential for a successful career in the American firm, and a Master's in Business Administration (MBA) increasingly required for the fast track as well, British business has traditionally placed little emphasis on management training and nearly as little on a university degree. Indeed, while Harvard has been graduating hundreds of MBAs annually for decades, and scores of business

schools now offer the credential that has become the sine qua non of corporate success in the U.S., Britain had no professional management schools
at all until the mid-1960s. Only then, and with misgivings continuing to the
present, did British business back the creation of two programs—the Manchester Business School and the London Graduate School of Business Studies—programs that still educate but a tiny fraction of the nation's future
managing directors.[18]

Fewer British managers receive a higher education and specialized
training than in any other advanced industrial society.[19] Nine separate surveys of top British management reveal that from only a third to a half the
directors had attended any university, whereas nearly as many U.S. surveys
show that better than three-quarters of top American management had
been enrolled.[20] While virtually no managing directors of large British firms
received postgraduate training, substantial numbers of their American counterparts had: two-fifths of the chief executives of the largest 800 U.S. firms
in 1980 held advanced degrees, primarily in business and law.[21] While
British managers remain skeptical of the need for any professional training,
American managers increasingly require it, making an MBA degree *the*
ticket to the top. Three-fifths of the chief executives of the top 800 American firms surveyed in 1980 regard the contributions of their managers holding MBAs to be superior to those without such degrees.[22] Specialized business training is still nearly unknown in the U.K. Surveying a wide range of
evidence including their own intensive study of business school graduates
in Britain, Richard Whitley, Alan Thomas, and Jane Marceau judge British
opinion to be highly uncertain and perhaps even backsliding on the issue
of professionalism in management. "Any formal management qualification,"
they conclude, "has continued to be regarded with ambivalence by substantial sections of British industry. . . . If anything there has been a tendency to reassert the importance of personality, attitudes, leadership ability,
and track-record against a background of increasing 'technicalization' of
management tasks."[23] Even the process of technicalization offers latent non-
technical advantages to mid-career industrialists who would seem to be
seeking the professional training they had always missed. A return to business school can compensate for the lack of not only the right skills, but the
right stuff as well. "If you happen to work in despised industry and, worse,
if you missed university of any kind, not to mention Oxbridge, then to pass
through" the London Business School, writes one observer of British management, "is to press a little closer to the extreme centre of concentric
British society."[24]

Comparative studies of British and American management and organizational styles consistently report that American firms are more formally
organized, more bureaucratic, more insistent on formal training—in a word,

more professionalized. A group of investigators led by J. H. K. Inkson, for instance, compared a sample of eighteen American manufacturing firms with a matched set of British firms. Holding size constant, they found that the American companies relied more upon written rules and procedures to ensure compliance, the British firms more upon informal custom.[25] In another study, Ian Jamieson, compared six American manufacturing companies operating in Britain with six carefully matched British firms. Even though the American firms are constantly exposed to British culture and though they employ many British nationals, the decision rules and procedures are far more explicit and elaborate in the American companies than in their British counterparts. When managers are recruited, American firms are less likely to rely upon personal contacts, more likely to utilize professional head hunters. The underprofessionalization of British management cannot be explained, concludes Jamieson, without reference to the continuing legacy of upper-class values. Managerial capitalism is still competing with the cultural products of an era whose organizational principles are in many ways antithetical to modern business. "In Britain the values of capitalism have always been faced with the opposite set of values emanating from the landed aristocracy," writes Jamieson. "In America on the other hand, the relative absence of such a tradition has made it more difficult for American capitalists to resist the forces of efficiency generated by the capitalist mode of production."[26]

The Aristocracy and Anti-industrial Culture

The failure of industrial organization to more fully sweep aside the family and precorporate relations is a product of reinforcing social, cultural, and economic factors. The most important social factor is the continuing presence of an aristocracy whose prominence, sense of mission, and right to rule remains an accepted fact within the business community. The influence of the upper class has long outlasted the ancient institutions on which it was formed. It is true, as Anthony Giddens and Philip Stanworth have argued, "that Britain made gentlemen of businessmen and businessmen of gentlemen," and that a "consolidated and unitary 'upper class' in industrial Britain" was the product,[27] but it is equally true that the merger was achieved on terms decided by the gentlemen.

High culture in England has never really recognized the power, let alone the value, of industrial activity.[28] Finance became a noble calling for the upwardly aspiring, but in sharp contrast to American patterns, bright young men have been encouraged to avoid careers in the seemingly mundane world of making products. Manufacturing remains a stigmatized option for the elite of the new generation. One director of a large British manufacturer, a graduate of Charterhouse, reflected on his days at Oxford's Balliol College:

> I had one friend who was determined to go into business. Everyone said, "you're a brilliant philosopher, what on earth do you want to go into business for." It was regarded as the most extraordinary eccentricity. The people I was with all went in the BBC, into journalism and are now Fleet Street editors. They're all in politics, the bar, the professions, the civil service. Peter Parker was an Oxford colleague and went into business [becoming head of British Rail], but he was one of the rare ones.

Although aspiring to a career in industry best be left unannounced, planning for a life in finance could be confessed. "Much of banking had a kind of glamour to bright graduates that manufacturing did not," continued this director. "If one wasn't in the civil service, the bar, journalism, or the BBC, it's just possible that one might be in merchant banking." His more intimate associates still consider his entry into manufacturing as a peculiar step demanding explanation. His observations and own experience are daily reproduced in conversation, writing, and ceremony wherever established people communicate. So strong is the ambiance that even successful business leaders succumb to its message, choosing to send their sons to public schools and then Oxford or Cambridge, knowing they will be encouraged to renounce their heritage and seek their fortunes elsewhere. "This antiindustrial culture" is so pervasive, observes historian Martin Wiener, that industrialists "breathed it in ever more deeply the higher they rose in social position."[29]

The failure of the visible hand to sweep aside family rule and the vestiges of precapitalist forms in Britain has also been attributed to a variety of economic factors. The explanations could not be more divergent in argument, but all converge in their conclusion that industrial organization remains a British stepchild. Some analysts attribute manufacturing's underperformance to the overperformance of finance, with industry forced to remain in the shadow of banking. Other explanations single out Britain's low rate of productivity, high rate of state welfare, excessive reliance on international trade, and the structural incapacity of the British political system to respond to changing industrial needs.[30]

The Aristocracy and Business Access to Government

Although British business never so fully entered the era of managerial capitalism that emerged supreme in the U.S., it has nonetheless evolved the classwide strands of institutional capitalism just as extensively as in the U.S. Indeed, the sinews that have always linked the aristocracy facilitated the foundation of the transcorporate network linking large companies, the hallmark of the appearance of institutional capitalism. Members of the aristocracy have long been favored for nonexecutive director appointment. They add instant luster to any board, but even more important they bring exceptional and influential connections.

The aristocracy's extended kinship adds an additional backbone to the higher circles of British business for which there is no counterpart in the U.S. Study of the shared directors among major British industrial and financial companies reveals considerable integration, but even greater intercorporate contact is evident if the overlay of kinship is studied as well. Bonds of kinship connect many of the largest companies otherwise without formal ties, and it is the aristocracy, not the nouveau directors, who maintain them.[31] Virtually all of the financial firms and nearly half of the industrial firms are linked in a single kinship network. Thus, as the intercorporate network expanded in Britain, its expansion was facilitated by preexisting transcorporate relationships derivative of the aristocracy's successful move into business.

The undiminished autonomous power of the British upper class has also facilitated the exchange of views between the highest levels of business and government. Though the recruitment base for the civil service has widened some in recent years, it still remains a special preserve of the British establishment. More than half of the senior civil servants had been Oxford or Cambridge educated, a fraction still characterizing new recruits to the civil service today.[32] And within the Conservative party, particularly among its Cabinet members when in power, the aristocracy remains very prominent.[33] The shared educational experience and social origins ease communication across the institutional gulf that inherently separates business and government. A residue of mutual respect and accessibility comes from the common schooling and culture, a closure that finds no ready parallel in the U.S. This difference is encoded in the business cultures of the two countries: for many American business leaders, civil servants represent an uncomprehending hostile force; for British directors, civil servants constitute a familiar and sympathetic, if not always responsive, body. The intimacy of London circles extends to Parliament as well. One British manager asserted that with the agency of "the old British system" he could informally reach virtually any member of the House of Commons. "It's a question of whether you're in the network," he said. "If you're in the network, you're bound to meet" whomever you seek. "Inevitably because Members of Parliament and leaders of the press and so on in this country come from a relatively small catchment area," said another industrial director, "we tend to have known them for a long time." An American executive, the veteran of years with the London office of his U.S. firm, put it this way: "The way a lot of things work in London is like a small town."

The special access that upper-class connections can provide British business leaders is evident if we compare the British and American managers and directors closely studied in our special data sets. Many of the British leaders are members of seven exclusive clubs known for their patrician and business ambiance: Marylebone Cricket Club (MCC), Brook's, White's, Pratt's, Boodle's, City of London, and the Carlton.[34] Such club memberships are both a product and producer of connections to government, and the evidence indicates that they do facilitate contact with government, above and beyond what company position otherwise provides. As indicators of access to government, we focus on two of the directors' experiences: service in an advisory role to the national government at some point during their career, and service on any of thirty-seven major government advisory boards in 1978–79.[35] To isolate the clubs' facilitating impact, the directors' multiple company positions are also taken into account by dividing the directors into two groups: those who serve on the board of a single large company and those who occupy two or more such positions.

The figures in Table 7.1 display the incremental value of select club membership in securing government appointment. Two estimates are given, with the true value in all likelihood between the two but probably closest to the B figure.[36] For those who serve on two or more company boards, belonging to an exclusive club adds very little to the probability that the director will be found serving as an advisor to government or on a public board in 1978–79. Using the B estimates, for instance, 8 percent of the multiple-company directors not in a club served on a public board, while 10 percent of the multiple directors with club membership were so appointed. However, among single company directors without a club, 2 percent served on a public board, but 11 percent of those with a club did so,

Table 7.1 Percentage of British company directors serving as government advisor, by number of company directorships and exclusive club memberships

Number of large-company directorships and exclusive club membership[a]	Government public board, 1978–79		Government advisor, career	
	A est.	B est.	A est.	B est.
One co. direc., no club mem.	4.7%	1.8%	10.6%	3.4%
One co. direc., one+ club	10.8	10.8	18.0	18.0
Two+ co. direc., no club mem.	12.7	7.7	28.7	18.1
Two+ co. direc., one+ club	10.1	10.1	26.9	26.9

SOURCE: Data compiled by author.

   [a] The numbers of directors on which the percentages are based for the A estimates are, in descending order, 425, 139, 181, and 119; the numbers for the B estimates are, 1415, 139, 299, and 199.

a percentage exceeding that for the multiple company directors and demonstrating the value of club connections. The analogous percentages for a government advisory position are 4 and 18. Similar disparities are apparent if A estimates are examined. Thus, club membership is associated with a sharp increase in government contact for single directors (better than fivefold by one estimate), but such membership predicts only a very modest increase for multiple directors. The informal social networks embedded in club memberships, networks with upper-class sinews, can compensate in part for the absence of involvement in the company network.

Such is not the case in the U.S. When an identical analysis is performed on the American data, the club connection achieves very little beyond what involvement in the intercorporate network does. The rates of service differ little once the number of company directorships is taken into account. Inner-circle connections facilitate government contact far more than does single-company position in both countries, but only in Britain does an upper-class identity still open doors for the businessman into the inner sanctum of the government.

The access paved by the upper-class connection contains an irony, however. Managing directors in the U.K. may find quicker hearing than in the U.S., but sometimes slower understanding. The lingering of anti-industrial values extends to senior civil servants; they are less impressed with the successful manufacturing firm, less eager to know about its inner working, and less prone to seek employment in it. Nonetheless, many businessmen would likely say that working with British ministries is far easier than with American agencies. The British lack of awe of the successful businessman is more than compensated for by an awareness of the superior capabilities of its civil service. "There's no comparison in the quality of the civil servants," lamented one American manager with extensive government contacts in both countries. "The British civil servant is generally among the better educated, he comes from a middle class or sometimes even an upper class family and therefore he has a more sophisticated cultural background." American civil servants by contrast, in his experience, "are frequently political appointees that are turned over rapidly, that are payoffs for campaign support. You turn up some people who may not necessarily be stupid, but sometimes are misdirected and frequently very poorly informed about their responsibilities." The product is "an absolute morass, a quagmire of administration." Though his judgment that there was simply "no comparison" between the two civil services may be factually overdrawn, it is an opinion widely shared within the American business community.[37]

As large British firms have sought better intelligence on their business and political environments, they have been able to rely in part on nonbusiness networks already in place. Thus, while American firms have depended on their senior officers for monitoring the environment, British firms have not been reluctant to use the intimate byways of the upper class to achieve the same. The difference is evident in the frequent, casual contact among London managing directors and senior civil servants. Luncheons, receptions, and dinners are continuous, and weekend retreats add special intimacy. "In one's normal social life one sees people everyday including politicians, top officials, businessmen, and bankers," offered the managing director of one merchant bank. Concerned that seeing was not always the same as hearing, however, he organized a series of occasional day-long meetings for financiers, civil servants, and some industrialists. Each of these "City/ Whitehall" seminars included ten invited senior civil servants and an equal number of business leaders; informal examination of key policy questions of mutual concern was the objective.

AGENDA AND PARTICIPANTS IN
CITY/WHITEHALL INFORMAL SEMINARS

Subject	Introducer
Seminar I. March, 1975	
The funneling of funds through the City into industry: the available facilities and constraints.	G.G. Williams Vice-Chairman, J. Henry Schroder Wagg & Co.
The supply of public funds for industry: the available facilities and constraints.	C. Benjamin, Assistant Secretary, Industrial Development Unit
The problem viewed by an industrial finance director.	A.W. John, Finance director, Unigate Limited
The effectiveness of British negotiations in the field of international competition.	D.R. Harrod, Economic Correspondent, B.B.C.
The problem of communication between the City and Whitehall: the misunderstandings that arise; the image each has of the other; possible solutions.	(no lead discussant)
Seminar II. January, 1976	
The differing attitudes and constraints of the City and Whitehall towards the funding of industry.	R. Fox, Kleinwort Benson Ltd.

AGENDA AND PARTICIPANTS IN
CITY/WHITEHALL INFORMAL SEMINARS (*Continued*)

Subject	Introducer
	R.J. Priddle, Department of Industry
Problems of export. Why does Britain find it so hard to produce a well co-ordinated policy between the City, Industry and Whitehall for selling abroad?	The Hon. Hugo Kindersley, Lazard Brothers & Co. J. T. Caff, Economic Advisor, H.M. Treasury
General policies of control of investment in the insurance and banking field.	P. Moody, Prudential Assurance Co. J.H.M. Solomon, Dept. of Prices and Consumer Protection

Seminar III. October, 1976

The restructuring of industry and its finance.	C. Benjamin, Dept. of Industry R. E. Artus, Prudential Assurance Co.
Living with floating rates.	P.S. Ardron, Barclays Bank Internatl. J.W. Hepburn, Ministry of Agriculture, Fisheries & Food

Seminar IV. September, 1977

The control of public expenditures and cash limits.	M. Fogden, Assistant Secretary, Department of Health and Social Security
How could Britain use North Sea oil revenue: primarily to create wealth, or primarily to prevent unemployment? Is there a dichotomy here?	W.J.A. Dacombe, Executive Director, Williams & Glyn's Bank

AGENDA AND PARTICIPANTS IN
CITY/WHITEHALL INFORMAL SEMINARS *(Continued)*

Subject	Introducer
Seminar V. June, 1978	
The value and future of exchange control regulations.	A. Britton, H.M. Treasury
Investment in industry, both governmental and institutional.	R. Quartano, Chief Executive, Post Office Super-annuation Fund
Seminar VI. March, 1979	
Major capital investment projects overseas are becoming so large that they exceed the financial capabilities of any single company. How important to Britain are these projects and why? What additional sources finance should be realized in order to supplement the existing conventional methods?	D.N. Royce, Under Secretary, Export Development Division, Department of Trade R.J.R. Owen, Director, Morgan Grenfell & Co.
It has been suggested that Britain is not well organized to obtain contracts in "dirigiste" and in particular, communist countries. With opportunities such as China may offer, what new useful structures might be developed, e.g. Whitehall forbidding competition between British firms, backing one firm with all its power?	A. Shipp, Director, Samuel Montagu & Co. R.W. Browning, Under Secretary, Commercial Relations Exports, Department of Trade

Since the aristocracy has long favored finance over industry, British banking and insurance enjoys a privileged intimacy with higher government circles that many industrial firms jealously regard from a distance. Yet the highest levels of many manufacturing firms do have entree. For the second ranking manager of a major industrial firm, "barely a week goes through without every one of my colleagues meeting some politician on some basis. It may be that we go to a reception somewhere, or it may be that we have them to lunch." But it is, he offered, "a much softer sell [than in the U.S.], really more a matter of trying to keep in touch and make sure that people are aware of the facts." The round of business luncheons for government officials is reported to be so intense that one is left wondering how the officials manage to accommodate so many invitations. At the end of an interview with a government minister whom numerous company directors said they knew intimately, and with whom they said they frequently dined, I asked how he was able to attend so many luncheons despite his extremely demanding schedule. He implied that the number of claimants may have far exceeded the number of actual hosts. But with a suppressed smile at the conclusion of the interview, the minister confessed he was on his way to the directors' dining room of a multinational manufacturing company.

American business is not without its informal contact as well. But it is less frequent, less intimate, less understanding. Its inadequate development is illustrated by a program of one politically oriented public relations firm in Washington that would never, and need never, be organized in London. For senior executives without their own informal access to policymakers, a substantial fee will reserve a seat at periodic prearranged luncheons with U.S. senators. The paying company is entitled to send its chief executive or designated replacement for an intimate exchange of views with a dozen executives and a prominent Republican member of the Senate. The program has no special appeal to the very largest American firms, whose contact is as blue chip as the best in London. But for the less than preeminent companies, it is a program that provides an opportunity that the absence of upper-class networks has otherwise denied.

These differences in business and government relations in the two countries, however, should not be allowed to disconfirm their fundamentally similar configurations. Just as in the U.S., the rise of institutional capitalism in Britain has been accompanied by a shift of control from family and firm to the classwide network. Management succession is increasingly determined not only by loyalty to owner and company, but also by acceptance into the broader corporate community. Moreover, because contact between large companies and government has become so crucial to the operation of the firm, acceptance by the inner circle and its state counterpart has also become an important criterion for seniormost company promotion. Asked if it were an unspoken company policy that top managers become involved in political and governmental channels of contact, the deputy chairman of a large British industrial company responded that "it isn't an unspoken policy, it's a bloody spoken one. It's an absolutely clear part of the top job of leadership in this company to be involved in the governmental and opinion-forming scene." For promotion to the top, then, "we would require the man to be an effective executive . . . but given that we had enough effective executives, on balance a guy who was able to do this would get a leg up before a guy who wasn't." He himself maintained continuous contact with those both in and out of power, making the personal acquaintance of virtually all government ministers and shadow ministers of the opposition Labour party. Within a year of the interview he was promoted to the top executive post of his industrial firm.

INSTITUTIONAL CAPITALISM AND CLASSWIDE POLITICS

The rise of institutional capitalism in the U.S. and U.K. contributed to the rise of more conservative political climates in the early 1980s. Though the new corporate political activity was not decisive, its significance should not be underestimated. A central objective of the business political mobilization on both sides of the Atlantic was to restore company profits to levels of an earlier decade. In pursuing "reindustrialization" and "recapitalizing capitalism," government spending was targeted as the chief impediment to such prosperity.[38] In the American case, excessive government restraint on business decisions was also named as a critical target; in Britain, government failure to resist and control organized labor was identified by business as another top priority. With differing emphasis both business communities pointed toward government reductions in social spending, the dismantling of agencies that regulate business, and the scaling back of programs beneficial to labor.

The electoral success and political thrust of the Thatcher and Reagan governments were in no small part products of this business venture into politics. Both governments did sharply reduce controllable social spending, lift controls on business, and cut back unemployment benefits, welfare and other programs of special interest to labor. The squeeze on the private sector was thus translated into a shrinking public sector, with the exception of military spending. The decline of the welfare state, the slowing of social spending, and the end of activist government in the U.S. and U.K. were thus not simply, and indeed not largely, a product of spontaneous public disaffection with the socially interventionist state. Nor were they the result of an unarticulated, inchoate response to the chronic stagnation of the "British disease" and its American strain. Nor did they derive from an unorganized aggregation of business protest against the seemingly antibusiness posture of the national government.

Rather, the rise of the new conservative forces that were among the pillars of the Republican and Conservative governments was a product of the formation on both sides of the Atlantic of informal and formal organizational networks linking together most large corporations. These networks facilitated the political mobilization of business—by helping business to identify the public policies most needed for its aggregate welfare, and by helping it to express its consensual preferences in electoral campaigns, government lobbying, and other forms of political intervention. There was for business, however, no certainty of outcome, for although both the Reagan administration and Thatcher government were in power in part because of their corporate allies, neither was particularly responsive to the changing calculus of business, nor even of the economy for that matter. In power, these governments were guided, as were previous administrations, by their own special agendas, each item on the agendas added in response to the needs or interests of constituency blocs. Thus were created agendas coincident only in part with what large corporations and their inner-circle leadership would have liked to see achieved. Still, business became more confident that it was able to articulate its message with these governments. A survey of the top executives of 600 of the largest U.S. firms in 1982, for instance, revealed their widespread belief that their effectiveness had substantially increased. More than two-thirds of the senior managers said that "business is much better organized now than five years ago to deal with politics"; 90 percent thought that "business is better able now to gets its message across in Washington than it was five years ago." Political action committees were viewed as one of the most important reasons. Corporate executives "are purring," concluded Louis Harris, the survey's director. "Business is much more self-confident about its power than it was."[39]

The formation of the classwide system of organization within the corporate communities is rooted in the emergence of institutional capitalism. While nascent and far from displacing managerial capitalism, the appearance of this new transcorporate form of corporate control requires reformulation in our ways of thinking about large corporations and how they enter politics. Those who focus on the pluralism within the corporate community and some neo-Marxist schools have developed models of business relationships with government based on the presumption that the corporate community is relatively disorganized and incapable of advancing a coherent, community-serving position in the political arena. We have seen that such a characterization is partly right and partly wrong. Yet a contrasting assumption shared by another neo-Marxist tradition and the elitist school of political analysis has fared little better when placed against the evidence. The characterization of the corporate community as relatively cohesive and organized is on the mark when applied to a select circle but off the mark when taken to describe the entire business community. Here is where anti-Marxist commentary finds easy ground for cogent criticism. In their portrait of the "American establishment," for instance, Leonard Silk and Mark Silk take such aim: "The Marxists believe that, when all is said and done, big business *is* the American establishment. But the actual relationship of big business to the establishment in America is far more complex than the Marxists suppose. Most businessmen are in no sense members of the establishment. What they are concerned about overwhelmingly is their own business." Nonetheless, conclude Silk and Silk, "there is a select group of business leaders" who help run the affairs of the country.[40] As we have argued here, they do so as and through the inner circle.

Though cognizant of an upper-class rationality in some areas of business decision making, most schools of analysis correctly portray that rationality as largely subordinate to corporate and classwide principles of social organization. The British aristocracy may have dictated the terms of entry into commerce and industry a century ago, but that the balance has shifted in favor of the demands of corporate and classwide rationalities is evident in Britain and even more certainly demonstrated in America. Moreover, careful study of the integration of patrician circles and corporate positions has revealed that the fusion has been most pronounced, if not largely limited to, the highest reaches of business management, primarily the inner circle. The hereditary titles and pedigrees of many of those most visible in this politically active circle, however, should not be mistaken for its foundation. The inner circle is rooted in the classwide economic and social relationships among large corporations and their executives, not in the exclusivity of the nation's first families, though it is true that a traceable genealogy is sometimes useful in assuring influence within the inner circle.

The classwide principle of organization is the product of inclusive and diffusely structured networks of intercorporate ownership and directorship linking ever concentrating units of economic activity. These networks define a segment of the business community whose strategic location and internal organization propel it into a political leadership role on behalf of the entire corporate community. John Porter's description of Canada's system of power could equally well have been developed for the American and British counterparts. He closes his study of the Canadian "vertical mosaic" with the conclusion that the multiple directors linking the country's large corporations "are the ultimate decisionmakers and coordinators within the private sector of the economy. It is they who at the frontiers of the economic and political systems represent the interests of corporate power. They are the real planners of the economy."[41]

The planning role in America and Britain is executed through the multiple directors' guidance of the major business associations, their role as gatekeepers for the formal and informal consultative circles linking the highest levels of business and government, and their direct participation in the governance of the nonprofit sector. Generalized challenges to big business, whether from labor or government, have further enhanced the capability of the inner circle to lead. Business weakness in the face of labor and government pressure, exacerbated by adverse profit trends, has led to a new business strength achieved through collective political mobilization.

As a result, more overall planning initiative is assumed by business, less by government. Rather than having to sift through the disparate demands of a thousand chief executives, government officials are presented with an integrated vision already developed by those members of the corporate community best positioned to reconcile the competing demands. Of course, government decision makers are subjected to numerous other constraints and pressures, and there is no certainty that any given business position will prevail. Indeed, many are certainly rejected. The Confederation of British Industry and the Business Roundtable were frequently at odds with the Thatcher and Reagan governments. Still, the classwide foundation of the inner circle makes their positions more authoritative and less easily ignored.

We also need to revise our thinking about the nature of the business firm. Under managerial capitalism, corporate principles prevail, and the firm is the primary unit of action. Professional management is fully in charge, the company's profits are the first and final order of business, and a Hobbesian competition of all against all is the environment. The thrust of corporate decisions and politics under managerial capitalism is quite different from what it was during the era of family capitalism, when upper-class principles prevailed and family was the central unit of action. The founding entrepreneur and kin then retained control, family fortunes were of guiding concern, and intermarriage could produce alliance and reduce competition.

But the emergence of institutional capitalism and classwide principles of organization have introduced still different rules. The firm remains a primary unit of action, but the transcorporate network becomes a quasi-autonomous actor in its own right. Company management is now less than fully in charge; classwide issues do intrude into company decisions; and competition is less pitched. Management decisions to underwrite political candidates, devote company resources to charitable causes, give advertising space to matters of public moment, and assume more socially responsible attitudes derive in part from an individual company calculus, but also in part from a classwide calculus. Promotion of managers into seniormost positions is based on their successful performance within the company, but also on their reputations within the inner circle and broader corporate community. The theories and models of pluralism, some brands of neo-Marxism, and the major schools of management science and organizational behavior have all tended to read only the patterns associated with managerial capitalism. While correct in form, these patterns now coexist with the new patterns of institutional capitalism. Any complete picture of the social organization of business and its political activity thus cannot fail to take these into account. In the uppermost reaches of both the British and American corporate communities, classwide principles are evident, and institutional capitalism is ascendent.

APPENDIX

BRITISH AND AMERICAN CORPORATIONS STUDIED

BRITISH FIRMS

A.J. Mills; A. Monk & Co.; Aberdeen Construction Group; Alexanders Discount Co.; Alfred Herbert; Allen Harvey & Ross; Alliance Trust Co.; Allied Breweries; Amalgamated Power Engineering; Amalgamated Metal Corp.; Antony Gibbs Holdings; Arbuthnot Latham Holdings; Armstrong Equipment; Arthur Lee & Sons; Atlas Electric & General Trust.

B. Elliott & Co.; Babcock & Wilcox; Bank of Scotland; Barclays Bank; Baring Bros. & Co.; Bass Charrington; B.A.T. Industries; Beecham Group; BICC; BOC International; Boots Co.; Bowater Corporation; Britannic Assurance Co.; British Assets Trust; British Enkalon; British Leyland; British Petroleum Co.; Brixton Estate; Brooke Bond Liebig; Brown Shipley Holdings; Burmah Oil Co.

C.T. Bowring & Co.; Cable Trust; Cadbury Schweppes; Capital & Counties Property Co.; Capper Neill; Caravans International; Cater Ryder & Co.; Central Manufacturing and Trading Group; Central & Sheerwood; Centrovincial Estates; Charterhouse Japhet; Clive Discount Holdings; Coats Patons; Commercial Union Assurance Co.; Consolidated Gold Fields; Cooperative Bank; Cooperative Insurance Society; Courtaulds; Crane Fruehauf.

Daejan Holdings; Dalgety; Distillers Co.; Dorada Holdings; Drake & Scull Holdings; Ductile Steels; Dunlop Holdings.

Eagle Star Insurance Co.; Edgar Allen Balfour; Edinburgh & Dundee Invest. Co.; EMI; English Property Corp.; Equity & Law Life Assurance Society.

F.C. Finance; Federated Chemical Holdings; First National Securities; Foreign & Colonial Investment Trust Co.; Friends Provident Life Office.

Gallaher; General Accident Fire & Life Assurance; General Electric Co.; George Wimpey & Co.; Gerrard & National Discount Co.; Gill & Duffus Group; Gillett

Brothers Discount Co.; Giltspur; Globe Investment Trust; Grand Metropolitan; Great Portland Estates; Great Universal Stores; Guardian Royal Exchange Assurance; Guest Keen & Nettlefolds; Guinness Mahon & Co.

H. Samuel; Hambro Life Assurance; Hambros; Harrisons & Crosfield; Haslemere Estates; H.A.T. Group; Hawker Siddeley Group; Hestair; Hewden Stuart Plant; Hickson & Welch; Hill Samuel Group.

Imperial Chemical Industries; Imperial Group; Inchcape & Co.; Industrial & General Trust; Inveresk Group; Investment Trust Corp.

J.E. Sanger; J. Lyons & Co.; J. Sainsbury; Jessel Toynbee & Co.

King & Shaxson; Kleinwort Benson Lonsdale.

Land Securities Investment Trust; Lankro Chemicals Group; Lazard Brothers & Co.; Legal & General Assurance Society; Liverpool Victoria Friendly Society; Lloyds and Scottish; Lloyds Bank; London & Overseas Freighters; Lonrho; Lucas Industries.

M.J. Gleeson; Marks & Spencer; Mccorquodale & Co.; Mears Bros. Holdings; MEPC; Metal Box; Metal Closures Group; Midland Bank; Morgan Grenfell Holdings.

National Westminster Bank; National & Commercial Banking Group; Norwich Union Insurance Group.

P & O Steam Navigation Co.; Pearl Assurance Co.; Phoenix Assurance Co.; Plessey Co.; Pritchard Services Group; Provident Financial Group; Prudential Assurance Co.

Ranks-Hovis-McDougall; Rea Brothers; Ready Mixed Concrete; Reckitt & Colman; Reed International; Refuge Assurance Co.; Revertex Chemicals; Richardsons Westgarth & Co.; Rio Tinto Zinc Corporation; Robertson Foods; Rolls Royce; Rothmans International; Royal Insurance Co.; Royal London Mutual Insurance Society.

S & W Berisford; S.G. Warburg & Co.; Sale Tilney & Co.; Samuel Montagu & Co.; Schroders; Scottish Amicable Life Assurance Society; Scottish Eastern Investment Trust; Scottish Widows' Fund and Life Assurance Society; Scottish & Universal Invs.; Sears Holdings; Seccombe Marshall & Campion; Sedgwick Forbes Holdings; Selincourt; Sheepbridge Engineering; Shell Transport & Trading; Smith St. Aubyn & Co.; Spillers; Staflex International; Standard Life Assurance Co.; Sun Alliance & London Insurance; Sun Life Assurance Society.

Tarmac; Tate & Lyle; Tesco Stores; Thomas Tilling; Thorn Electrical Industries; Town & City Properties; Tozer Kemsley & Millbourn; Travis & Arnold; Trident Television; Tube Investments.

Ultramar Co.; Unigate; Unilever Ltd.; Union Discount Co. of London; United Biscuits; United Dominions Trust.

Ward White Group; Whitecroft; Wilkins & Mitchell; Wm. Collins & Sons.

Y.J. Lovell

AMERICAN FIRMS

Aetna Life & Casualty; Amarada Hess; American Airlines; American Chain & Cable; American Electric Power; American Express; American General Insurance; American Hoist & Derrick; American Telephone & Telegraph; American United Life; Arcata National; Armstrong Rubber; Ashland Oil; Atlantic Richfield.

Baldwin United; Bancohio Corp.; Bank of New York Co.; Bankamerica Corp.; Bankers Life; Bankers Life & Casualty; Bankers Trust New York Corp.; Bausch & Lomb; Beatrice Foods; Belco Petroleum; Bethlehem Steel; Boeing; Briggs & Stratton; Broadview Financial Corp.; Burlington Northern; Butler Manufacturing.

C.I.T. Financial; Caterpillar Tractor; Charter New York Corp.; Chase Manhattan Corp.; Chemical New York Corp.; Chrysler; Citicorp; Cities Service; Citizens & Southern Nat. Bank; Colgate Palmolive; Columbia Pictures Industries; Commonwealth Life; Congoleum; Connecticut General Life; Connecticut Mutual; Continental; Continental Group; Continental Illinois Corp.; Continental Oil; Cook Industries; Country Life; Crocker National Corp.

Dairylea Cooperative; Deere; Dennison Manufacturing; Dow Chemical.

E.I. Du Pont de Nemours; Eastman Kodak; Economics Laboratory; EG&G; Equitable Life Assurance; ERC Corp.; Esmark; Exxon.

Fairchild Industries; Farmers Group; Federal Paper Board; Financial Corp. of Santa Barbara; Firestone Tire & Rubber; First Bank System Inc.; First Charter Financial; First Chicago Corp.; First Int. Bancshares Inc.; First National Boston Corp.; First Pennsylvania Corp.; Ford Motor; Foxboro.

General American Life; General Electric; General Foods; General Motors; General Telephone & Electronics; Georgia Pacific; Gerber Products; Girard Co.; Globe Union; Goodyear Tire & Rubber; Government Employees Insurance; Great Atlantic & Pacific Tea; Great Western Financial; Greyhound; Gulf & Western Industries; Gulf Oil.

H.F. Ahmanson; Handy & Harman; Harcourt Brace Jovanovich; Houdaille Industries; Hyster.
IBM; Idle Wild Foods; Imperial Corp. of America; INA; Inland Container; Insilco; International Harvester; International Paper; International Telephone & Telegraph.

J.C. Penney; J.P. Morgan & Co.; John Hancock Mutual; Johnson Controls; Jonathan Logan.

K Mart; Kemper; Koehring; Kraft.

Lincoln National Life; Loews; LTV.

Manufacturers Hanover Corp.; Manufacturers National Corp.; Marathon Oil; Marine Midland Banks Inc.; Maryland Cup; Massachusetts Mutual; Mattel; McCormick; Mellon National Corp.; Mercantile Texas Corp.; Merrill Lynch & Co.; Metropolitan; Midland Cooperatives; Minnesota Mining & Manufacturing; Mobil; Monfort of Colorado; Monsanto; Monumental; Mutual Benefit; Mutual of New York.

National City Corp.; National Detroit Corp.; National Semiconductor; National Starch & Chemical; Nationwide Life; New England Mutual; New York Life; Northwest Bancorp; Northwestern Mutual; Northwestern Nation.

Occidental Petroleum; Olinkraft.

P.R. Mallory; Pacific Gas & Electric; Pacific Resources; Peabody International; Penn Mutual; Phillip Morris; Phillips Petroleum; Pilot Life; Pittsburgh National Corp.; Procter & Gamble; Prudential.

R.J. Reynolds Industries; Rainier Bancorp; Ralston Purina; Rath Packing; RCA; Republic of Texas Corp.; Rockwell International; Roper.

Safeway Stores; Scott & Fetzer; Sears Roebuck; Security Pacific Corp.; Shell Oil; Southern Company; Southern Pacific; Standard Oil (Ind.); Standard Oil of California; Sun.

Talley Industries; Tenneco; Texaco; Texas Commerce Bancshares Inc.; Trans World Airlines; Transamerica; Travelers Corp.; Tyler.

U.S. Bancorp; U.S. Steel; UAL; Union Carbide; Union Central; Union Mutual; Union Oil of California; Union Pacific; United Parcel Service; United Technologies.

Valley National Bank of Arizona; Varian Associates.

W.R. Grace; Walter E. Heller International; Warnaco; Weeden Holding Corp.; Wells Fargo & Co.; Western Bancorp; Western Electric; Western Financial; Westinghouse Electric; Westmoreland Coal; Wm. Wrigley Jr.

Xerox.

Notes

CHAPTER ONE: ORGANIZING BUSINESS

1. Coleman 1982.
2. A sampling of the commentary on these contrasting elements can be found in Almond (1956), Turner (1960), Almond and Verba (1963), Lipset (1963), Institute of Directors (1965), Hopper (1968), Granick (1972), Granick (1973), Treiman and Terrell (1975), Marwick (1980).
3. Channon 1973; Jamieson 1980; Bank of England 1981; Feldstein et al. 1982.
4. Domhoff 1974, p. 109; 1967; 1970; 1972; 1979.
5. Miliband 1969, p. 47.
6. Berg and Zald 1978, p. 137.
7. Bell 1962, pp. 62–63.
8. Silk and Vogel 1976, p. 181.
9. Stanworth and Giddens 1974, p. 100.
10. Westergaard and Resler 1975, p. 346.
11. Scott 1979, pp. 125–26.
12. Nettl 1965, p. 23.
13. Grant 1980, p. 146.
14. Szymanski 1978, p. 39.
15. Rothman 1978, p. 89.
16. Duberman 1976, p. 74.
17. Buchholz 1982, pp. 58–59.
18. Steiner and Steiner 1980, p. 9.
19. Many elements of the several perspectives are summarized in Alford (1975). The less well-known intra-Marxist debate is described within or exemplified by the works of Miliband (1969), Offe (1973), O'Connor (1973), Poulantzas (1973), Gold et al. (1975), Jessop (1977), Domhoff (1979), Whitt (1980, 1982), and Skocpol (1980).
20. Giddens 1974, p. xi.
21. Rubinstein 1977, p. 125.
22. Other principles are described in Useem (1980).
23. See, for instance, Cole (1955), pp. 101–23; Guttsman (1963); Perrott (1968); Sampson (1971); Johnson (1973); Giddens (1976).

24. Baltzell 1958, 1964, 1966, 1979; Domhoff 1967, 1970, 1974, 1979; Collins 1971, 1979; Silk and Silk 1980.
25. Baltzell 1966, p. 273.
26. Bedardia 1979, pp. 202–4.
27. Westhues (1976) provides a description of this approach.
28. Wiener 1981, p. 24. Discussion of this interpretation can be found in Burrage (1969), Dubin (1970), Granick (1972), Coleman (1973), Channon (1973), Stanworth (1980), and Jamieson (1980).
29. Vogel 1978a, p. 68.
30. Offe 1973, p. 111.
31. *Business Week* 1981 (a special issue on "Reindustrialization in America").
32. Steckmest 1982, p. 265.
33. Stein 1978.
34. The British directors are drawn from the data set numbered (2) in the section later in this chapter entitled "Information on Corporations and Their Managers and Directors." The description of this data set is entitled "British Corporate Executives and Directors and Their Firms"; the American directors are selected from data set (1) "American Corporate Executives and Directors and Their Firms."
35. The gallery of office photographs showing the great Himalayan peaks this director had ascended suggested that it was not the first time visitors were long delayed in meeting with him.
36. *Fortune* 1978.
37. The identities of the six top officers (typically, the chairman of the board, the president, and several senior and executive vice-presidents) were obtained from conventional sources, primarily Dun and Bradstreet's 1977–78 edition of the *Million Dollar Directory*. In cases where the top six officers were all on the board of directors, two nondirector officers were also sampled. In addition, all nonexecutive directors were drawn for study when they were in total ten or fewer, and ten were randomly selected when the total number of outside directors exceeded ten.
38. Dun and Bradstreet's *Reference Book of Corporate Management;* Standard and Poor's *Register of Corporations, Directors and Executives;* Marquis's *Who's Who in America* (several editions); *Who's Who in Finance and Industry; Who's Who in the World; Who's Who in the East; Who's Who in the West, Who's Who in the Midwest; Who's Who in the South, Who's Who in Law,* and *Who's Who in Government.*
39. The identities of the 212 American firms appear in the Appendix.
40. An accessible account of the role of these various financial institutions can be found in Committee to Review the Functioning of Financial Institutions (1980). On accepting houses, a useful account is provided by Lisle-Williams (1981).
41. Foreign-owned subsidiaries of other enterprises and a few companies for which the identities of the directors could not be determined after searching several standard sources were excluded. The 60 largest manufacturers range from the company ranked first by turnover on the *Times* list to the firm ranked 80th; 11 of the firms deleted from the *Times* 80 to constitute our top 60 were foreign owned, 5 retail companies were removed to form a separate sectoral category, and four other firms were dropped for lack of adequate public information about them. The 50 lesser industrials range from the firm

ranked 454th by the *Times* to number 550; this spread was due to the large number of foreign-owned and retail enterprises in this range of the *Times* list. Life insurance companies are ranked by life funds, and 23 of the top 24 are included (number 20 was dropped for lack of an adequate list of directors). Fifteen of the largest 16 accepting houses (similar to American investment banks) ranked by total assets are included (the 14th was a subsidiary of another company). Our 10 large investment trusts consist of the top 5 ranked by investments at market value, and those ranked 13 to 17. Similarly, the top 10 large property companies, ordered according to capital employed, include the top 5 and numbers 13 to 17. The set of large finance houses is made up of those ranked 2, 6, 7, 13, and 14, according to outstanding balances (other firms above or between these ranks were owned by various banks and thus excluded). Finally, all seven clearing banks have been included, as have the top 11 discount houses (ranked by gross deposits) and the 5 largest retail companies (ranked by turnover).

42. Shelbourne later left merchant banking to serve as chairman of the British National Oil Corporation.

43. Additional detail on the sampling and sources can be found in Useem and McCormack (1981). A complete list of the British firms appears in the Appendix.

44. From the May, 1970 issue of *Fortune*.

45. The identities of all 8,623 directors of the 797 firms were compiled by Michael Schwartz and Peter Mariolis from standard sources (primarily Standard and Poor's *Register of Corporations, Directors, and Executives*).

46. We utilized the 1976–77 edition of *Who's Who in America;* a complete listing of all federal advisory committees compiled for 1976 by a U.S. Senate subcommittee (Subcommittee on Reports, Accounting and Management, U.S. Senate, Committee on Government Affairs, 1977); and membership lists for 16 business associations and 20 clubs obtained by G. William Domhoff for the period from the mid-1960s to the early 1970s (Bonacich and Domhoff, 1981). Links, Pacific Union, and Metropolitan are among the clubs included in the latter; the Committee for Economic Development, Council on Foreign Relations, Business Council, the Conference Board, and the Business Roundtable are among the business policy groups. Additional details on these sources and the sampling can be found in Useem (1979).

47. Patrick and Eells 1969; Sanderson 1972.

48. The survey was conducted by Hartnett (1969) under the auspices of the Educational Testing Service. The nation's 2,231 colleges and universities in 1966–67 were divided into six broad groupings, from which a disproportionate stratified cluster sample was taken. The 654 sampled schools were asked to provide a list of their governing board members; the names of 10,036 trustees were compiled from the 82 percent of the institutions that cooperated. An extensive questionnaire was sent to these trustees in 1968, and a usable response rate of 52.5 percent was obtained. General financial and student information on the sampled institutions was acquired from the eleventh edition of the American Council on Education's guide to colleges and universities, which reports information on the 1970–72 period (Furniss 1973). Data on the baccalaureate degrees and the social composition of student bodies were obtained from Astin's (1965) mid-1960s school profiles. The amount of business aid to each of the schools was acquired from annual surveys for

1966–67 and 1967–68 conducted by the Council for Financial Aid to Education (1968, 1969). Further information about the survey and institutional data is available in Hartnett (1969), and Useem (1978, 1981a).

CHAPTER TWO: THE ECONOMIC AND SOCIAL FOUNDATION

1. In the discussion that follows, we concentrate on relations among British companies operating in the U.K. and American companies operating within the U.S. Relations among multinational companies—British and American multinationals included—in other countries are important subjects but such an examination is beyond the focus of this inquiry. So too are relations of American and British corporations with Japanese, European, and other foreign firms operating within the American and British economies. Since the American and British firms are still far more influential in American and British politics than are foreign companies of comparable size doing business in either country, we have chosen to focus on these domestic firms only.
2. Arguments on behalf of various alternative priorities can be found in Kaysen (1957), Baumol (1967), and Galbraith (1971).
3. Berle and Means 1967 (first published in 1932), p. 66.
4. McEachern 1975, pp. 7–20; Leibenstein 1979, pp. 478–79.
5. Parsons 1953, p. 69.
6. Kaysen 1957, p. 313.
7. Parsons 1970, p. 23.
8. Means 1967, p. xxix.
9. Galbraith 1971, p. xvii.
10. Committee to Review the Functioning of Financial Institutions, 1980, p. 249.
11. The studies are, respectively, Villarejo (1961), Gordon (1945), Sheehan (1967), and Burch (1972); Berle and Means (1967); Goldsmith and Parmelee (1940, pp. 99–114), Chevalier (1969), Burch (1972), Zeitlin (1974), Pedersen and Tabb (1976), and Kotz (1978); Larner (1970), Palmer (1972), and Herman (1981, pp. 53–68). Discussion of these investigations is available in Zeitlin (1974), Berg (1979), Useem (1980), Greer (1980), and Herman (1981).
12. Herman 1981, p. 66.
13. Nyman and Silberston 1978. Florence (1961, p. 153) reports an earlier study of English enterprise; Scott and Hughes (1976, 1980) describe an assessment of Scottish company control, and a useful interpretive discussion can be found in Scott (1979, pp. 60–68).
14. Herman 1981, p. 93.
15. See Fox (1978), and Blumberg (1978).
16. Lewellen 1971, p. 2; also see Lewellen 1968, 1975.
17. This argument is advanced by Baumol (1967), and substantiating evidence is reported in Roberts (1959), McGuire et al. (1962), and Ciscel (1974).
18. Larner 1970, p. 59; Lewellen and Huntsman 1970; Masson 1971; also see Cox and Shauger 1973; Smyth et al. 1975, pp. 60–79.
19. James and Soref 1981.
20. Allen 1981; Allen and Panian 1982.
21. Lieberson and O'Connor 1972.

22. Pahl and Winkler 1974, p. 118. Italics in original.
23. Francis 1980.
24. Silk and Vogel 1976, pp. 136–40.
25. Kross 1970, p. 382.
26. Seider 1977, p. 123.
27. Monsen et al. 1968; Boudreaux 1973; Stano 1976; McEachern 1976.
28. Boudreaux 1973.
29. Kamerschen 1968; Hindley 1970; Larner 1970; Elliott 1972; Sorenson 1974; Stano 1975; Ware 1975; Gogel 1977, pp. 185–87; Zeitlin and Norich 1979; Herman 1981, pp. 326–31; Radice 1971; Holl 1975.
30. Zeitlin and Norich 1979.
31. Galbraith 1971, p. xvii.
32. Herman 1981, p. 113.
33. Hannah 1976, p. 216.
34. Whittington 1972, p. 31; Shepherd 1972; Meeks and Whittington 1975; Prais 1976.
35. Committee to Review the Functioning of Financial Institutions 1980, pp. 407–8, 598.
36. Shepherd 1972; Organization for Economic Co-operation and Development 1979.
37. Marris 1979, p. 33.
38. Leonard 1976.
39. Greer 1980.
40. Organization for Economic Co-operation and Development 1979, p. 86.
41. Green and Buchsbaum 1980, p. 68.
42. Tobias 1976.
43. Rumelt 1974, 1977; Honeycutt and Zimmerman 1976.
44. Committee to Review the Functioning of Financial Institutions 1980, pp. 496–500; King 1977, p. 36; Royal Commission on the Distribution of Income and Wealth 1975, pp. 6–19.
45. Koch 1978, p. 65; U.S. Senate Committee on Government Operations 1974, pp. 143–61.
46. Corporate Data Exchange 1977, pp. 224–25.
47. Corporate Data Exchange 1977, 1978, 1980.
48. Discussion of and reference to most of the relevant literature can be found in Kotz (1978), Scott (1979), Herman (1981), and Mintz and Schwartz (1981).
49. Committee to Review 1980, pp. 248–56; Herman 1981, pp. 146–54.
50. See Simison (1981). The fears expressed by one of the American executives interviewed as part of the present study overstate the views of most managers, but they are indicative of the widespread and adamant opposition to any movement away from the traditional board composition: the British unions, he said, "control the Labour party, and some of them are communists, to make matters worse. The first step in this country is this fellow Fraser getting on the Chrysler board, which is a terrible mistake. The board of directors represents the shareholders and this is where the capital expenditures are made, which may or may not be in conflict with what the employees want. That's the last place where the labor people can be effective," for the simple fact is, concluded the executive, "Fraser is a socialist."
51. Harris and Associates 1977, p. 5.

52. Heidrick and Struggles 1980; also see Bacon 1973, p. 29.

53. The analysis is based on the 1969 U.S. data set and reported in Useem (1979).

54. The analysis is based on the U.K. data set. Large firms are defined for the present purpose to include all quoted U.K. industrial companies and all non-industrial companies appearing on the lists of large financial and property firms compiled by the 1977 edition of *The Times 1000: Leading Companies in Britain and Overseas, 1977–78* (London: Times Books, 1977). Also see Committee of Inquiry on Industrial Democracy 1977; Bacon and Brown 1977; and Bank of England 1979a.

55. Giddens and Stanworth 1978.

56. Stanworth and Giddens 1975.

57. Whitley 1974, p. 73.

58. Johnson and Apps 1979.

59. Mizruchi 1982.

60. Allen 1974.

61. Bearden et al. 1975; Mariolis 1975.

62. Mariolis 1975; Mizruchi 1982.

63. Pfeffer 1972, p. 222.

64. Allen 1974, p. 403.

65. For a sampling of studies, see Dooley 1969; Allen 1974; Kotz 1978; Pennings 1980; Burt et al. 1980; Burt 1981.

66. The main elements of this financial control thesis can be found in the work of Aaronovitch (1961), Fitch and Oppenheimer (1970), Kotz (1978), Herman (1981, pp. 114–61), Mintz and Schwartz (1981), and other sources cited therein.

67. Koenig et al. 1979.

68. Palmer 1983.

69. Similar conclusions emerge from a study by Ornstein (1980) of turnover in Canadian shared directorships.

70. Gogel and Koenig 1981.

71. Bacon and Brown 1977, p. 93.

72. Korbin 1982; Task Force on Corporate Social Performance 1980; Fleming 1981; Windsor and Greanias 1982.

73. Bauer et al. 1972, p. 470.

74. Mintzberg 1975.

75. Burck 1976, and data kindly provided by *Fortune* magazine.

76. Harris and Associates 1977, p. 5.

77. Heidrick and Struggles 1980.

78. It must be stressed that this conclusion applies only to directorships among the largest firms. Ties between large firms and medium-sized or smaller corporations are less often derived from business-scan considerations, and are more often a product of resource-exchange concerns.

CHAPTER THREE: INNER-CIRCLE ORGANIZATION

1. Mills 1956.

2. Burck 1976, p. 173.

3. Mills 1956, p. 121.

4. Mills 1956, p. 121.

5. Mills 1956, p. 122.
6. Zeitlin 1974, p. 1,112.
7. U.S. House Committee on the Judiciary, 1965, Antitrust Subcommittee, pp. 225–26. Other statements of congressional concern over potentially adverse consequences of corporate concentration, intercorporate ownership, and shared directorships can be found in U.S. House Committee on Banking and Currency, 1968, Subcommittee on Domestic Finance; U.S. Senate Committee on Government Operations, 1974, Subcommittee on Intergovernmental Relations, and Budgeting, Management, and Expenditures; U.S. Senate Committee on Government Operations, 1976, Subcommittee on Reports, Accounting, and Management; U.S. Senate Committee on Governmental Affairs, 1978, Subcommittee on Reports, Accounting, and Management; U.S. Senate Committee on Governmental Affairs 1980.
8. Zeitlin et al. 1974, p. 4.
9. A helpful conceptualization of class segments within the business community can be found in Zeitlin et al. (1976).
10. Oberschall 1973.
11. Perrucci and Pilisuk 1970; Koch and Labovitz 1976.
12. Baltzell 1964, pp. 362–74; Powell 1969; Domhoff 1974; Sampson 1962, pp. 66–75.
13. Large British firms are defined to include all quoted U.K. industrial companies and all nonindustrial companies appearing on the lists of the largest financial firms compiled by the *Times*.
14. Each of the nearly 2,000 British directors' main-board directorships have been determined through the joint use of three information sources. The 1978 and 1979 editions of *Who's Who* and the 1978 edition of the *Directory of Directors* identified additional company directorships, if any, held by each director. Since the latter volume indistinguishably lists subsidiary along with main-board positions, use of a concurrent edition of *Who Owns Whom* was required to separate the two. (*Who's Who 1978, 1979,* London: Adam and Charles Black, 1978, 1979; *Directory of Directors 1978,* East Grinstead, West Sussex: Thomas Skinner Directories, 1978; *Who Owns Whom: United Kingdom and Republic of Ireland 1978–79,* London: Dun and Bradstreet, 1979).
15. Many of the directors, of course, also hold additional directorships with smaller firms. If all company directorships are included in the count, not simply those with large enterprises, the number of single directors by this criterion is reduced to 1,272 (from 1,554), the number of double directors remains, coincidentally, the same at 264, but the number of many-board directors increases to 436 (from 154). The immediately ensuing analysis has also been undertaken using this more relaxed criterion for inclusion in the inner circle, and the results are, in essence, no different from those reported here using the more stringent specification of the inner-circle boundary. A similar conclusion emerges from the results of several alternative analyses of the American data, suggesting that the basic findings do not depend on the particular method of analysis.
16. Large firms are defined as the one thousand biggest industrial companies and the fifty largest companies in each of six other sectors—commercial banking, insurance, diversified financial, retail, transportation, and utilities. We followed the 1977 *Fortune* magazine listing of the largest firms as of the end of 1976. The outside directorships held by American executives and directors are

determined through the use of nearly a dozen sources reporting board memberships and another source identifying main firms and their subsidiaries. These include Dun and Bradstreet, *Reference Book of Corporate Managements, 1977–78;* Standard and Poor's *Register of Corporations, Directors and Executives 1978* and *1980;* Marquis's *Who's Who in America 1976–1977* and *1978–1979;* and nine other Marquis directories identified in note 38, chapter 1; and National Register's *Directory of Corporate Affiliations 1979.*

17. For terminological consistency, this label is carried over from the British data, even though a fraction of the American single directors are not on a main board at all. This difference reflects the slightly variant sampling strategies dictated by the divergent management structures (as described in Chapter 1). Virtually all top executives in British firms are also on their own boards, which led to the decision to restrict the British sample to directors only. By contrast, often no more than four or five of the senior officers in American corporations also sit on their own boards, and this factor made necessary the decision to include a few top managers who held no directorships, either in their own company or others. Even though they are thus not directors, these senior managers are placed in the single-director category for the analysis that follows.

18. Though not precisely identical, this club list closely corresponds to lists of other clubs found in several other studies to be the favored haunts of business leaders (Lupton and Wilson 1959; Sampson 1962; Whitley 1973, 1974; Fidler 1981).

19. In examining differences between single, double, and many-board directors, two estimates are calculated here. Two estimates will also often be offered in later analyses of the British information and, on occasion, in treatments of the American data. These estimates place boundaries on the true rate, which in some instances cannot be directly extracted from available data. This stems from the fact that information on some of the directors' characteristics and experiences could only be obtained from the standard biographical directories. Membership in British clubs, for example, was obtained from such sources, though in the American case actual membership rosters of the premier clubs had become available. Using biographical references creates a special problem, however: many directors are not featured, and, even more worrisome, the likelihood of a listing often correlates with the characteristics of interest. Among the British single directors, for instance, only 36 percent were deemed worthy of feature by the reference editors, whereas attention was bestowed on 64 percent of the double directors and 85 percent of the many-board directors; comparable differentials characterize the American executives and directors as well. These figures themselves confirm one of the predictions derived from the inner-circle thesis, namely, that the inner circle is far more prominent and visible than the remainder of the corporate elite. But the figures also imply that if we compare their rates of exclusive club memberships using only those directors appearing in the biographical references, we will underestimate the actual differences, since those single directors least likely to be included in the reference are those most often without club membership. On the other hand, if we base the analysis on all directors, using the tentative (though probably largely correct) assumption that all directors not in a reference are not in a club either, we will overestimate the actual difference. The true rate, thus, lies somewhere between the figure based on only the

directors described in a biographical reference—henceforth the *A estimate*—and the figure based on all directors in the data set—the *B estimate*. The true rate is generally closer to the latter.

20. Bendix 1956; Lipset and Bendix 1959; Keller 1963; Warner and Abegglen 1955a, 1955b; Newcomer 1955; *Scientific American* 1965; Diamond 1970; Useem and Miller 1975; Burck 1976; Useem 1980.

21. Copeman 1971; The Director 1965; Heller 1973; Fidler 1981.

22. See, for instance, Guttsman 1963; Johnson 1973.

23. Whitley 1973.

24. Sampson 1971, p. 135.

25. Discussion of the higher origins of those enrolled in elite American boarding schools can be found in Baltzell 1958, pp. 292–319, McLachlan (1970), Baird (1977), Levine (1980). Studies of the family background of students in the most prominent English boarding schools are conveniently summarized in MacDonald (1977); an ethnographic portrayal has been provided by Gathorne-Hardy (1977).

26. There were at least 25 alumni of each, though Eton, as in virtually all established domains of British life, dominated the field with nearly 200 alumni. Identities of the public school graduates was obtained from the standard biographical directories for Eton, Marlborough, and Rugby; however, for Harrow and Winchester, complete lists of their alumni had become available. The inclusion of only five schools among those that "count" is necessarily somewhat arbitrary, but this particular division has no significant bearing on the outcome of the analysis, for the results are in essence the same whether we include the top five, ten, or fifteen British schools. Though not always explicitly indicated in the following pages, whenever a conceptual measure could be created in several plausible alternative fashions, analysis has also been checked with the alternatives to ensure that the conclusions reached do not depend on the specific indicator employed.

27. Each of these counted at least ten alumni among the ranks of the American corporate elite. Identities of the graduates of the American boarding schools were directly obtained from the alumni directories published by each of the schools.

28. Baltzell 1966, p. 267. Studies of the American upper class by E. Digby Baltzell and G. William Domhoff provide ample validation of this meaning of the index; any other definition of upper-class status generates family names highly coincident with those in the register (Baltzell 1966; Domhoff 1967, 1970).

29. Brittain 1978; Rubinstein 1981.

30. Directors and executives of large corporations only are included in the analysis. The only indicator of company size in the survey was whether the firm was listed on a stock exchange, but this is a reasonably accurate measure. Shares of fewer than 3,000 firms were publicly traded on any of the fourteen stock exchanges in 1970, the largest proportion listed with the New York Stock Exchange. The average firm on this exchange reported assets of $590 million in 1968. While New York Stock Exchange firms represented 0.1 percent of the total number of U.S. corporations in 1970, they accounted for 36 percent of all corporate assets and 91 percent of all profits. Virtually all the major, publicly traded corporations are listed on one of the exchanges, and few small firms are listed with any (New York Stock Exchange 1972).

31. Projector and Weiss 1966.

32. In 1966, for instance, two-thirds of the income of those earning over $100,000 came, on average, from stock dividends and capital gains (Ackerman et al. 1972).

33. Even among the managers, evidence suggests the same ordering of events. If the wealth of a manager is largely retained personal income rather than inherited assets, our proxy measure for wealth should demonstrate a strong correlation with the manager's age. But in fact, it does not (the correlation coefficient is .106). The strong wealth differences between those inside and outside the inner circle are virtually the same whatever the age of the corporate managers, implying that the wealth disparities had been fixed long before they had had an opportunity to add their own differences. (Multiple correlation procedures were utilized for the last result; details are provided in Useem 1978).

34. For a sampling of the studies, see Blank (1973), Shoup and Minter (1977), Grant and Marsh (1977), Domhoff (1979, pp. 61–127), McQuaid (1980), Green and Buchsbaum (1980), and other investigations cited therein.

35. "A nasty split in industry's ranks," *World Business Weekly*, December 1, 1980.

36. Grant and Marsh 1977, p. 209; Commission of Inquiry into Industrial and Commercial Representation 1972; Grant 1980.

37. British Institute of Management 1979, p. 3.

38. Kilborn 1982.

39. Kohlmeier 1981.

40. The business-association membership and leadership positions are gauged as follows. The identities of most of the Confederation of British Industry's chief participants were not a matter of public record until 1982 (*Times* 1982). Fortunately, however, the CBI's central office in London kindly made available its files on council and all committee memberships for 1980, and involvement in one or more of these is taken as an indication of recognition and leadership within the CBI. For the British Institute of Management, a complete roster of council and committee memberships and fellows was provided for 1979, and election to the council, committees, or fellow status is considered to signify leadership and recognition within the BIM. The identities of the members and leadership in the American organizations were obtained from a variety of sources, some public, others less so. The least accessible roster is that of Business Roundtable members, but a copy had been obtained and published by Green and Buchsbaum (1980). For the Business Roundtable, we use their 1979 membership list; for the Business Council, the 1977 and 1979 membership rosters are utilized; for the Committee on Economic Development, service as a trustee in 1978 is recorded; for the Conference Board, we include the trustees and officers for 1976, 1977, and 1979; and for the Council on Foreign Relations, we examine the 1978 membership.

CHAPTER FOUR: THE LEADING EDGE OF BUSINESS POLITICAL ACTIVITY

1. Our focus is on the inner circle's national political activities. Though the patterns are not identical at the local and regional levels, there is an analogous special presence of the locally and regionally based corporate inner circles in the political life of these communities. This can be seen, for instance, in a study of the St. Louis metropolitan region directed by Richard Ratcliff (Ratcliff et al. 1980).

2. Steck 1975, p. 245; U.S. Senate Committee on Governmental Affairs, 1977, Subcommittee on Reports, Accounting and Management.
3. Civil Service Department 1978.
4. Hanson and Walles 1975, p. 187; Beer 1965, pp. 337–39.
5. Jenkins 1959, p. 41–44.
6. This annual listing, perhaps too revealing of private participation in public governance, was discontinued in 1977. (U.S. Senate Committee on Governmental Affairs, Subcommittee on Reports, Accounting and Management 1976, 1977).
7. At least one of our directors served on thirty-seven of these boards. (*Whitaker's Almanack 1979* and *Whitaker's Almanack 1980*, London: J. Whitaker & Sons, 1978 and 1979).
8. Using the special American data set for 1969.
9. Details can be found in Useem 1979.
10. While the general characteristics of inner-circle structure are largely unvarying with time, there is, of course, continuous movement and turnover of occupants within the structure. Thus, illustrative personal profiles throughout this study are necessarily time bound; that of Mr. Chappell is constructed for 1980. It and other profiles identifying specific individuals or companies are taken entirely from public records.
11. Kolko 1969; Dye and Pickering 1974; Freitag 1975; Burch 1980.
12. See, for instance, Farnsworth (1981).
13. Jackson 1981.
14. Crittenden 1982.
15. Business Roundtable 1981.
16. See Hartnett (1969) for university governing boards, DiMaggio and Useem (1978) for arts organization ruling bodies, and Landau (1977) for hospital trustees.
17. The British universities are far smaller in number and more nationally oriented than are American universities. To introduce more comparability, we limit the U.S. institutions to those thirty-nine of greatest national prominence; their selection was based on previous studies of elite universities (summarized in Pierson [1969] and Useem and Miller [1975]) and evidence compiled in the present study (these are the institutions that had most often been attended by corporate officers and directors in the U.S. set). The institutions are: Boston University, Brown University, University of California, University of Chicago, Columbia University, Cornell University, Dartmouth College, Duke University, Harvard University, University of Illinois, Indiana University, University of Iowa, Johns Hopkins University, University of Kansas, Lehigh University, Massachusetts Institute of Technology, University of Michigan, Michigan State University, University of Minnesota, New York University, University of North Carolina, Northwestern University, University of Oklahoma, University of Pennsylvania, Pennsylvania State University, University of Pittsburgh, Princeton University, Purdue University, Rutgers University, Stanford University, University of Tennessee, Tufts University, University of Virginia, Virginia Polytechnic Institute, Washington University, Western Reserve University, Williams College, University of Wisconsin, and Yale University.
18. For British foundations, we used the *Directory of Grant-Making Trusts 1979* (Elizabeth Skinner (ed.), Tonbridge, Kent: Charities Aid Foundation, 1978). This source lists members of the boards of trustees for more than 2,000 char-

itable trusts. Trusts with incomes exceeding £1,000 and for which adequate information is available are included in the directory. For American foundations, we utilized the 1977 and 1979 comprehensive listing of foundation trustees, *Trustees of Wealth: The Taft Guide for Philanthropic Decision Makers* (New York: Taft Corporation, 1977 and 1979).

19. This conclusion from cursory inspection of the table is also sustained by more systematic treatment. If an analysis of variance is conducted with an expanded fund-raising measure as the criterion variable (the dollar amount is coded in seven steps: under $1,000; $1,000 to $9,999; $10,000 to $29,999; $30,000 to $99,999; $100,000 to $499,999; $500,000 to $999,999; and $1 million and over), the directorship dimension yields a highly significant F ratio ($p<.001$), while the executive-status dimension and the interaction between the two variables generate F values that fail to meet minimum levels of statistical significance ($p>.05$).

20. This is a subset of the colleges and universities included in the study of American trustees. Two-year colleges were excluded due to the absence of sufficient data on the institutional traits of a majority, and schools with fewer than five trustees were excluded as well. Details on the sample and measures utilized in this analysis can be found in Useem (1981).

21. The period includes the academic years of 1966–67 and 1967–68, the years closest to the time of the survey. The corporate contribution data are obtained from a standard annual listing published by the Council for Financial Aid to Education (1968, 1969).

22. Although the details are not identical, these patterns are, in essence, the same if in place of total corporate support we use either corporate support per student (which adjusts for varying university size) or total university endowment (an indirect measure, in part, of past corporate subvention).

23. Descriptions of corporate political action committees can be found in Epstein (1980a, 1980b).

24. Burck (1976), and information furnished by *Fortune* magazine. While only one in seventeen of the chief executives in this survey had held elective office, this rate is far higher than that for most other occupations. A few of the top executives had reached their corporate office by succeeding in electoral politics first, but for nearly all those elected, a political calling came only on top of long and distinguished corporate careers.

25. Moore 1980, p. 47.

26. Citizens' Research Foundation 1973.

27. Citizens' Research Foundation 1973.

28. A study of campaign financing by Koenig (1979), also for the 1972 election, reveals similar results. Examining the political contributions of the directors of the largest 800 corporations in 1969 and 1972, he also finds that multiple directors were more active. Thus, 5 percent of those serving on a single board of the top 800 firms contributed to the campaigns of both the incumbent, Richard Nixon, and a Democratic candidate, whereas 14 percent of those on three or more of the major boards sent money to both camps.

29. Ratcliff et al. 1980.

30. Butcher 1980.

31. Moore 1980, p. 47.

32. Shapiro 1979.

33. A manager of one British firm, for instance, denied my request for an inter-

view, explaining that it was company policy to reject such inquiries. At nearly the same moment, his managing director was accepting my invitation.
34. This proposal emerged at a meeting of U.S. corporate executives sponsored by the Conference Board for the purpose of allowing a candid exchange of views on the changing social and political role of American business. (Silk and Vogel 1976, p. 184). Further discussion of business views of the media can be found in Banks (1978) and Rubin (1977).
35. Rothman and Lichter 1982.
36. Citation information is drawn from *The New York Times Annual Index* for 1975, 1976, and 1977.
37. June 11, 1981, p. 1.
38. Harris and Klepper 1977, p. 1749.
39. Burck 1976.
40. McGrath 1976; Buchholz, 1980.
41. Buchholz 1980.
42. Cited in Steckmest 1982.
43. Pfeffer (1977), Kanter (1977), Useem (1980), Swinyard and Bond (1980), and other sources cited therein identify some of the main elements.
44. Guttsman 1963, 1974; Kelsall 1974; Johnson 1973.
45. Stages on the way to the inner circle are further described in Useem (1981b, 1981c).
46. Partridge 1979, p. 3.
47. *Reader's Digest* and the Business Roundtable, "Free Enterprise—Is This Any Way to Live?" (appearing in *Reader's Digest*, September, 1975).
48. Fuerbringer 1982.
49. Russett and Hanson 1975; also see Lieberson 1971 and Lo 1982.
50. Kilborn 1982.
51. Green and Buchsbaum 1980.
52. Green and Buchsbaum 1980, p. 154.
53. Lodge 1975; Martin and Lodge 1975.
54. Sethi 1978.
55. Post 1979.
56. Barton 1982.
57. An extended defense of the need for compromise in business political activity can be found in a report for the Business Roundtable prepared by Francis Steckmest (1982).
58. Kolko 1963; Weinstein 1968.
59. Barratt Brown 1973, p. 77.
60. Banks 1970, p. 223.
61. Lindblom 1977, p. 175.

CHAPTER FIVE: CLASSWIDE POLITICS AND CORPORATE DECISION-MAKING

1. Descriptions of this perspective can be found in Westhues (1976) and Scott (1981).
2. Advertisements sponsored by the Corporate Fund for the Performing Arts at the Kennedy Center, 1977.
3. Conference Board 1978.
4. Business Committee for the Arts, 1980.

5. Barratt et al. 1980.
6. Barratt et al. 1980; Sedgwick 1980; Otten 1981; Rattner 1981.
7. Association for Business Sponsorship of the Arts, statement, 1979.
8. Conference Board 1980.
9. Conference Board 1980.
10. Walsh 1979, p. 77.
11. Brooks 1976.
12. White 1980.
13. Ermann 1979.
14. Galaskiewicz and Rauschenbach 1979.
15. Otten 1981.
16. Scotese 1978, pp. 21–22; Graham 1979.
17. The company is Philip Morris; the declaration appeared in advertisements placed in *Business Week* (November 24, 1980) and elsewhere. Nearly a third of Philip Morris's several million dollar annual contribution budget is devoted to the arts, most of it to the visual arts, making it a leader of the corporate field (Salmans 1981; Sinclair 1981).
18. Sedgwick 1980.
19. To illustrate: the London Mozart Players receives a large annual company donation because the company's chief executive had long been an ardent Mozart admirer. The London Philharmonic Orchestra enjoys corporate beneficence because the managing director of another firm is an old acquaintance of the artistic director, Sir Georg Solti.
20. Chase Manhattan Bank 1980.
21. The presidents and chairmen of 378 large corporations responding to one survey report that they devote over three hours per week of their own time to public service activities, but also more than three hours weekly of their company time (Harris and Klepper 1976, p. 11).
22. Chairman of Commercial Union Assurance and director of various major companies.
23. Dillon 1969, p. 49; Stanton 1974, p. 9; additional commentary can be found in Gingrich 1969; Koch 1979.
24. Sinclair (1981, p. 2). Equitable is the third largest U.S. insurer.
25. Harris and Klepper 1976, p. 16.
26. Conference Board 1978. All figures are based on domestic assets and income, but the same patterns prevail if worldwide numbers are used instead.
27. Conference Board 1978; Council for Financial Aid to Education 1979.
28. Burt 1981.
29. Ermann 1979.
30. Levy and Shatto 1980.
31. Burt 1981.
32. Large firms are defined as in Chapter 3, pp. 10–12. Firms vary some in the size of the boards, and it is arguable that the average rather than total number of ties should be used as the measure. Reanalysis of the results presented here with average number of ties used in place of total number yields results that are virtually the same. American firms with "many" ties are those with more than 19; "some" ties are those with 16 to 18; and "few" ties are those with less than 15. The number of U.S. firms in the three categories is 74, 61, and 72, respectively. British firms with many ties are those with more than 18; some ties are those companies with 9 to 17; and few ties are those cor-

porations with less than 8. The number of companies in the three categories is 62, 66, and 68.

33. Membership in Business Committee for the Arts is recorded for 1978. Identification of the leading arts contributors is based on a guide to corporate giving prepared by the American Council for the Arts. More than 1,700 large firms were asked to release information on their arts contributions, and details were provided by 359. Though some leading arts supporters declined to participate, those responding are from the most active ranks of the cultural underwriters, and inclusion in the guide is thus a reasonably suitable indicator (Wagner 1978). Since 1966, annual awards have been made to businesses for "noteworthy programs in support of the arts," at first by *Esquire Magazine*, and since 1968 by the Business Committee for the Arts as well. It is not an honor bestowed only on companies in the BCA; 85 percent of the recipients are from outside. The number of awards received between 1966 and 1978 is obtained from Business Committee for the Arts (1976) and various issues of *Arts Business,* a newsletter published by the BCA. The Council for Financial Aid to Education (CFAE), founded in 1952, promotes corporate support for higher education. Companies whose executives serve on the board of directors or board of advisors of the CFAE in 1978 or 1979 are termed members here. The CFAE publishes an annual "casebook" describing the programs of "leading business concerns" in the field of education. Those included in the casebook have strong programs and are willing to have them publicly described, and this provides another useful, though imperfect measure of strong philanthropic commitment (we draw on the tenth edition; Council for Financial Aid to Education, 1978).

34. Obtained by direct consultation of the annual reports of the 196 firms for these years.

35. ABSA membership is for 1979, and the awards are for 1978. Information is obtained from membership lists of the ABSA and Association for Business Sponsorship of the Arts (1979).

36. Size is measured by 1977 sales. The differences remain when size is introduced as a covariate adjuster in an analysis of variance. The same conclusions emerge if regression-based technique are employed instead. The introduction of other likely correlates, such as net income or profits, further diminishes the differences, but the basic gap remains even after controlling for all these firm-level factors.

37. Roderick 1982.

38. Corporate-level factors such as size, income, and sector play a more determining role in donation decisions for isolated than for connected firms.

39. The estimate is by Leading National Advertisers' Multi-Media Services; cited in Henry (1980). The flattening of the growth rate is indicated by a study of the Association of National Advertisers, cited in Dougherty (1981).

40. Association of National Advertisers, 1982.

41. Advertisement, *The New York Times,* July 31, 1981, p. A3.

42. *Newsweek,* September, 1980.

43. *Wall Street Journal,* February 26, 1981, pp. 12–13.

44. *The New York Times,* March 12, 1981, p. 26.

45. Union Carbide (1980).

46. "A modest proposal," *Wall Street Journal,* November 4, 1981, p. 2. Also see Molander 1980, pp. 209–23.

47. Ladd 1978; Lipset and Schneider 1978; Lipset and Schneider 1981.
48. Bell 1976; Berger 1981.
49. Dreier 1982.
50. Pittman 1977. Other forms of company political activity, such as congressional lobbying, efforts to influence regulatory bodies, and trade association efforts, are also driven in part by direct company stakes in an issue. As reported in various studies, companies more at risk from a legislative or policy decision are also far more politically active on a variety of fronts (Bauer et al. 1972; Brenner 1980).
51. Labour Research 1979; Miller and Minns 1981.
52. Pinto-Duschinsky 1981, p. 229.
53. Descriptions of the Economic League and the other organizations may be found in Economic League (1979), Labour Research (1979, 1980), and State Research (1978).
54. Epstein 1979; 1980a; 1980b.
55. Boyce 1982.
56. Boyce 1982.
57. Boyce 1982.
58. Farney 1982.
59. Epstein 1979, 1980a, 1980b; Alexander 1981; Mulkern et al. 1981.
60. Ratcliff et al. 1980.
61. Determined through multiple regression techniques. The coefficient of determination exceeded 0.6 with bank size, bank connections with other firms, and bank directors' ties to locally prominent social organizations included in the equation. The banks' connections to other corporations was the single, most powerful predictor of both Republican and Democratic contributions.
62. Koenig 1979.
63. Data are drawn from records of the Federal Election Commission (1980).
64. Public Affairs Council 1979.
65. Epstein 1980a, p. 146. Italics in original.
66. In this analysis, the number of shared directorships was further weighted by the size of the other companies with which they were held.
67. Ratcliff et al. 1980.
68. Vogel (1978b) and Bradshaw and Vogel (1981) offer surveys of the lobbying efforts of these groups in the United States.
69. Quoted in Rodgers (1978).
70. Jensen 1978a, 1978b; Rodgers 1978; *Business Week* 1980.
71. Quoted in Jensen (1978b).
72. Sturdivant and Ginter 1977.
73. Alexander and Buchholz 1978.
74. Kedia and Kuntz 1981.
75. Preston 1981, p. 9; Aldag and Bartol 1978; Kedia and Kuntz 1981.
76. In Chapter 2.
77. Hayes and Abernathy 1980, p. 70.

CHAPTER SIX: THE CHALLENGE OF PROFITS, LABOR, AND GOVERNMENT

1. Keim 1981; Murray 1982.
2. The Government's Expenditure Plans 1980–81 (London: Her Majesty's Stationery Office, 1977), p. 2. Quoted in Walker 1980.

3. Clinard and Yeager 1980.
4. Glyn and Sutcliffe 1972; Gordon 1975; King 1975; Castells 1980.
5. Bank of England 1979b, 1981; Williams 1981.
6. Nordhaus 1974; Feldstein and Summers 1977; Holland and Myers 1980; Feldstein, et al. 1982.
7. Feldstein and Summers 1977.
8. Feldstein et al. 1982.
9. Holland and Myers 1980.
10. Blumstein 1982.
11. Price and Bain 1976.
12. Committee of Inquiry on Industrial Democracy 1977, p. 16–19.
13. Pinto-Duschinsky 1981, p. 238.
14. Ulman 1968; Caves 1980; Smith 1980; Robinson 1981.
15. Alford 1963; Greenstone 1969; Middlemas 1979.
16. Middlemas 1979, p. 456; Pinto-Duschinsky 1981, p. 237.
17. Hibbs 1978.
18. Lipset 1963; Fox and Miller 1966; Granick 1973; Caves 1980; Jamieson 1980; Marwick 1980.
19. Channon 1973, p. 45.
20. Labour Party 1973, p. 9.
21. Confederation of British Industry 1978, p. 49.
22. Middlemas 1979, p. 455.
23. Staber 1982.
24. Development of the distinction between the two forms of federal regulation can be found in Lilley and Miller (1977), MacAvoy (1979), McQuaid (1980), and Herman (1981, pp. 172–84).
25. Weidenbaum 1978.
26. Arthur Andersen 1979.
27. MacAvoy 1979, p. 88.
28. Sommers 1978; Comptroller General 1977; DeFina 1977; Weidenbaum 1977; Data Resources 1979; Green and Waitzman 1980.
29. MacAvoy 1979, p. 92.
30. Weaver 1978.
31. Silk and Vogel 1976.
32. Post 1977.
33. McQuaid 1980, pp. 57–58.
34. Schumacher 1979, p. 1.
35. Kahn 1981.
36. California Roundtable 1978.
37. Mohl 1981.
38. Massachusetts Business Roundtable 1980a, 1980b.
39. California Roundtable 1979a, 1979b.
40. Coser 1956.
41. Vogel 1980.
42. Hibbs 1976.
43. Ouchi 1981.
44. *The Wall Street Journal,* March 5, 1982, p. 8, and March 8, 1982, p. 4.

CHAPTER SEVEN: FAMILY, MANAGERIAL, AND INSTITUTIONAL CAPITALISM

1. Descriptions of both the first families of family capitalism and its more generic features can be found in Bell (1962), Collier and Horowitz (1976), Kolko (1967), Baltzell (1958, 1964, 1979), Lundberg (1968), Ingham (1978), Davis (1978), Hersh (1978).
2. Bell 1962, Chapter 2.
3. Chandler 1977, p. 10.
4. Herman 1981.
5. Described in Chapter 2.
6. Allen 1981; Allen and Panian 1982.
7. Whyte 1956; Riesman 1950.
8. Maccoby 1976.
9. Kanter 1977.
10. Margolis 1979.
11. Engelbourg 1980.
12. DiMaggio 1982.
13. Baltzell 1979, p. 254; Story 1980.
14. Baltzell 1979, p. 258.
15. McGrath 1936.
16. Recommendations of the Resource and Review Committee, Business Round-table, 1982, published in Steckmest 1982.
17. Channon 1973.
18. Whitley et al. 1981.
19. Granick 1972, 1973.
20. Summarized in Melrose-Woodman (1978) and Useem and Miller (1975).
21. Arthur Young 1980.
22. Arthur Young 1980.
23. Whitley et al. 1981, p. 58.
24. Mant 1979, p. 161.
25. Inkson et al. 1970.
26. Jamieson 1980, p. 222.
27. Giddens and Stanworth 1978, p. 100.
28. See Burrage 1969; Channon 1973; Bedardia 1979; Wiener 1981; Kumar 1981.
29. Wiener 1981, p. 159.
30. Blank 1977, 1979; Gamble 1981.
31. Whitley 1974.
32. Kelsall 1974.
33. Guttsman 1963, 1974; Johnson 1973.
34. These clubs are the subject of an earlier description and analysis in Chapter 3.
35. Career service was obtained from *Who's Who 1978, Who's Who 1979,* and *Who's Who in Finance 1975/6.* The 1978–79 public board service information and source is described in Chapter 4.
36. The A and B estimating procedures are described in Chapter 3.
37. Silk and Vogel (1976) also find a general business distrust of government officials in the U.S.
38. Etzioni 1982; Miller and Tomaskovic-Devey 1983.
39. *Business Week* 1982.
40. Silk and Silk 1980, pp. 226–27. Italics in original.
41. Porter 1965, p. 255.

References

Aaronovitch, Sam. 1961. *The Ruling Class: A Study of British Finance Capital.* London: Lawrence and Wishart.

Ackerman, Frank, Howard Birnbaum, James Wetzler, and Andrew Zimbalist. 1972. "The extent of income inequality in the United States." Pp. 207–218 in *The Capitalist System*, Richard C. Edwards et al., eds. Englewood Cliffs, N.J.: Prentice-Hall.

Aldag, Ramon J., and Kathryn M. Bartol. 1978. "Empirical studies of corporate social performance and policy: a survey of problems and results." Pp. 165–199 in *Research in Corporate Social Performance and Policy, 1978*, Lee E. Preston, ed. Greenwich, Ct.: JAI Press.

Alexander, Gordon J., and Rogene A. Buchholz. 1978. "Corporate social responsibility and stock market performance." *Academy of Management Journal* 21: 479–486.

Alexander, Herbert E. 1981. "Corporate political behavior." In *Corporations and Their Critics*, Thornton Bradshaw and David Vogel, eds. New York: McGraw-Hill.

Alford, Robert. 1963. *Party and Society: The Anglo-American Democracies.* Chicago: Rand McNally.

Alford, Robert. 1975. "Paradigms of relations between state and society." In *Stress and Contradiction in Modern Capitalism*, Leon Lindberg et al., eds. Lexington, Ma.: Heath.

Allen, Michael P. 1974. "The structure of interorganizational elite cooptation: interlocking corporate directorates." *American Sociological Review* 39: 393–406.

Allen, Michael P. 1981. "Managerial power and tenure in the large corporation." *Social Forces* 60: 482–494.

Allen, Michael, and Sharon K. Panian. 1982. "Power, performance and succession in the large corporation." Unpublished manuscript, Washington State University.

Almond, Gabriel. 1956. "Comparative political systems." *Journal of Politics* 18: 406–408.

Almond, Gabriel, and Sidney Verba. 1963. *The Civic Culture: Political Attitudes and Democracy in Five Nations.* Boston: Little, Brown.

Arthur Andersen. 1979. *The Costs of Government Regulation Study*. New York: Business Roundtable.

Arthur Young Executive Resource Consultants. 1980. *The Chief Executive: Background and Attitude Profile*. New York: Arthur Young Executive Resource Consultants.

Association for Business Sponsorship of the Arts. 1979. "Business Support for the Arts, April 1978 to March 1979." Bath: Association for Business Sponsorship of the Arts.

Association of National Advertisers. 1982. *Current Company Practices in the Use of Corporate Advertising*. New York: Association of National Advertisers.

Astin, Alexander. 1965. *Who Goes Where to College?* Chicago: Science Research Associates.

Bacon, Jeremy. 1973. *Corporate Directorship Practices: Membership and Committees of the Board*. New York: Conference Board.

Bacon, Jeremy, and James K. Brown. 1977. *The Board of Directors: Perspectives and Practices in Nine Countries*. New York: Conference Board.

Baird, L. L. 1977. *The Elite Schools: A Profile of Prestigious Independent Preparatory Schools*. Lexington, Ma.: Heath.

Baltzell, E. Digby. 1958. *Philadelphia Gentlemen: The Making of a National Upper Class*. New York: Free Press.

Baltzell, E. Digby. 1964. *The Protestant Establishment: Aristocracy and Caste in America*. New York: Random House.

Baltzell, E. Digby. 1966. " 'Who's Who in America' and 'The Social Register': elite and upper class indexes in metropolitan America." Pp. 266–275 in *Class, Status, and Power*, Reinhard Bendix and Seymour Martin Lipset, eds. New York: Free Press, 2nd edition.

Baltzell, E. Digby. 1979. *Puritan Boston and Quaker Philadelphia*. New York: Free Press.

Bank of England. 1979a. "Composition of company boards." *Bank of England Quarterly Bulletin* 19: 392–393.

Bank of England. 1979b. "The profitability of UK industrial sectors." *Bank of England Quarterly Bulletin* 19: 394–401.

Bank of England. 1981. "Profitability and company finance." *Bank of England Quarterly Bulletin* 21: 228–231.

Banks, J. A. 1970. *Marxist Sociology in Action*. London: Faber and Faber.

Banks, Louis. 1978. "Taking on the hostile media." *Harvard Business Review*, March–April.

Barratt Brown, Michael. 1973. "The controllers of British industry." In *Power in Britain*, J. Urry and J. Wakeford, eds. London: Heinemann.

Barratt, P. C., S. L. Fates, and K. J. N. Meek. 1980. "Corporate donations and sponsorship as sources of income for arts organizations in Great Britain." In *Charity Statistics 1979/80*. Tonbridge, Kent: Charities Aid Foundation Publications.

Barton, Allen H. 1982. "Determinants of attitudes in the American business elite." Paper presented at the World Congress of Sociology, Mexico City.

Bauer, Raymond A., Ithiel de Sola Pool, and Lewis Anthony Dexter. 1972. *American Business and Public Policy*. 2nd ed. New York: Atherton Press.

Baumol, William J. 1967. *Business Behavior, Value, and Growth*, rev. ed. New York: Macmillan.

Bearden, James, William Atwood, Peter Freitag, Carol Hendricks, Beth Mintz, and Michael Schwartz. 1975. "The nature and extent of bank centrality in corporate networks." Presented at the Annual Meeting of the American Sociological Association.

Bedardia, Francois. 1979. *A Social History of England, 1851–1975*. A. S. Foster, trans. London: Methuen.

Beer, Samuel. 1965. *Politics in The Collectivist Age*. New York: Norton.

Bell, Daniel. 1962. *The End of Ideology*. New York: Free Press.

Bell, Daniel. 1976. *The Cultural Contradictions of Capitalism*. New York: Basic Books.

Bendix, Reinhard. 1956. *Work and Authority in Industry: Ideologies of Management in the Course of Industrialization*. New York: Wiley.

Berg, Ivar. 1979. *Industrial Sociology*. Englewood Cliffs, N.J.: Prentice-Hall.

Berg, Ivar, and Mayer N. Zald. 1978. "Business and society." *Annual Review of Sociology* 4: 115–143.

Berger, Peter L. 1981. "New attack on the legitimacy of business." *Harvard Business Review* 59 (September–October): 82–89.

Berle, Adolf, Jr., and Gardiner C. Means. 1967. *The Modern Corporation and Private Property*. Reprint. ed. New York: Harcourt, Brace and World.

Blank, Stephen. 1973. *Industry and Government in Britain: The Federation of British Industries in Politics, 1945–65*. Lexington, Ma.: Heath.

Blank, Stephen. 1977. "Britain: the politics of foreign economic policy, the domestic economy, and the problem of pluralist stagnation." *International Organization* (Fall): 673–721.

Blank, Stephen. 1979. "Britain's economic problems: lies and damn lies." In *Perspectives on the British Crisis*, Issac Kramnick, ed. Ithaca, N.Y.: Cornell University Press.

Block, Fred. 1977. "The ruling class does not rule: notes on the Marxist theory of the state." *Socialist Review* 33 (May–June): 6–28.

Blumberg, Paul I. 1978. "Another day, another $3,000: executive rip-off in corporate America." *Dissent* 25: 157–178.

Blumenthal, Sidney. 1981. "Whose side is business on, anyway?" *New York Times Magazine*, October 25, pp. 29 ff.

Blumstein, Michael. 1982. "Hard-hit company profits reach lowest levels in perhaps 5 years." *New York Times*, August 4, 1982, pp. 1 ff.

Bonacich, Phillip, and G. William Domhoff. 1981. "Latent classes and group membership." *Social Networks* 3: 175–196.

Boudreaux, K. J. 1973. "Managerialism and risk-return performance." *Southern Economics Journal* 29: 366–372.

Boyce, Tracey. 1982. "Corporate PACs and the Delicate Balance." Department of Sociology, Northeastern University.

Bradshaw, Thornton, and David Vogel, eds. 1981. *Corporations and Their Critics: Issues and Answers to the Problems of Corporate Social Responsibility*. New York: McGraw-Hill.

Brenner, Steven N. 1980. "Corporate political activity: an exploratory study in a developing industry." Pp. 197–236 in *Research in Corporate Social Performance and Policy, 1980*, Lee E. Preston, ed. Greenwich, Ct.: JAI Press.

British Institute of Management. 1979. *Annual Report*. London: British Institute of Management.

Brittain, John A. 1978. *Inheritance and the Inequality of Material Wealth*. Washington, D.C.: The Brookings Institution.

Brooks, John. 1976. "Fueling the arts, or, Exxon as Medici." *New York Times,* January 25, pp. D1 ff.

Buchholz, Rogene A. 1980. *Business Environment/Public Policy: Corporate Executive Viewpoints and Educational Implications.* St. Louis: Center for the Study of American Business, Washington University.

Buchholz, Rogene A. 1982. *Business Environment and Public Policy: Implications for Management.* Englewood Cliffs, N.J.: Prentice-Hall.

Burch, Philip H., Jr. 1972. *The Managerial Revolution Reassessed: Family Control in America's Large Corporations.* Lexington, Ma.: Heath.

Burch, Philip H., Jr. 1980. *Elites in American History: The New Deal to the Carter Administration.* New York: Holmes and Meier Publishers.

Burck, Charles G. 1976. "A group profile of the Fortune 500 chief executive." *Fortune,* May, pp. 173ff.

Burrage, Michael. 1969. "Culture and British economic growth." *British Journal of Sociology* 20: 117–133.

Burt, Ronald S. 1981. *Corporate Profits and Cooptation.* Berkeley, Calif.: Survey Research Center, University of California, Berkeley.

Burt, Ronald S., Kenneth P. Christman, and Harold C. Kilburn, Jr. 1980. "Testing a structural theory of corporate cooptation: interorganizational directorates as a strategy for avoiding market constraints on profits." *American Sociological Review* 45: 821–841.

Business Committee for the Arts. 1976. "Business in the Arts" *Awards: A Ten Year History, 1966–1975.* New York: Business Committee for the Arts.

Business Committee for the Arts. 1980. *Triennial Survey of Business Support of the Arts.* New York: Business Committee for the Arts.

Business Roundtable. 1981. "The Business Roundtable Urges Corporations to Increase Philanthropy." New York: Business Roundtable.

Business Week. 1980. "Is the J. P. Stevens war over?" June 9, pp. 85, 87.

Business Week. 1981. "Managers who are no longer entrepreneurs." *Business Week,* June 30, p. 78.

Business Week. 1982. "How business is getting through to Washington." *Business Week,* October 4, p. 16.

Butcher, Willard C. 1980. "Going public for the private enterprise system." New York: The Chase Manhattan Bank.

California Roundtable. 1978. "Statement of Purpose." Burlingame, Ca.: The California Roundtable.

California Roundtable. 1979a. *California Tax Study: An Analysis of Taxes and Expenditures of State and Local Governments in California.* Burlingame, Ca.: California Roundtable.

California Roundtable. 1979b. "1978 Activities." Burlingame, Ca.: California Roundtable.

Castells, Manuel. 1980. *The Economic Crisis and American Society.* Princeton, N.J.: Princeton University Press.

Caves, Richard E. 1980. "Productivity differences among industries." In Richard E. Caves and Lawrence B. Krause, eds., *Britain's Economic Performance.* Washington, D.C.: The Brookings Institution.

Chandler, Alfred D. 1977. *The Visible Hand: The Managerial Revolution in America.* Cambridge, Mass.: Harvard University Press.

Channon, Derek F. 1973. *The Strategy and Structure of British Enterprise.* Boston: Harvard University Graduate School of Business Administration.

Chase Manhattan Bank. 1980. *In Support of Heroes*. New York: Chase Manhattan Bank.

Chevalier, J.-M. 1969. "The problem of control in large American corporations." *Antitrust Bulletin* 14: 163–180.

Ciscel, D. H. 1974. "Determinants of executive compensation." *Southern Economic Journal* 40: 613–617.

Citizens' Research Foundation. 1973. *Political Contributors and Lenders of $10,000 or More in 1972*. Princeton, N.J.: Citizens' Research Foundation.

Civil Service Department. 1978. *A Directory of Paid Public Appointments Made by Ministers*. London: H.M. Stationery Office.

Clinard, Marshall B., and Peter C. Yeager. 1980. *Corporate Crime*. New York: Free Press.

Cole, G. D. K. 1955. *Studies in Class Structure*. London: Routledge and Kegan Paul.

Coleman, D. C. 1973. "Gentlemen and players." *The Economic History Review* 26: 92–116.

Coleman, James S. 1982. *The Asymmetric Society*. Syracuse, N. Y.: Syracuse University Press.

Collier, P., and D. Horowitz. 1976. *The Rockefellers: An American Dynasty*. New York: Holt, Reinhart and Winston.

Collins, Randall. 1971. "Functional and conflict theories of educational stratification." *American Sociological Review* 36: 1002–1019.

Collins, Randall. 1979. *The Credential Society: An Historical Sociology of Education and Stratification*. New York: Academic Press.

Commission of Inquiry Into Industrial and Commercial Representation. 1972. Report. London: Association of British Chambers of Commerce and Confederation of British Industry.

Committee of Inquiry on Industrial Democracy. 1977. Report. London: H.M. Stationery Office.

Committee to Review the Functioning of Financial Institutions. 1980. Report. London: H.M. Stationery Office.

Comptroller General. 1077. *Government Regulatory Activity: Justifications, Processes, Impacts, and Alternatives*. Washington, D.C.: General Accounting Office.

Confederation of British Industry. 1978. *Britain Means Business, 1978*. London: Confederation of British Industry.

Conference Board. 1978. *Annual Survey of Corporate Contributions, 1976*. New York: Conference Board.

Conference Board. 1980. *Annual Survey of Corporate Contributions, 1978*. New York: Conference Board.

Copeman, George. 1971. *The Chief Executive and Business Growth: A Comparative Study in the United States, Great Britain and Germany*. London: Leviathan House.

Corporate Data Exchange. 1977. *CDE Stock Ownership Directory: Transportation*. New York: Corporate Data Exchange.

Corporate Data Exchange. 1978. *CDE Stock Ownership Directory: Agribusiness*. New York: Corporate Data Exchange.

Corporate Data Exchange. 1980. *CDE Stock Ownership Directory: Banking and Finance*. New York: Corporate Data Exchange.

Coser, Lewis A. 1956. *Functions of Social Conflict*. New York: Free Press.

Council for Financial Aid to Education. 1968. *Voluntary Support of Education, 1967–1968*. New York: Council for Financial Aid to Education.

Council for Financial Aid to Education. 1969. *Voluntary Support of Education, 1968–1969*. New York: Council for Financial Aid to Education.

Council for Financial Aid to Education. 1978. *Aid-to-Education Programs of Leading Business Concerns*. 10th ed. New York: Council for Financial Aid to Education.

Council for Financial Aid to Education. 1978. *The Casebook: Aid-to-Education of Leading Business Concerns*. New York: Council for Financial Aid to Education.

Council for Financial Aid to Education. 1979. *Corporate Support of Higher Education, 1978*. New York: Council for Financial Aid to Education.

Cox, S. R., and D. Shauger. 1973. "Executive compensation, firm sales and profitability." *Intermountain Economic Review* 4: 29–39.

Crittenden, Ann. 1982. "Aide reflects Schultz style." *New York Times*, July 21, p. D1.

Data Resources. 1979. *The Macroeconomic Impact of Federal Pollution Control Programs, 1978 Assessment*. Washington, D.C.: Council on Environmental Quality.

Davis, J. H. 1978. *The Guggenheims: An American Epic*. New York: William Morrow.

DeFina, Robert. 1977. *Public and Private Expenditures for Federal Regulation of Business*. St. Louis, Mo.: Washington University Center for the Study of American Business.

DiMaggio, Paul. 1982. "Cultural entrepreneurship in nineteenth-century Boston: the creation of an organizational base for high culture in America." *Media, Culture and Society* 4: 33–50.

DiMaggio, Paul, and Michael Useem. 1978. "Cultural property and public policy: emerging tensions in government support for the arts." *Social Research* 45: 356–389.

Diamond, R. S. 1970. "A self-portrait of the chief executive." *Fortune* 81 (May): 181, 320, 328.

Dillon, C. Douglas. 1969. "The corporation, the arts and the ghetto." Pp. 48–51 in *Business and the Arts: An Answer to Tomorrow*, A. Gingrich, ed. New York: Eriksson.

Domhoff, G. William. 1967. *Who Rules America?* Englewood Cliffs, N.J.: Prentice-Hall.

Domhoff, G. William. 1970. *The Higher Circles: The Governing Class in America*. New York: Random House.

Domhoff, G. William. 1972. *Fat Cats and Democrats: The Role of the Big Rich in the Party of the Common Man*. Englewood Cliffs, N.J.: Prentice-Hall.

Domhoff, G. William. 1974. *The Bohemian Grove and Other Retreats: A Study of Ruling-Class Consciousness*. New York: Harper and Row.

Domhoff, G. William. 1979. *The Powers That Be: Processes of Ruling-Class Domination in America*. New York: Random House.

Dooley, Peter C. 1969. "The interlocking directorate." *American Economic Review* 59: 314–323.

Dougherty, Philip H. 1981. "Advertising: corporate ads show growth." *New York Times*, October 7, 1981, p. D17.

Dreier, Peter. 1982. "Capitalists vs. the media: an analysis of an ideological mobilization among business leaders." *Media, Culture & Society* 4.

Dreier, Peter. 1982. "The position of the press in the U.S. power structure." *Social Problems* 29: 298–310.

Duberman, Lucile. 1976. *Social Inequality: Class and Caste in America.* New York: Lippincott.

Dubin, R. 1970. "Management in Britain—impressions of a visiting professor." *Journal of Management Studies* 7: 183–198.

Dye, Thomas R. and J. W. Pickering. 1974. "Governmental and corporate elites: convergence and differentiation." *Journal of Politics* 36: 900–925.

Economic League. 1979. *59th Annual Review.* London: Economic League.

Elliott, J. W. 1972. "Control, size, growth, and financial performance in the firm." *Journal Financ. Quantitative Analysis* 7: 1309–1320.

Engelbourg, Saul. 1980. *Power and Morality: American Business Ethics, 1840–1914.* Westport, CT: Greenwood Press.

Epstein, Edwin M. 1979. "The emergence of political action committees." In *Political Finance,* Herbert E. Alexander, ed. Beverly Hills, Calif.: Sage.

Epstein, Edwin M. 1980a. "Business and labor under the Federal Campaign Act of 1971." In *Parties, Interest Groups and Campaign Finance Laws,* Michael J. Malbin, ed. Washington, D.C.: American Enterprise Institute.

Epstein, Edwin M. 1980b. "The PAC phenomenon: an overview." *Arizona Law Review* 22: 355–372.

Ermann, David. 1979. "Corporate contributions to public television." *Social Problems* 25: 505–514.

Etzioni, Amitai. 1982. *An Immodest Agenda: Reconstructing America Before the 21st Century.* New York: McGraw-Hill.

Farney, Dennis. 1982. "A liberal congressman turns conservative: did PACs do it?" *Wall Street Journal,* July 29, pp. 1 ff.

Farnsworth, Clyde H. 1981. "All the President's Businessmen." *New York Times,* January 4, 1981, pp. F1, 22.

Federal Election Commission. 1980. *Party and Non-Party Political Committees, Final Report 1977–1978.* Washington, D.C.: Federal Election Commission.

Feldstein, Martin, James Poterba and Louis Dicks-Mireaux, 1982. "The effective tax rate and the pretax rate of return." Cambridge, Ma.: National Bureau of Economic Research.

Feldstein, Martin, and Lawrence Summers. 1977. "Is the rate of profit falling?" In Arthur M. Okun and George L. Perry, eds., *Brookings Papers on Economic Activity,* No. 1. Washington, D.C.: The Brookings Institution.

Fidler, John. 1981. *The British Business Elite: Its Attitudes to Class, Status and Power.* London: Routledge and Kegan Paul.

Fitch, Robert, and Mary Oppenheimer. 1970. "Who rules the corporations? Part I." *Socialist Revolution* 1 (July–August): 73–107.

Fleming, John E. 1981. "Public issues scanning." Pp. 155–173 in *Research in Corporate Social Performance and Policy, 1981,* Lee E. Preston, ed. Greenwich, Ct.: JAI Press.

Florence, P. S. 1961. *Ownership, Control and Success of Large Companies.* London: Sweet and Maxwell.

Fortune. 1978. *The Fortune 1978 Double 500 Directory.* New York: Fortune Magazine.

Fox, H. 1978. *Top Executive Compensation, 1978 Edition.* New York: Conference Board.

Fox, Thomas, and S. M. Miller. 1966. "Intra-country variations: occupational stratification and mobility." Pp. 574–581 in *Class, Status, and Power,* Reinhard Bendix and S. M. Lipset, eds. 2nd ed. New York: Free Press.

Francis, Arthur. 1980. "Company objectives, managerial motivations and the behaviour of large firms: an empirical test of the theory of 'managerial' capitalism." *Cambridge Journal of Economics* 4: 349–361.

Frederick, William C. 1981. "Free market vs. social responsibility: decision time at the CED." *California Management Review* 23 (Spring): 20–28.

Freitag, Peter J. 1975. "The cabinet and big business: a study of interlocks." *Social Problems* 23: 137–152.

Fuerbringer, Jonathan. 1982. "Reagan tax rise: business divided." *New York Times,* August 18, pp. D1, D20.

Furniss, W. Todd. 1973. *American Universities and Colleges.* 11th Edition. Washington, D.C.: American Council on Education.

Galaskiewicz, Joseph, and Barbara Rauschenbach. 1979. "Patterns of interinstitutional change: an examination of linkages between cultural and business organizations in a metropolitan community." Paper presented at the annual meeting of the American Sociological Association.

Galbraith, John Kenneth. 1971. *The New Industrial State.* Boston: Houghton Mifflin.

Gamble, Andrew. 1981. *Britain in Decline.* London: Macmillan.

Gathorne-Hardy, Jonathan. 1977. *The Old School Tie: The Phenomenon of the English Public School.* New York: Viking Press.

Giddens, Anthony. 1974. "Preface." In *Elites and Power in British Society,* Philip Stanworth and Anthony Giddens, eds. London: Cambridge University Press.

Giddens, Anthony. 1976. "The Rich." *New Society* 38 (October): 63–66.

Giddens, Anthony, and Philip Stanworth. 1978. "Elites and privilege." In Philip Abrams, ed., *Work, Urbanism and Inequality.* London: Weidenfeld and Nicolson.

Gingrich, A., ed. 1969. *Business and the Arts: An Answer to Tomorrow.* New York: Eriksson.

Glyn, A. and B. Sutcliffe. 1972. *British Capitalism, Workers and the Profits Squeeze.* Harmondsworth: Penguin.

Gogel, Robert M. 1977. *Interlocking Directorships and the American Corporate Network.* Ph.D. dissertation, University of California, Santa Barbara.

Gogel, Robert, and Thomas Koenig. 1981. "Commercial banks, interlocking directorates and economic power: an analysis of the primary metals industry." *Social Problems* 29: 117–128.

Gold, David A., Clarence P. H. Lo, and Erik Olin Wright. 1975. "Recent developments in Marxist theories of the capitalist state." *Monthly Review* 27 (October): 29–43.

Goldsmith, R. W., and R. C. Parmelee. 1940. "The distribution of ownership in the 200 largest nonfinancial corporations." Pp. 1–1557 in *Investigation of Concentration of Economic Power,* Monograph 29. Washington, D.C.: U.S. Government Printing Office.

Gordon, David M. 1975. "Recession is capitalism as usual." *The New York Times Magazine,* April 25.

Gordon, Robert A. 1945. *Business Leadership in the Large Corporation.* Berkeley, Ca.: University of California Press.

Graham, Roberta. 1979. "Business and the arts make a perfect match." *Nation's Business,* April, pp. 57–60.

Granick, David. 1972. *Managerial Comparisons of Four Developed Countries: France, Britain, United States and Russia.* Cambridge, Ma.: MIT Press.

Granick, David. 1973. "Differences in educational selectivity and managerial behavior in large companies: France and Britain." *Comparative Educational Review* 17: 350–361.

Grant, Wyn. 1980. "Business interests and the British Conservative Party." *Government and Opposition* 15: 143–161.

Grant, Wyn, and David Marsh. 1977. *The CBI.* London: Hodder and Stoughton.

Green, Mark, and Andrew Buchsbaum. 1980. *The Corporate Lobbies: Political Profiles of the Business Roundtable and the Chamber of Commerce.* Washington, D.C.: Public Citizen.

Green, Mark, and Norman Waitzman. 1980. "Costs, benefit, and class." *Working Papers for a New Society* 7 (May/June): 39–51.

Greenstone, J. David. 1969. *Labor in American Politics.* New York: Knopf.

Greer, Douglas F. 1980. *Industrial Organization and Public Policy.* New York: Macmillan.

Guttsman, W. L. 1963. *The British Political Elite.* London: MacGibbon and Kee.

Guttsman, W. L. 1974. "The British political elite and the class structure." Pp. 22–44 in *Elites and Power in British Society,* Philip Stanworth and Anthony Giddens, eds. London: Cambridge University Press.

Hannah, Leslie. 1976. *The Rise of the Corporate Economy.* London: Methuen.

Hanson, A. H., and M. Walles. 1975. *Governing Britain.* London: Fontana.

Harris, James F., and Anne Klepper. 1976. *Corporate Philanthropic Public Service Activities.* New York: Conference Board.

Harris, James F., and Anne Klepper. 1977. "Corporate philanthropic public service activities." In *Research Papers, The Commission on Private Philanthropy and Public Needs.* Washington, D.C.: U.S. Department of the Treasury.

Harris, Louis, and Associates. 1977. *A Survey of Outside Directors of Major Publicly Owned Corporations.* New York: Louis Harris.

Hartnett, Rodney T. 1969. *College and University Trustees: Their Backgrounds, Roles and Educational Attitudes.* Princeton, N.J.: Educational Testing.

Hayes, Robert H., and William J. Abernathy. 1980. "Managing our way to economic decline." *Harvard Business Review* (July–August): 67–77.

Heidrick and Struggles, Inc. 1980. "The changing board, 1980 update: a profile of the board of directors." Chicago: Heidrick and Struggles.

Heller, R. 1973. "The state of British boardrooms." *Management Today,* May.

Henry, J. S. 1980. "From soap to soapbox: the corporate merchandising of ideas." *Working Papers for a New Society* 7 (May–June): 55–57.

Herman, Edward S. 1981. *Corporate Control, Corporate Power.* New York: Cambridge University Press.

Hersh, B. 1978. *The Mellon Family: A Fortune in History.* New York: William Morrow.

Hibbs, Douglas A., Jr. 1976. "Industrial conflict in advanced industrial societies." *American Political Science Review* 70: 1033–1058.

Hibbs, Douglas A., Jr. 1978. "Political parties and macroeconomic policy." *American Political Science Review* 71: 1467–1487.

Hindley, B. 1970. "Separation of ownership and control in the modern corporation." *Journal of Law and Economics* 13: 185–222.

Holl, P. 1975. "Effect of control type on the performance of the firms in the U.K." *Journal of Industrial Economics* 23: 257–271.

Holland, Daniel M., and Stewart C. Myers. 1980. "Profitability and capital costs for manufacturing corporations and all nonfinancial corporations." *American Economic Review* 70: 320–325.

Honeycutt, T. C., and D. L. Zimmerman. 1976. "The measurement of corporate diversification: 1950–1967." *Antitrust Bulletin* 21: 509–535.

Hopper, Earl I. 1968. "A typology for the classification of educational systems." *Sociology* 2: 29–46.

Ingham, John N. 1978. *The Iron Barons: A Social Analysis of an American Urban Elite, 1874–1965.* Westport, Ct.: Greenwood Press.

Inkson, J. H. K., J. P. Schwitter, D. C. Pheysey and D. J. Hickson. 1970. "A comparison of organizational structure and managerial roles: Ohio, USA, and Midland, England." *Journal of Management Studies* 7: 347–363.

Institute of Directors. 1965. "The anatomy of the board." *The Director* (January): 87–91.

Jackson, Brooks. 1981. "Close encounter: Samuel Pierce meets the mayors." *Wall Street Journal,* January 28, p. 20.

James, David R., and Michael Soref. 1981. "Managerial theory: unmaking of the corporation president." *American Sociological Review* 46: 1–18.

Jamieson, Ian. 1980. "Capitalism and culture: a comparative analysis of British and American manufacturing organizations." *Sociology* 14: 217–245.

Jenkins, C. 1959. *Power at the Top: A Critical Survey of the Nationalized Industries.* London: MacGibbon and Kee.

Jensen, Michael C. 1978a. "Chairman of Avon resigns from J. P. Stevens Board." *New York Times,* March 22.

Jensen, Michael C. 1978b. "Union strategist on Wall Street." *New York Times,* March 26, sect. 3, p. 5.

Jessop, Bob. 1977. "Recent theories about the capitalist state." *Cambridge Journal of Economics* 1: 353–373.

Johnson, P. S., and R. Apps. 1979. "Interlocking directorates among the UK's largest companies." *Antitrust Bulletin* 24: 357–369.

Johnson, R. W. 1973. "The British political elite, 1955–1972." *European Journal of Sociology* 14: 35–77.

Kahn, E. J., III. 1981. "The day the banks saved Boston." *Boston Magazine,* November, pp. 161 ff.

Kamerschen, D. R. 1968. "The influence of ownership and control on profit rates." *American Economic Review* 58: 432–447.

Kanter, Rosabeth Moss. 1977. *Men and Women of the Corporation.* New York: Basic Books.

Kaysen, Carl. 1957. "The social significance of the modern corporation." *American Economic Review* 47: 311–319.

Kedia, Banwari L., and Edwin C. Kuntz. 1981. "The context of social performance: an empirical study of Texas banks." Pp. 133–154 in *Research in Corporate Social Performance and Policy, 1981,* Lee E. Preston, ed. Greenwich, Ct.: JAI Press.

Keim, Gerald D. 1981. "Foundations of a political strategy for business." *California Management Review* 23 (Spring): 41–48.

Keller, Suzanne. 1963. *Beyond the Ruling Class: Strategic Elites in Modern Society*. New York: Random House.

Kelsall, R. K. 1974. "Recruitment to the higher civil service: how has the pattern changed?" Pp. 170–184 in *Elites and Power in Britain*, Philip Stanworth and Anthony Giddens, eds. London: Cambridge University Press.

Kessler, Ellen Terry. 1980. "Social conscience or self-interest." *Magazine Age* 1 (June): 26–33.

Kilborn, Peter T. 1982. "Business chiefs see need to cut military spending to trim deficit." *New York Times*, October 11, pp. 1, 11.

King, M. A. 1975. "The United Kingdom profits crisis: myth or reality?" *Economic Journal* 85: 33–54.

King, Mervyn. 1977. *Public Policy and the Corporation*. London: Chapman and Hall.

Koch, A., and S. Labovitz. 1976. "Interorganizational power in a Canadian community: a replication." *Sociological Quarterly* 17: 3–15.

Koch, Frank. 1979. *The New Corporate Philanthropy: How Society and Business Can Profit*. New York: Plenum Press.

Koenig, Thomas. 1979. "Interlocking directorates among the largest American corporations and their significance for corporate political activity." Unpublished Ph.D. Dissertation, University of California, Santa Barbara.

Koenig, Thomas, Robert Gogel, and John Sonquist. 1979. "Models of the significance of interlocking corporate directorates." *American Journal of Economics and Sociology* 38: 173–186.

Kohlmeier, Louis M. 1981. "The big businessmen who have Jimmy Carter's ear." *New York Times*, February 5, Section 3, p. 1.

Kolko, Gabriel. 1963. *The Triumph of Conservatism: A Reinterpretation of American History, 1900–1916*. New York: Free Press.

Kolko, Gabriel. 1967. "Brahmins and business, 1870–1914: a hypothesis on the social basis of success in American history." Pp. 343–363 in *The Critical Spirit*, Kurt H. Wolff and Barrington Moore, eds. Boston: Beacon Press.

Kolko, Gabriel. 1969. *The Roots of American Foreign Policy*. Boston: Beacon.

Korbin, Stephen J. 1982. *Managing Political Risk Assessment: Strategic Response to Environmental Change*. Berkeley, Ca.: University of California Press.

Kotz, David M. 1978. *Bank Control of Large Corporations in the United States*. Berkeley, Ca.: University of California Press.

Kristol, Irving. 1977. "On corporate philanthropy." *Wall Street Journal*, March 21.

Kross, H. E. 1970. *Executive Opinion: What Business Leaders Said and Thought on Economic Issues, 1920s–1960s*. Garden City, N.J.: Doubleday.

Kumar, Krishan. 1981. "Culture and the condition of Britain." *Times Higher Education Supplement*, May 8.

Labour Party Study Group on Banking and Insurance. 1973. *Banking and Insurance Green Paper*. London: The Labor Party.

Labour Research. 1979. "Political donations in 1978." *Labour Research* 68 (November): 234–236.

Labour Research. 1980. "The anti-union league." *Labour Research* 69 (March).

Ladd, Everett Carll. 1978. "What the voters really want." *Fortune* 98 (December, 18): 40–48.

Landau, David. 1977. "Trustees: the capital connection." *Health/PAC Bulletin* 74: 1–23.

Larner, Robert J. 1970. *Management Control and the Large Corporation.* New York: Dunellen.

Leibenstein, H. 1979. "A branch of microeconomics is missing: micro-macro theory." *Journal of Economic Literature* 17: 477–502.

Leonard, William N. 1976. "Mergers, industrial concentration and antitrust policy." *Journal of Economic Issues,* June.

Levine, Steven B. 1980. "The rise of American boarding schools and the development of a national upper class." *Social Problems* 28: 63–94.

Levy, Ferdinand K., and Gloria M. Shatto. 1980. "Social responsibility in large electric utility firms: the case for philanthropy." Pp. 237–249 in *Research in Corporate Social Performance and Policy, 1980,* Lee E. Preston, ed. Greenwich, Ct.: JAI Press.

Lewellen, W. G. 1968. *Executive Compensation in Large Industrial Corporations.* New York: National Bureau of Economic Research.

Lewellen, W. G. 1971. *The Ownership Income of Management.* Princeton, N.J.: Princeton University Press.

Lewellen, W. G. 1975. "Recent evidence on senior executive pay." *National Tax Journal* 28: 159–172.

Lewellen, W. G., and B. Huntsman. 1970. "Managerial pay and corporate performance." *American Economic Review* 60: 710–720.

Lieberson, Stanley. 1971. "An empirical study of military-industrial linkages." *American Journal of Sociology* 76: 562–84.

Lieberson, Stanley, and J. F. O'Connor. 1972. "Leadership and organizational performance: a study of large corporations." *American Sociological Review* 37: 117–130.

Lilley, William III, and James C. Miller III. 1977. "The new social regulation." *The Public Interest* 47 (Spring).

Lindblom, Charles E. 1977. *Politics and Markets: The World's Political-Economic Systems.* New York: Basic Books.

Lipset, S. M., and Reinhard Bendix. 1959. *Social Mobility in Industrial Society.* Berkeley, Ca.: University of California Press.

Lipset, Seymour Martin. 1963. *The First New Nation: The United States in Historical and Comparative Perspective.* New York: Basic Books.

Lipset, Seymour Martin, and William P. Schneider. 1981. *The Confidence Gap: How Americans View Their Institutions.* New York: Macmillan.

Lipset, Seymour Martin, and William Schneider. 1978. "How's business: what the public thinks." *Public Opinion* 1 (July–August): 41–47.

Lisle-Williams, Michael. 1981. "Continuities in the English financial elite, 1850–1980." Nuffield College, Oxford University.

Lo, Clarence. 1982. "Theories of the state and business opposition to increased military spending." *Social Problems* 29: 424–438.

Lodge, George C. 1975. *The New American Ideology.* New York: Alfred A. Knopf.

Lundberg, Ferdinand. 1968. *The Rich and the Super-Rich.* New York: Lyle Stuart.

Lupton, Tom, and C. S. Wilson. 1959. "The social background and connections of 'top decision makers.'" *The Manchester School* 28: 30–51.

MacAvoy, Paul W. 1979. *The Regulated Industries and the Economy.* New York: Norton.

MacDonald, M. 1977. *The Education of Elites*. London: The Open University.

Maccoby, Michael. 1976. *The Gamesman*. New York: Simon and Schuster.

Malott, Robert H. 1978. "Corporate support of education: some strings attached." *Harvard Business Review* (July–August): 133–138.

Mant, Alastair. 1979. *The Rise and Fall of the British Manager*. Rev. ed. London: Pan Books and Macmillan.

Margolis, Diane Rothbard. 1979. *The Managers: Corporate Life in America*. New York: William Morrow and Company.

Mariolis, Peter. 1975. "Interlocking directorates and control of corporations: the theory of bank control." *Social Science Quarterly* 56: 425–439.

Marris, R. 1979. *Theory and Future of the Corporate Economy and Society*. Amsterdam: North-Holland.

Martin, William F., and George Cabot Lodge. 1975. "Our society in 1985— business may not like it." *Harvard Business Review* 53 (November-December): 143–152.

Marwick, Arthur. 1980. *Class: Image and Reality in Britain, France and the USA Since 1930*. New York: Oxford University Press.

Massachusetts Business Roundtable 1980a. "Task Forces." Boston: Massachusetts Business Roundtable.

Massachusetts Business Roundtable 1980b. "Statement of Mission and Goals." Boston: Massachusetts Business Roundtable.

Masson, R. T. 1971. "Executive motivations, earnings, and consequent equity performance." *Journal of Political Economy* 79: 1278–1292.

McEachern, William A. 1975. *Managerial Control and Performance*. Lexington, Ma.: Heath.

McGrath, E. J. 1936. "The control of higher education in America." *Educational Record* 17: 259–272.

McGrath, Phyllis S. 1976. *Managing Corporate External Relations: Changing Perspectives and Responses*. New York: Conference Board.

McGuire, J. W., J. S. Y. Chiu, and A. E. Elbing. 1962. "Executive incomes, sales and profits." *American Economic Review* 52: 753–761.

McLachlan, J. 1970. *American Boarding Schools: A Historical Study*. New York: Scribner's.

McQuaid, Kim. 1980. "Big business and public policy in contemporary United States." *Quarterly Review of Economics and Business* 20: 57–68.

Means, Gardiner C. 1967. "Implications of the corporate revolution in economic theory." In *The Modern Corporation and Private Property*, Adolf A. Berle and Gardiner C. Means. Reprint ed. New York: Harcourt, Brace and World.

Meeks, Geoffrey, and Geoffrey Whittington. 1975. "Giant companies in the United Kingdom 1948–69." *The Economic Journal* 85: 824–843.

Melrose-Woodman, J. E. 1978. *Profile of the British Manager*. London: British Institute of Management.

Middlemas, Keith. 1979. *Politics in Industrial Society: The Experience of the British System Since 1911*. London: Andre Deutsch.

Miliband, Ralph. 1969. *The State in Capitalist Society*. New York: Basic Books.

Miller, Francine, and Richard Minns. 1981. "Well banked." *New Statesman*, p. 4.

Miller, S. M., and Donald Tomaskovic-Devey. 1983. *The Recapitalization of Capitalism*. London: Routledge and Kegan Paul.

Mills, C. Wright. 1956. *The Power Elite*. New York: Oxford University Press.

Millstein, Ira M., and Salem M. Katsh. 1981. *The Limits of Corporate Power.* New York: Macmillan.

Mintz, Beth, and Michael Schwartz. 1981. "Interlocking directorates and interest group formation." *American Sociological Review* 46: 851–869.

Mintzberg, Henry. 1975. "The manager's job: folklore and fact." *Harvard Business Review,* July–August: 49–61.

Mizruchi, Mark S. 1982. *The American Corporate Network.* Beverly Hills, Ca.: Sage.

Mohl, Bruce A. 1981. "The UN of the business view." *Boston Globe,* January 11, 1981, pp. 48 ff.

Molander, Earl A. 1980. *Responsive Capitalism: Case Studies in Corporate Social Conduct.* New York: McGraw-Hill.

Monsen, R. J., J. S. Chiu, and D. E. Cooley. "The effects of separation of ownership and control on the performance of the large firm." *Quarterly Journal of Economics* 82: 435–451.

Moore, David G. 1980. *Politics and the Corporate Executive.* New York: Conference Board.

Mulkern, John R., Edward Handler, and Lawrence Godtfredsen. 1981. "Corporate PACs as fundraisers." *California Management Review* 23 (Spring): 49–55.

Murray, Edwin A., Jr. 1982. "The public affairs function: report on a large scale research project." Pp. 129–155 in *Research in Corporate Social Performance and Policy, 1982,* Lee E. Preston, ed. Greenwich, Ct.: JAI Press.

Myers, Desaix III. 1980. *U.S. Business in South Africa: The Economic, Political, and Moral Issues.* Bloomington, Ind.: Indiana University Press.

Nettl, J. P. 1965. "Consensus or elite domination: the case of business." *Political Studies* 8: 22–44.

New York Stock Exchange. 1972. *1972 Fact Book.* New York: New York Stock Exchange.

Newcomer, Mabel. 1955. *The Big Business Executive: The Factors That Made Him, 1900–1950.* New York: Columbia University Press.

Nordhaus, William D. 1974. "The falling share of profits." In Arthur M. Okun and George L. Perry, eds., *Brookings Papers on Economic Activity, No. 1.* Washington, D.C.: The Brookings Institution.

Nyman, Steve, and Aubrey Silberston. 1978. "The ownership and control of industry." *Oxford Economic Papers* 30: 74–101.

O'Connor, James. 1973. *The Fiscal Crisis of the State.* New York: St. Martin's Press.

Oberschall, Anthony. 1973. *Social Conflicts and Social Movements.* Englewood Cliffs, N.J.: Prentice-Hall.

Offe, Claus. 1973. "The abolition of market control and the problem of legitimacy (I)." *Kapitalistate* 1: 109–116.

Organization for Economic Co-Operation and Development. 1979. *Concentration and Competition Policy.* Paris: Organization for Economic Co-Operation and Development.

Ornstein, Michael D. 1980. "Assessing the meaning of corporate interlocks: Canadian evidence." *Social Science Research* 9: 287–306.

Otten, Alan L. 1981. "English Corporations: Art's New Tudors?" *Wall Street Journal,* April 3.

Ouchi, William. 1981. *Theory Z: How American Business Can Meet the Japanese Challenge.* Reading, Ma.: Addison-Wesley.

Pahl, R. E., and J. T. Winkler. 1974. "The economic elite: theory and practice." Pp. 102–22 in *Elites and Power in British Society,* Philip Stanworth and Anthony Giddens, eds. London: Cambridge University Press.

Palmer, Donald. 1983. "Broken ties: interlocking directorates and intercorporate coordination." *Administrative Science Quarterly* 28: 40–55.

Palmer, John P. 1972. "The separation of ownership from control in large U.S. industrial corporations." *Quarterly Review of Economics and Business* 12: 55–62.

Parsons, Talcott. 1953. "A revised analytical approach to the theory of stratification." Pp. 92–128 in *Class, Status and Power,* Reinhard Bendix and S. M. Lipset, eds. New York: Free Press.

Parsons, Talcott. 1970. "Quality and inequality in modern society, or social stratification revisited." *Sociological Inquiry* 40: 13–72.

Partridge, Sir John. 1979. "Preface." In *Understanding British Industry, Annual Review, 1978–79.* London: CBI Educational Foundation.

Patrick, Kenneth G., and Richard Eells. 1969. *Education and the Business Dollar: A Study of Corporate Contributions Policy and American Education.* New York: Macmillan.

Pedersen, L., and W. K. Tabb. 1976. "Ownership and control of large corporations revisited." *Antitrust Bulletin* 21: 53–66.

Pennings, Johannes H. 1980. *The Interlocking Directorates.* San Francisco: Jossey-Bass.

Perrott, Roy. 1968. *The Aristocrats.* London: Weidenfeld and Nicolson.

Perrucci, Robert, and Marc Pilisuk. 1970. "Leaders and ruling elites: the interorganizational bases of community power." *American Sociological Review* 35: 1040–1057.

Pfeffer, Jeffrey. 1972. "Size and composition of corporate boards of directors: the organization and its environment." *Administrative Science Quarterly* 17: 218–228.

Pfeffer, Jeffrey. 1977. "Toward an examination of stratification in organizations." *Administrative Science Quarterly* 22: 553–567.

Pfeffer, Jeffrey, and Gerald R. Salancik. 1978. *The External Control of Organizations: A Resource Dependence Perspective.* New York: Harper and Row.

Pierson, George W. 1969. *The Education of American Leaders: Comparative Contributions of U.S. Colleges and Universities.* New York: Praeger.

Pinto-Duschinsky, Michael. 1981. *British Political Finance, 1830–1980.* Washington, D.C.: American Enterprise Institute.

Pittman, Russell. 1977. "Market structure and campaign contributions." *Public Choice* 31 (Fall): 37–58.

Porter, John. 1965. *The Vertical Mosaic: An Analysis of Social Class and Power in Canada.* Toronto: University of Toronto Press.

Post, James E. 1979. "The internal management of social responsiveness: the role of the public affairs department." School of Management, Boston University.

Post, James E. 1977. "Strategy and orientation as determinants of patterns of corporate response to social conflict." Research Program in Management and Public Policy, Boston University.

Poulantzas, Nicos. 1973. *Political Power and Social Classes.* Timothy O'Hagen, trans. London: New Left Books, and Sheed Ward.

Powell, Reed M. 1969. *Race, Religion, and the Promotion of the American Executive.* Columbus, Oh.: College of Administrative Science, Ohio State University.

Prais, S. J. 1976. *The Evolution of Giant Firms in Britain.* London: Cambridge University Press.

Preston, Lee E. 1981. "Corporate power and social performance: approaches to positive analysis." Pp. 1–16 in *Research in Corporate Social Performance and Policy, 1981,* Lee E. Preston, ed. Greenwich, Ct.: JAI Press.

Price, Robert, and George S. Bain. 1976. "Union growth revisited: 1948–1974." *British Journal of Industrial Relations* 14: 339–355.

Projector, Dorothy S., and Gertrude S. Weiss. 1966. *Survey of Financial Characteristics of Consumers.* Washington, D.C.: Federal Reserve Board.

Public Affairs Council. 1979. "Political actions committees," *PAC News,* n. 7, July 27, 1979.

Radice, H. K. "Control type, profitability and growth in large firms: an empirical study." *Economic Journal* 81: 547–562.

Ratcliff, Richard E. 1980. "Banks and corporate lending: an analysis of the impact of the internal structure of the capitalist class on the lending behavior of banks." *American Sociological Review* 45: 553–570.

Ratcliff, Richard E., Mary Beth Gallagher, and David Jaffee. 1980. "Political money and ideological clusters in the capitalist class." Annual meeting of the American Sociological Association, New York.

Rattner, Steven. 1981. "The arts in Britain are pennypinching, too." *New York Times,* September 13.

Riesman, David. 1950. *The Lonely Crowd: A Study of the Changing American Character.* New Haven, Ct.: Yale University Press.

Roberts, D. R. 1959. *Executive Compensation.* New York: Free Press.

Robinson, Derek. 1981. "British industrial relations research in the sixties and seventies." In *Industrial Relations in International Perspective,* Peter B. Doeringer, ed., London: Macmillan.

Roderick, David M. 1982. "A few practical concerns." *American Arts,* March, 1982.

Rodgers, Wilfrid C. 1978. "Textile union strategy brings 2 resignations." *Boston Globe,* September 13, p. 47.

Rothman, Robert A. 1978. *Inequality and Stratification in the United States.* Englewood Cliffs, N.J.: Prentice-Hall.

Rothman, Stanley, and S. Robert Lichter. 1982. "Media and business elites: two classes in conflict?" *Public Interest* 69: 117–125.

Royal Commission on the Distribution of Income and Wealth. 1975. *Income from Companies and Its Distribution.* London: H.M. Stationery Office.

Rubin, Bernard, ed. 1977. *Big Business and the Mass Media.* Lexington, Ma.: Heath.

Rubinstein, W. D. 1977. "Wealth, elites and the class structure of modern Britain." *Past and Present* 76: 99–126.

Rubinstein, W. D. 1981. *Men of Property: The Very Wealthy in Britain Since The Industrial Revolution.* New Brunswick, N.J.: Rutgers University Press.

Rumelt, R. P. 1974. *Strategy, Structure, and Economic Performance.* Cambridge, Mass.: Harvard University Press.

Rumelt, R. P. 1977. "Diversity and profitability." *Working Paper MGL-51.* University of California, Los Angeles.

Russett, Bruce M., and Elizabeth C. Hanson. 1975. *Interest and Ideology: The Foreign Policy Beliefs of American Businessmen*. San Francisco: Freeman.

Salmans, Sandra. 1981. "Philip Morris and the arts." *New York Times*, November 11: D1–6.

Sampson, Anthony. 1962. *Anatomy of Britain*. London: Hodder and Stoughton.

Sampson, Anthony. 1971. *The New Anatomy of Britain*. London: Hodder and Stoughton.

Sanderson, Michael. 1972. *The Universities and British Industry, 1850–1970*. London: Routledge and Kegan Paul.

Schumacher, Edward. 1979. "Top business executives in city act to speak with a single voice." *New York Times*, December 19, pp. 1, B3.

Scientific American. 1965. *The Big Business Executive, 1964: A Study of His Social and Educational Background*. New York: Scientific American.

Scotese, Peter G. 1978. "Business and art: a creative, practical partnership." *Management Review*, October, pp. 20–23.

Scott, John. 1979. *Corporations, Classes and Capitalism*. London: Hutchinson.

Scott, John, and Michael Hughes. 1976. "Ownership and control in a satellite economy: a discussion from Scottish data." *Sociology* 10: 21–42.

Scott, John, and Michael Hughes. 1980. "Capital and communication in Scottish business." *Sociology* 14: 29–47.

Scott, W. Richard. 1981. *Organizations: Rational, Natural and Open Systems*. Englewood Cliffs, N.J.: Prentice-Hall.

Sedgwick, Alastair. 1980. "Industry and the arts." *Management Today*, February, pp. 67–72.

Seider, M. S. 1977. "Corporate ownership, control and ideology: support for behavioral similarity." *Sociology and Social Research* 62: 113–128.

Sethi, S. Prakash. 1978. "Dimensions of corporate social responsibility: an analytical framework." *California Management Review* 17: 58–64.

Shapiro, Irving. 1979. "Business and the public policy process." Harvard University Symposium on Business and Government, May 9.

Sheehan, Robert J. 1967. "Proprietors in the world of big business." Fortune 15 (June): 178–183, 242.

Shepherd, William G. 1972. "Structure and behavior in British industries, with U.S. comparisons." *Journal of Industrial Economics* 21: 35–54.

Shoup, Laurence H., and William Minter. 1977. *Imperial Brain Trust: The Council on Foreign Relations and United States Foreign Policy*. New York: Monthly Review Press.

Silk, Leonard, and David Vogel. 1976. *Ethics and Profits: The Crisis of Confidence in American Business*. New York: Simon and Schuster.

Silk, Leonard, and Mark Silk. 1980. *The American Establishment*. New York: Basic Books.

Simison, Robert L. 1981. "Chrysler lauds strong performances of UAW's Fraser as board member." *Wall Street Journal*, March 12, p. 25.

Sinclair, Stephen. 1981. "Why business gives to the arts." *Cultural Post* 7 (December): 1–5.

Skocpol, Theda. 1980. "Political response to capitalist crisis: Neo-Marxist theories of the state and the case of the New Deal." *Politics and Society* 10: 155–201.

Smith, David C. 1980. "Trade union growth and industrial disputes." In Richard E. Caves and Lawrence B. Krause, eds., *Britain's Economic Performance*. Washington, D.C.: The Brookings Institution.

Smyth, D. J., W. J. Boyes, and D. E. Peseau. 1975. *Size, Growth, Profits in the Large Corporation: A Study of the 500 Largest United Kingdom and United States Industrial Corporations.* New York: Holmes and Meier.

Sommers, Paul. 1978. "The economic costs of regulation: report for the American Bar Association, Commission on Law and the Economy." Department of Economics, Yale University.

Sorensen, R. 1974. "The separation of ownership and control and firm performance: an empirical analysis." *Southern Economic Journal* 41: 145–148.

Staber, Udo Hermann. 1982. The Organizational Properties of Trade Associations. Cornell University, unpublished Ph.D. dissertation.

Stano, M. 1975. "Executive ownership interests and corporate performance." *Southern Economic Journal* 42: 272–278.

Stano, M. 1976. "Monopoly Power, ownership control, and corporate performance." *Bell Journal of Economics* 7: 672–679.

Stanton, Frank. 1974. "To benefit the community as a whole." New York: Business Committee for the Arts.

Stanworth, Philip. 1980. "Trade, gentility, and upper-class education in Victorian Britain." *International Studies of Management and Organization* 10: 46–70.

Stanworth, Philip, and Anthony Giddens. 1974. "An economic elite: a demographic profile of company chairmen." In *Elites and Power in British Society,* Philip Stanworth and Anthony Giddens, eds. London: Cambridge University Press.

Stanworth, Philip, and Anthony Giddens. 1975. "The modern corporate economy: interlocking directorships in Britain, 1906–1970." *Sociological Review* 23: 5–28.

State Research. 1978. "The Economic League." *Bulletin* No. 7 (August-September): 135–145.

Steck, Henry J. 1975. "Private influence on environmental policy: the case of the National Industrial Pollution Control Council." *Environmental Law* 5: 241–281.

Steckmest, Francis W. 1982. *Corporate Performance: The Key to Public Trust.* New York: McGraw Hill.

Stein, Herbert. 1978. "Businessmen of the world unite." *Wall Street Journal,* June 12.

Steiner, George A., and John F. Steiner. 1980. *Business, Government, and Society: A Managerial Perspective.* New York: Random House.

Story, Ronald. 1980. *The Forging of an Aristocracy: Harvard and the Boston Upper Class, 1800–1870.* Middletown, Ct.: Wesleyan University Press.

Sturdivant, Frederick D., and James L. Ginter. 1977. "Corporate social responsiveness: management attitudes and economic performance." *California Management Review* 19, 3: 30–39.

Swinyard, Alfred W., and Floyd A. Bond. 1980. "Who gets promoted?" *Harvard Business Review.* September-October, pp. 6–18.

Szymanski, Albert. 1978. *The Capitalist State and the Politics of Class.* Cambridge, Ma.: Winthrop Publishing Company.

Task Force on Corporate Social Performance. 1980. *Business and Society: Strategies for the 1980's.* Washington, D.C.: U.S. Department of Commerce.

The Director. 1975. "Anatomy of the board." January.

Tobias, Andrew. 1976. "The merging of the 'Fortune 500.'" *New York Magazine,* December 20: 23–25, 49, 67.

Treiman, Donald J., and Kermit Terrell. 1975. "The process of status attainment in the United States and Great Britain." *American Journal of Sociology* 81: 563–583.

Turner, Ralph. 1960. "Sponsored and contest mobility and the school system." *American Sociological Review* 25: 855–67.

U.S. House Committee on Banking and Currency. 1968. Subcommittee on Domestic Finance. *Commercial Banks and Their Trust Activities: Emerging Influence on the American Economy.* Washington, D.C.: U.S. Government Printing Office.

U.S. House Committee on the Judiciary. 1965. Antitrust Subcommittee. *Interlocks in Corporate Management.* Washington, D.C.: U.S. Government Printing Office.

U.S. Senate Committee on Government Affairs. 1977. Subcommittee on Reports, Accounting and Management. *Federal Advisory Committees.* Washington, D.C.: U.S. Government Printing Office.

U.S. Senate Committee on Government Operations. 1974. *Disclosure of Corporate Ownership.* Washington, D.C.: U.S. Government Printing Office.

U.S. Senate Committee on Government Operations. 1976. Subcommittee on Reports, Accounting, and Management. *Institutional Investors' Common Stock, Holdings and Voting Rights.* Washington, D.C.: U.S. Government Printing Office.

U.S. Senate Committee on Government Operations. 1974. Subcommittees on Intergovernmental Relations, and Budgeting, Management and Expenditures. *Disclosure of Corporate Ownership.* Washington, D.C.: U.S. Government Printing Office.

U.S. Senate Committee on Governmental Affairs. 1978. Subcommittee on Reports, Accounting and Management. *Voting Rights in Major Corporations.* Washington, D.C.: U.S. Government Printing Office.

U.S. Senate Committee on Governmental Affairs. 1980. *Structure of Corporate Concentration.* Washington, D.C.: U.S. Government Printing Office.

Ullman, Lloyd. 1968. "Collective bargaining and industrial efficiency." In *Britain's Economic Prospects,* Richard Caves, ed. Washington, D.C.: Brookings Institution.

Union Carbide. 1980. *The Vital Consensus: American Attitudes on Economic Growth.* New York: Corporate Communications Department, Union Carbide.

Useem, Michael. 1978. "The inner group of the American capitalist class." *Social Problems* 25: 225–240.

Useem, Michael. 1979. "The social organization of the American business elite and participation of corporation directors in the governance of American institutions." *American Sociological Review* 44: 553–572.

Useem, Michael. 1980. "Corporations and the corporate elite." In *Annual Review of Sociology,* Alex Inkeles, Neil J. Smelser, and Ralph Turner, eds. Palo Alto, Ca.: Annual Reviews.

Useem, Michael. 1981. "Business segments and corporate relations with American universities." *Social Problems* 29: 129–141.

Useem, Michael. 1981b. "Route to the Inner Circle." *New York Times,* January 4 (Sunday): Business Section, p. 22.

Useem, Michael. 1981c. "Blue Chip Guide to the Inner Circle." *The Guardian,* August 5, p. 13.

Useem, Michael. 1982. "Classwide rationality in the politics of managers and directors of large corporations in the United States and Great Britain." *Administrative Science Quarterly* 27: 199–226.

Useem, Michael, and Arlene McCormack. 1981. "The dominant segment of the British business elite." *Sociology* 15: 381–406.

Useem, Michael, and S. M. Miller. 1975. "Privilege and domination: the role of the upper class in American higher education." *Social Science Information* 14 (6): 115–145.

Villarejo, D. 1961. "Stock ownership and the control of the corporation." *New University Thought* 2: 33–77.

Vogel, David. 1978a. "Why businessmen distrust their state: the political consciousness of American corporate executives." *British Journal of Political Science* 8: 45–78.

Vogel, David. 1978b. *Lobbying the Corporation: Citizen Challenges to Business Authority*. New York: Basic Books.

Vogel, David. 1980. "Businessmen unite." *Wall Street Journal*, January 14.

Wagner, Susan E. (ed.). 1978. *A Guide to Corporate Giving to the Arts*. New York: American Council for the Arts.

Walker, Alan. 1980. "A right turn for the British welfare state?" *Social Policy* 23 (March/April): 47–51.

Walsh, John. 1979. "Where are the Medicis of the British boardroom?" *Director* 32 (October): 77–80.

Ware, R. F. 1975. "Performance of manager- versus owner-controlled firms in the food and beverage industry." *Quarterly Journal of Economics and Business* 15: 81–92.

Warner, W. L., and J. C. Abegglen. 1955a. *Occupational Mobility in American Business and Industry, 1928–1952*. Minneapolis: University of Minnesota Press.

Warner, W. L., and J. C. Abegglen. 1955b. *Big Business Leaders in America*. New York: Harper and Brothers.

Weaver, Paul H. 1978. "Regulation, social policy, and class conflict." In *Regulating Business: The Search for an Optimum Solution*. San Francisco: Institute for Contemporary Studies.

Weidenbaum, Murray L. 1977. *Business, Government, and the Public*. Englewood Cliffs, N.J.: Prentice-Hall.

Weidenbaum, Murray L. 1978. *The Impact of Government Regulation*. St. Louis, Mo.: Center for the Study of Business, Washington University.

Weinstein, James. 1968. *The Corporate Ideal and the Liberal State, 1900–1918*. Boston: Beacon.

Westergaard, John, and Henrietta Resler. 1975. *Class in Capitalist Society: A Study of Contemporary Britain*. London: Heinemann.

Westhues, Kenneth. 1976. "Class and organization as paradigms in social science." *The American Sociologist* 11: 38–49.

White, Arthur H. 1980. "Corporate philanthropy: impact on public attitudes." Pp. 17–19 in *Corporate Philanthropy in the Eighties*. Washington, D.C.: National Chamber Foundation.

Whitley, Richard. 1973. "Commonalities and connections among directors of large financial institutions." *Sociological Review* 21: 613–632.

Whitley, Richard. 1974. "The City and industry: the directors of large companies, their characteristics and connections." In Philip Stanworth and Anthony Giddens, eds., *Elites and Power in British Society*. London: Cambridge University Press.

Whitley, Richard, Alan Thomas, and Jane Marceau. 1981. *Masters of Business? Business Schools and Business Graduates in Britain and France*. London: Tavistock Publications.

Whitt, J. Allen. 1980. "Can capitalists organize themselves?" In *Power Structure Research*, G. William Domhoff, ed. Beverly Hills, Ca.: Sage.

Whitt, J. Allen. 1982. *Urban Elites and Mass Transportation*. Princeton, N.J.: Princeton University Press.

Whittington, G. 1972. "Changes in the top 100 quoted manufacturing companies in the United Kingdom 1948 to 1968." *Journal of Industrial Economics* 21: 17–34.

Whyte, William H. 1956. *The Organization Man*. New York: Simon and Schuster.

Wiener, Martin J. 1981. *English Culture and the Decline of the Industrial Spirit, 1850–1980*. New York: Oxford University Press.

Williams, N. P. 1981. "Influences on the profitability of twenty-two industrial sectors." *Discussion Paper* No. 15. London: Bank of England.

Windsor, Duane, and George Greanias. 1982. "Strategic planning systems for a politicized environment." Pp. 77–104 in *Research in Corporate Social Performance and Policy, 1982*, Lee E. Preston, ed. Greenwich, Ct.: JAI Press.

Zeitlin, Maurice. 1974. "Corporate ownership and control: the large corporation and the capitalist class." *American Journal of Sociology* 79: 1073–1119.

Zeitlin, Maurice, Richard Earl Ratcliff, and Lynda Ann Ewen. 1974. "The 'Inner Group': interlocking directorates and the internal differentiation of the capitalist class in Chile." Presented at the annual meeting of the American Sociological Association.

Zeitlin, Maurice, W. Lawrence Newman, and Richard Earl Ratcliff. 1976. "Class segments: agrarian property and political leadership in the capitalist class in Chile." *American Sociological Review* 41: 1006–1029.

Zeitlin, Maurice, and Samuel Norich. 1979. "Management control, exploitation, and profit maximization in the large corporation: an empirical confrontation of managerialism and class theory." *Research in Political Economy*.

Index